HOPE, PROMISE AND BETTER FUTURE FOR MANKIND

The Complete Encyclopedia of
Verses of Social Thoughts
(Volume II)

BUU-VAN AJAREYAJEMIR RASIH

Copyright © 2021 by Buu-Van AjareyaJemir Rasih.

ISBN   978-1-953821-09-6 Ebook
ISBN   978-1-953821-08-9 Paperback

All rights reserved. No part of this publication may be reproduced, distributed, or transmitted in any form or by any means, including photocopying, recording, or other electronic or mechanical methods without the prior written permission of the publisher. For permission requests, solicit the publisher via the address below through mail or email with the subject line "Attention: Publication Permission".

The EC Publishing LLC books may be ordered
through booksellers or by contacting:

EC Publishing LLC
116 South Magnolia Ave.
Suite 3, Unit F
Ocala, FL 34471, USA
Direct Line: +1 (352) 644-6538
Fax: +1 (800) 483-1813
http://www.ecpublishingllc.com/

Ordering Information:
Quantity sales. Special discounts are available on quantity purchases by corporations, associations, and others. For details, contact the publisher at the address above.

Printed in the United States of America

"Hope, Promise and Better Future for Mankind: The Complete Encyclopedia of Verses of Social Thoughts (Volume II)
Copyright © 2021 by Buu-Van AjareyaJemir Rasih

"Out of Darkness Comes Light: America's New Triumph" 21st Century Encyclopedia of Verses of Social Thoughts (Volume I)
Copyright © 2010 by Buu-Van AjareyaJemir Rasih
1102930499
"My Journey to America" Copyright © 2019 by Buu-Van AjareyaJemir Rasih 795691
"Mi Viaje a América"
My Journey to America in Spanish
30038637785
All rights reserved. Printed in United States of America.
No part of these 3 books above may be used or reproduced in any manner whatsoever without permission except in case of brief quotations embodies in critical articles and reviews. For information, address America's New Triumph(AM)Books, Library & Monument
P.O. BOX 722002
San Diego, CA 92172
U.S.A.

Library of Congress Cataloging-in-Publication
ISBN-: 978-1-5434-7294-3 Paperback
ISBN-: 978-1-7960-2875-1 Paperback
ISBN-: 978-1-7960-4619-9 Hard Cover
ISBN-: 978-1-7960-2874-4 EBook
ISBN-: 978-1-4535-2553 Paperback
ISBN-: 987-179-6040-623 Spanish
ISBN-: 987-179-6040-616 eTextbook

3 BOOKS BY
American Citizen Maker Buu-Van AjareyaJemir Rasih

"Out of Darkness Comes Lights: America's New Triumph" 21st Century
Encyclopedia of Verses of Social Thoughts (Volume I)
Subtitle: New Creation of New America and New World in Six-Day.

Hope, Promise and Better Future for Mankind: The Complete Encyclopedia of
Verses of Social Thoughts (Volume II)

"My Journey to America" and
in Spanish "Mi Viaje a América"

DEDICATION

"Hope, Promise and Better Future for Mankind: The Complete Encyclopedia of Verses of Social Thoughts" is dedicated to The America's New Triumph(AM) the genius of the American Spirit and to "AjareyaJemir" Who He Triumphs.

May His light shine upon us all. This book is a journey of Hope and committed to the preservation and enjoyment of the "America's New Triumph(AM)".

This book is dedicated to my Nguyễn parents, Nguyen grandparents and Nguyen great-great grandparents, wife, children and grandchildren. To my co-founders, instructors and associates of the Rasih Citizenship Education Institute and 1,440 citizenship graduate students who are new naturalized citizens of the United States. To thank David Nguyen, Lisa Atkinson, Kelsey Rodriguez, Blake Anderson, Blake Brown, Duat Nguyen, Cúc Phan, Quyen Tran, Chau Ho, Michael B. Nguyen, Dr. Jon Highum, Dr. Kefah Dwabe, M.D. Somnet Chanthapannha, Vannasone Keodara, Kingsavanh Pathammavong, Nikki Summa, Nickie Foulks, Jantima Danford, Leonard Novarro, Rosalynn Carmen, Sư Nguyen Ke Pham and Nguyet VanAnh Nguyen for your friendship, love and support over 4 decades.

CREDITS AND ACKNOWLEDGEMENTS

The author thanks the following business associates & partners, editors, endorsement agencies, book investors/ publishers, book critic/ reviewers, individuals, newspapers/ magazines & poetry editors, marketing campaign distributors, movies producers, organizations/ foundations & institutions, publicists, radio interviewers/ syndicators/ broadcasters and their following names are:

Ajareya-Jemir, America's New Triumph, Al Cole, Alexa Johnson, SLA.com, America's Thai Chamber of commerce San Diego, Amy Chanthaphavong, Amy Le, Anthony Delellis, J.D, APAC, Arthur Thares, Asian Heritage Society, Asia Media America, Barnes & Nobles, Benji Cole, Blake Anderson, Blake Brown, CalState University San Marcos, CBS Radio, Champa Maokhamphiou, Chau Ho, Chau Quy, Choi Sovidaray, Cúc Phan, Dan Chuc Mai, Danny Truong, Debra Márston, Doug Perkins, Duat Nguyen, EBay, EC PublishingLLC.com, FaceBook, Famous Poets Press, Global Childe, Gloria McCall, Google.com, HarperCollins, Hoa Truong, Hollywood book Reviews, Hong Vi, International Society of Poets, Irrigation Dev. institute of Pakkred, Thailand, Jantima Danford, Jareya Bartolome, Jeff Marston, Jon Highum, M.D., Ke Pham, Kefah Dwabe, M.D., Kieryn Zieglar, Kim Kennedy, Kingsavanh Pathammavong, Lao Community Cultural Center of San Diego, Laura Gunderson, Lavender Aurora, Leonard Novarro, Liberty Ellis Island Foundation, Los Angeles Times, Lycée de Luangprabang, Lycée de Vientiane, Lucas Evans, Luke Davis, Marquis Who's Who, Mio The Nguyen, Michael B.Nguyen, Mitz Lee, Monica Conn, NameCheap.com, New York Times, Nguyet VanAnh Nguyen, Nickie Foulks, Nikki Summa, PRWeb.com, Pete Wilson, phuc Bao, Quyen Tran, Quynh Nga Natalie, Radio Free Asia, Rasih Citizenship Education Institute, Rasih Institute, Reza Athari, Ron Roberts, Rosalynn Carmen, San Diego City for Human Relations Commission, San Diego Republicans. Org, San Diego superior court, San Diego Union Tribune, Scott Peters, Shirley Weber, Ph.D., silverLiteraryAgency.com, Sao Bang, Somnet Inthapannha, Soutsada Sirattana, Su Nguyễn, Suphaphorn Wannawan, Todd Gloria, Toni G. Atkins, Tom Sayarath, Tran Truong, Tuan Van, Tuyen Pham, Uyen Tran, URLink Publishing Company, USAID, U.S. Catholic Conference, USCIS, Vannasone Keodara, Voice of America, Wildlife World Fund, Xlibris, YouTube, ZooAmerica.

FOREWORD BY LEONARD NOVARRO

With an Everyman sense of world angst and a zen-like rapier spirit, Buu-Van Rasih tackles Life in all its manifestations, from ire at the Internal Revenue Service to the purpose of labor caught in the drift of uncertainty.

Along with his previous work" Out of Darkness Comes Light," Buu-Van is a model for a new America, an immigrant poet from a proud tradition in Laos, Vietnam and Thailand, who chose to make a career out of helping others adapt to the United States and embrace their new country That is America. This is much their book as his- an amalgam of spirit and love for an adopted country you will rarely see- a quality Lonh absent from our own landscape.

When he says" Concessions. I used to cringe at that word," he believe it. When he says "We ate in knowledge-worker world. If you were building me a building, I could measure the number of bricks," he has lived it. When he says that "science discovers lots of stuff which later on is always disapproved," he embraces it. With topics ranging from the future of baby boomers and Gen Xers to the state of our military and the wonders of kinship, at the heart of his work is commitment to an ideal that is greater than the sum of its parts.

That ideal is America. Whether starting his outrage or speaking softly, he expresses an unsettled vision for an unsettled landscape- but a landscape with hope, promise and a better future.

Leonard Novarro
Co-founder Asia Media America,
Asia Heritage Society

Acid Attack

JUSTICE

*"The starting point
for grievous
bodily harm
is twelve years,
but this
is only a guideline."*

Despicable act.
Intent on causing
really serious harm.

The sentence
was considered
by many
to be surprisingly lengthy
and to some,
even excessive,
upon closer consideration
it isn't.
In my view the sentences
have to act as a deterrent
in society.
This has been one closely watched
by the public
and it is very much a message
being sent out to people
who carry acid.
You cannot get away with this,
which will be tolerated in England.

The starting point
for grievous
bodily harm
is twelve years,
but this
is only a guideline.
When deciding
the length
of the prison sentence
to impose,
the judge will consider
a number of aggravating
and mitigating factors.
Firstly,
in this case
the offense

was premeditated.
The fact
that somebody has planned,
armed themselves
and deliberately set out
with the specific intention
to cause planned
and serious harm,
significantly increases
the prison sentences.
The judge specifically commented
that he showed none.
If he had shown remorse,
it may have been reflected
in the sentence.

These injuries were,
in several cases,
lifechanging,
I think given the number
of victims,
the nature of the injuries
and that this was an acid attack,
even if Arthur
had no previous convictions,
the sentence
would not have been very different.

Note: Grievous Bodily Harm (often abbreviated to GBH) is a technical term used in English criminal law which has become synonymous with the offences that are created by sections 18 and 20 of the Offences Against the Person Act of 1861.

JUSTICE

Acid Attacks

Acid Survivors Trust International (ASTI)
Corrosive fluid.
Severe discomfort.
It's a growing problem,
there's no question,
corrosive substances are extremely
easy to get ahold of.
You can buy them from hardware stores
and don't have to register
why you're purchasing it
or what you want to use it for.

If you throw acid in
someone's face,
it's going to affect their eyes
and eyesight so you have a high
chance of getting away with it.
It's a very easy thing to do.
You can ride up to someone
on a bike
and throw it at them.

I ended up in the middle
of this fight
and I was thrown over the barrier
near the bar with all of my stuff,
getting up I could feel
my arm was burning.
It was like boiling water
had been poured over me,
but like I was cut as well.
I have never experienced
anything like it,
it was excruciating.
We saw six other girls
who had it in their eyes,
faces
and chest areas.
They were screaming

and crying.

I have nightmares…
I see it every day,
every hour,
like it was yesterday,
more than half of my life
I'm gonna have to
live like this…
sometimes I wish I was dead
and didn't survive.

Affair

SOCIETY

Virtual

I caught him cuddling a woman
on a sofa in the game,
it looked very affectionate.
He confessed that he had been talking
to this woman
player in America
for one
or two weeks;
had said our marriage was over
and that he didn't love me anymore.
Single.
In RL.
Real Life.

For awhile
there was this impression
that as long as it's online,
it doesn't matter,
but research has shown
it's not a separate world.

Real-Life Marriage Create Personality in Second Life Avatar: Three-dimensional virtual world with millions of users.

Aging

SOCIETY

Baby Boomers
It's about performance,
competence
and engagement,
not chronological age;
that's absurd
and indefensible.

There are Chief Executive Officers
operating well into their 70's
and beyond,
who are awesome.
You could argue
you're doing the company a disservice
by removing them at 65,
in our work we try
and advise boards hiring CEOs
to take age off the table.
Yes,
there can be concerns
that older CEOs
may be more concerned
with preserving their legacies,
but you could also argue
that older,
seasoned CEOs
will help a company avoid mistakes.

You need to take a step back
from executive function,
but continue to lend
your pattern recognition skills,
while serving as an effective partner
to someone younger.
Maybe five
or so years ago,
boards would fight activist investors,
but now they look to see
if maybe a change needs to be made.

Boards,
who are influenced by shareholders,
are much more mindful
of the ages of CEOs
at publicly traded companies,
you could easily have a case
where a 70-year old CEO
is doing a great job,
but most boards will still look at that
carefully.
Even if a lot of that talk
won't play out publicly.

With people like Redstone
and Murdoch
and so many others,
their persona
and personality
is so firmly attached
to the company itself
that quite often the lines get blurred.
Every organization
at some point deserves
a fresh injection of Leadership.

MILITARY

Air Force

What we've done
is put requirement
on the table that says
'if we're going to do the mission
you're going to ask us to do,
it will require this kind of investment,'
failing that,
we take what is
already a geriatric Air Force
and we drive it
for another twenty years
into an area of uncertainty,
if you want to accept
that today we're doing an adequate job
with this sort of patchwork
of airplanes,
when are we no longer
able to do an adequate job?
What's the next thing
that's going to happen?

The Air Force
is going to be confronting
a major procurement crisis,
because it can't buy
all the things
that it absolutely needs,
it's going to force us to rethink,
yet again,
what is the strategy we want?
What can we give up?

One of the reasons
their equipment has aged
so much is,
because they continue
to move ahead
with the development

and presumed acquisition
of new weapon systems
that cost two to three times
as much as the systems
they are replacing,
it's like replacing a Toyota
with a Mercedes.

Wish list.
There's no justification for it.
Period.
End of story,
until someone constrains
their budget requests,
the hunger for more
will charge ahead unchecked.

We are literally flying
the wings off
these two airplanes,
manageable crisis.
Anytime you have a small number
of airplanes
that the appetite
for continually increases,
it's hard to meet the demand,
if we don't wrestle with this now,
it's a looming problem out there.

Alaska

COMMUNITY

Happy Birthday Bop-Bop,
Happy Birthday Siti-Girl.
Cake mixes are the center of our little universe,
I have four damn shelves full.
Subsistence.
Cake lady.
Sometimes you don't have a lot of stuff
to make a regular cake,
maybe you don't have butter
or you don't have milk.

I mixed orange Jell-O
with two cups of bright orange salmonberries.
I poured it on top of that cake
and I threw it in the fridge,
people were just like,
'Wow, can you make that again for me?'

It's a festive environment
even though it's a sad time,
you should see the cakes;
they are so beautiful.
Village bakers are so brilliant.
I can't remember the last time
I paid the Amazon Prime fee,
we don't have any bakeries.
We have restaurants,
people really crave the fresh cake.
I was like the camp queen!
Middle of nowhere,
eating cake.

Albert Einstein

AMERICA'S NEW TRIUMPH

A calm
and modest life
brings more happiness
than the pursuit of success
combined with constant relentless,
when there's a will,
there's a way.

What we're doing here
is painting the portrait
of Albert Einstein–
the man,
the scientist,
his effect on the world–
through his writings,
this is a stone
in the mosaic.

There is probably no physicist
living today
whose name
has become so widely known
as that of Albert Einstein.
Calm
and modest.

Alcohol

COMMUNITY

It's grimy local politics
at its best,
the store became too successful.

Ceased to be a procedural,
legal filing issue
and become one of other problems...
it got all out of hand,
wet.
Eating-place beer,
Eating-place beer.
Cottagers,
I'm all for small business
and I like to drink beer,
granted,
if you put a bar in someone's backyard
it certainly diminishes property values.

When it was brought up
both times it was very divisive,
we're dry,
that's it.
People think it's kind of cool
being a dry town.

Clear mandate,
a signal to both
the State Liquor Authority
and local government
that Barrington
is willing to join
the 21st century amendment.

Algebra

SOCIETY

At a mediocre level.
The sharp falloff in mathematics
achievement in the United States begins
as students reach late middle school;
where,
for more
and more students
algebra course work begins.
Students who complete Algebra II
are more than twice as likely
to graduate from college
compared to students with
less mathematical preparation.
To prepare students for algebra,
the curriculum must simultaneously
develop concepts that understand
computational fluency
and problem-solving skills.
Debates regarding the relative
importance of those aspects
of mathematical knowledge are misguided.
The capabilities are mutually supportive.

There is no basis in research
for favoring teacher-based
or student-centered instruction,
people may retain their strong
philosophical inclinations,
but the research doesn't show
that either is better than the other.
Buys the nation from
cognitive science
that kids have to know the facts.

Plastics.
The graduate.
Fractions.
For all content areas,
practice allows students to achieve

automate of basic skill—
the fast,
accurate,
and effortless processing
of content information,
which frees up the working memory
for more complex aspects
of problem solving,
talent-driven approach to math,
that either you can
or you can't do it;
like playing the violin.

Algorithms

SOCIETY

Torture.
Fake news.
Don't regulate us,
we'll improve our behavior.
Trade secrets.
Online public square.
We are on to this,
white protest.
Children of the revolution.
Conservative nationalists.
Liberal conservatives.

Law and Justice's victory was a result
of wide frustrations.
A return to a pre-2015 period
is not desirable.

Al_Qaeda

COMMUNITY

Al-Qaeda is extreme
active,
captive:

My time as a prisoner
of the Taliban
and in Afghanistan
Al-Qaeda has a lot more influence
in the rural areas
and among the very poor
and among the deeply religious elements.
Flash in the pan.
No intellectual standing.

Game Changers:
Going local
to defeat violent extremists,
may actually have the long game figured out
in Syria
is more about working by,
with,
and through
local populations.

Amazon's Second Head Quarters

COMMUNITY

Key preferences
and decision drivers.
Site
and building,
paramount importance.

Amazon has the opportunity
to help build
and shape a city
and region,
that's easier in a Detroit
than a San Francisco.
It's much different
than just tapping the talent
that's already there.
Amazon will attract people
and other companies that are inspired by that.

Incentives,
high priority.
Amazon's first obligation
is to its investors,
the most cost-effective city
in which to locate
a second headquarters,
will produce the most value
for the company.

Competitive Alternatives.
Labor Force.
Tech Talent,
critically important,
community cultural fit,
community quality of life.
A diverse population.
Excellent Institutions of Higher Education.

America on Line (AOL)

COMMUNITY

We feel we can get back
into the leadership position
in social media
and the community,
which is our heritage of AOL.

America On Line was in danger
of becoming your father's Oldsmobile
this acquisition is designed
to prevent that.
It's a way for AOL
to get some skin in the game.

Game-changing.
Kate modern,
Bebo had the potential
of learning a valuable asset
to America On Line
if AOL manages it well
and executes it well,
then it's unclear
if they will be able to.

American Idol

VENUES

American Idol,
American Idol.
A moment like this.
Who's that sweaty, pregnant girl singing?
Oh snap,
that's me,
hahaha.
American Idol.

Idol.
American Idol's Greatest Hits,
pants on the ground guy.
Idol Rockers,
Idol.

American Veterans

MILITARY
World War II

Things got a little screwy,
because everyone was so busy celebrating.
Girls,
people always say to me
'*thank you for your service.*'
I tell them I did it willingly,
but I can't say it was enjoyable;
don't ask me to do it again.

This is the best thing I get to do
in my job,
there is a common humility
among these men
who gave so much
to their country,
so if there's a way I can give back to them,
it's an honor to do that.

He had some terrible experiences,
but they inspired him
to make a better life for himself,
he's an excellent ambassador
for coming back
and turning a bad experience around
into something positive.

All hands man your battle stations…
real planes,
real bombs,
no sh_ _!
Panic was growing,
some were screaming,
some were cursing
and one called repeatedly for help
from Mommy.

I remember as I stepped out
on the weather deck

to go to my battle station,
I saw a plane heading towards us,
our guys were all firing at him
and they were hitting him.
Pieces of the plane were falling off
into the water.
I thought,
'*Well,*
he's going to make it.',
but he didn't.

Americans With Disability Act (ADA)

JUSTICE

It's an amazing thing to watch
non-disabled people use the ramp
instead of the steps,
when given the option.
Some architects will say,
"Screw the steps.
We will just do the ramp."
You could be wheeling half a mile,
it's a work out.
If someone was coming,
I couldn't see them
until I was around the corner,
that ramp was an afterthought.

It's like you know you need
to have windows
and you have to have doors,
we think about it
from the very beginning.

They are everywhere...
built to fit into the terrain
more sensitive to the geography
that surrounds them,
because ramps take a lot of space...
The entire project becomes more costly,
it traces the route of the stairway,
so you don't miss the procession of people,
it became an opportunity
for a people-watching experience.

The ramp was a response
to the Americans with Disability Acts
and design issues,
it worked out nicely.

A little four-inch curb
can be like a mountain,
we want to have access

to the same things
as everybody else does.
You don't know
if it's around the block
or through the garage,
it's really frustrating.
It's a lot easier
if I'm meeting
at another lawyer's office,
I assume
I will have complete access;
ten years ago,
I could not have been assured
of that.

It's like being put in the back
of the bus,
it is important to have the ramp
be a regular way into the building,
instead of having to go all the way
to the side
or the back.

Animal Rights

ZOOAMERICA

This is a small town,
but this is not a small-town issue.
It's a national issue,
cats were killed at a shelter.
It's like going into a church
and killing;
that's last on certain people around.
Farmers just let their cats breed,
they are there
to keep the rodent population down.
A lot of them
don't really care much.
the suffering that goes on
is just tremendous.
Their population control
is diseased
and wandering off.
We wanted to create a sanctuary.

It is a very dramatic occurrence
in just the sheer number of animals.
It's really disturbing
and quite compelling.
If it's taken seriously
and prosecuted
to the fullest extent of the law.
It's a precedent.
The kind of trauma
they'd have if they got hit by a car
or were in Du Tornado,
this could be a make
or break moment for these kids;
you don't want to give
these teenagers a slap
on the wrist.
Fairfield is divided
about fifty-fifty,
their problem
is just a bottling of anger,

they need to change
their diet
so they keep their thinking level
and they need to cut their stress.

They should be practicing
Transcendental medication.
Got off light.
I hope some judge
doesn't order community service
I pray they get the max!
I agree what they did was wrong,
but to go to prison?
… how many things
did you
and I do growing up
that we wished
we hadn't done?
I think it's a thing
that boys have.
You used to see these out hunting,
targeting cats with 223.
Mediators.
Mediators.
They're...
...different,
real,
real different.

If I'd been out that night,
I would have helped,
I just don't like cats,
they scratch me.
They bite me.
When they find a cat
or a dog in the fields,
they tend to think
it's somebody else's problem
that got dumped out there.

Animal Shelters

COMMUNITY

Last year,
we dealt with over thirty-one thousand
animals in our department alone,
but we don't have thirty-one thousand
people knocking at our door
to adopt every single one of those animals.
The sad truth
is that we have to put more than half
of those animals to sleep.
We euthanized over seventeen thousand animals
last year.
The rest were either adopted
or claimed.
We try to move as many as we can,
but there is a surplus
amount of animals out there.
These are the unwanted
or as we call them,
'throwaway pets.'
We have to euthanize them,
which is unfortunate,
but we look at it this way:
if we did not perform
euthanasia,
which is a painless death,
on these seventeen thousand,
they would be out on the street,
abused,
hit by cars
and starved to death.

So we try our hardest
to adopt out as many as we can,
but the ones
that we can't adopt out,
we have a responsibility
to ensure that they're going
to have a painless death.
Ten,

fifteen years ago,
we were probably euthanizing
about twenty
or thirty thousand animals.
Age,
health,
temperament,
and spacing—
those are the criteria.
I only have so many
adoption kennels.
Sometimes we will double up
the animals in them,
but there are only so many
that can go into adoption.
This means the others
are going to have to be put to sleep,
because there are no more spaces left.
I can't put more in there.
That's the spacing requirement.
Then there are the age
and health requirements;
can't adopt out a nine
or 10-year-old German
that has gray around the muzzle
and a hip problem.
Temperament;
I can't adopt out aggressive dogs.
If we knowingly adopt out
a dog that has a bad temperament,
that will bite you,
bite your neighbor,
or maul some dog
down the street,
the county has a liability
issue.

These are ready to be adopted.
They've already had a health check
and they're ready
to be spayed.
We're waiting for someone
to come in
and say

'That's the one that I want.'
All they have to do
is pay their fees
and off they go.
We have a large adoption rate
on our cats,
because we ship a lot out
to pet stores.
People come in
during our litter season.
We adopt out a lot of kittens.
Kitten season
is anywhere between March
and all the way through summer.
Right about that time
you have a breeding season,
and we get a lot
of newborn kittens
that come through.

We have rabbits,
guinea pigs
and we have iguanas—
we have a man coming in
to adopt
our iguanas tomorrow.
You name it,
we deal with it.
This is not just a dog pound.
That's why they changed
the term—
about thirty years ago
to animal shelter.

This is our medical building,
we're refurnishing it.
The whole building
is going to be revamped.
There's going to be a new surgery center,
and there's going to be a recovery area
for the animals,
that have been neutered.

We try to spay
every animal that leaves here
prior to adoption.
Unfortunately,
sometimes we don't have the staffing
or a veterinarian
to provide that service to
every single animal that leaves.
We try to do that,
but we only have so much
staff to work with.

We do,
on occasion,
allow animals to be adopted
on what we call a voucher.
This means they pay
for the spay
or neuter.
They take the voucher
to one of our contract veterinarians
and they will provide the surgery.
We don't adopt to them.
We're not
in the business
of putting animals
back on the street
to reproduce.
We're trying
to control
the animal
population.
That's our primary responsibility;
if we're not concerned
with the overpopulated
pet problem,
our euthanasia rate goes up
and quite honestly,
we're tired of euthanizing.

We have a dead dog in here,
this is the euthanasia room;
this is where we euthanize
all the animals.

It's done by injection,
the same method
that veterinarians use.
The injection is of pentobarbital,
which is injected
into one of the major veins,
they're dead
within ten seconds,
very painless.
The people who work here
are people who care about animals.
We have a compassion for animals
and it's very difficult to come in
and perform euthanasia
and to euthanize seventeen
thousand animals a year;
it's not an easy task.

Anniversary

AMERICA'S NEW TRIUMPH

Where should we go after a lovely anniversary?
and retirement party?
A week ago on April 2nd,
we celebrated our 39th
wedding anniversary
and a retirement party,
we will go away
for a weekend
in Lake Tahoe
and Reno,
Nevada on May 1st.

Reduce Poverty,
increase education.
Their hopes
and dreams
became a reality
in the heavenly
and beautiful
Lake Tahoe.
Clear
and cobalt blue lake
where California
and Newark meet
and discover Reno,
300 days of sunshine a year.

Anti-Abortion Curriculum

JUSTICE

    For the purpose of achieving
    an abortion free society.
    My caucus
    wants to do all we can
    to reduce the number of abortions
    in Oklahoma,
    the goal is to alleviate
    any fiscal impacts
    to our school districts,
    about the humanity
    of a child in utero.

    It's virtually important
    to help people understand
    before such time
    that a girl might become pregnant
    that this is a living human being
    growing within her.
    That new human life
    deserves respect
    and protection.

    You're starting
    a book at the end,
    a student in Oklahoma
    would learn about abortion
    and gestational cycles,
    but there would be no guarantee
    that they would learn about sex
    and pregnancy.
    Adding yet another mandate
    on them
    and forcing them
    to have those very emotional
    and political conversations
    with young people
    just taking away instructional time
    from other areas.

Archery

SPORTS

The thing was,
we weren't 100 percent prepared
for that type of pressure
and it's a special type of pressure.
Basically,
one fraction of an inch
can be the difference
between you qualifying a team
and not qualifying a team.
That's something
we continue to work on.
My goal
is by the time we get to Turkey,
we're the most prepared team
at handling that type of pressure.
It's going to come down that day
to who handles the pressure the best.

I wasn't too far off,
but I needed to learn a few things
at the World Championship trials
and I did,
that's where some of my success
has come from recently,
learning from times when I didn't win
and becoming better from that.
It's really important sometimes
to learn hard lessons.
It was discouraging at the time.
It was definitely heartbreaking
not to make the team,
but I was grateful for it later.

A little bit,
but it's not like the crushing pressure,
like:
Now we have this
so we have to make it up to them
at the Olympics.

There may be a slight added pressure,
but I don't think it's anything more
than it has been.
It's more:
We have this awesome thing
so let's use it to our advantage
and help us get better.

I don't feel any extra expectations
or pressure from our organization,
because of our facility;
as the women's head coach,
I obviously feel some pressure
for us to perform,
but a lot of that
is my own desire
for us to beat the living crap
out of everyone we go against.

Architectural Designer

NATURE

Pheromones

Form follows pheromone!
I was thinking,
as I was devouring
my meatball sandwich,
about how we could use robotic arms
to spit out pheromones
guiding bees to template honeycombs
in the absence of queens.
The robots,
you see,
could master the hive.
We are sending bees to outer space,
we've got a little cell
on Jeff Bezos's Blue Origin mission.
We treat design more like gardening practice.

If I was the Terminator,
Neri is Terminator 2.
I was crappy titanium parts,
but she's like liquid metal.

She's not afraid of formal elegance,
the reason why she is a gift
to the field of architecture
and design is that her science works,
her aesthetics work
and her theory works.
It's been interesting
to see scientists respond.
They welcome the collaboration,
because they know the research
they develop with her team
is going to be accepted by their peers
and it might be beautiful.
I'm not afraid to use that word,
by the way.

I used to be a coke enthusiast,
but now I'm addicted to E. Coli.

What does it mean
to design a living object?
How do we accommodate
for dimensional mismatches
between environmental constraints,
light,
lead,
da,
da,
da
and the material?
How can you have a single material system
that is multifunctional,
that is not made of parts
and that can vary over space
and time for different conditions?
Can you make architecture
that behaves like a tree.
Look,
we haven't gone this far
to sell glass-painted light fixtures
on Amazon,
we are here
and remain committed
because we are able to design
an architectural 'skin'
as an optical lens,
thereby opening up possibilities
for harnessing solar energy
on urban scales.
These technologies
should not be trivialized
for entertainment purpose alone,
through potentially profitable solutions
through potentially profitable solutions
such as a biodegradable Pellegrino bottle
may well help us cut out plastic.
One has to start somewhere
without compromising soul.

I sang a song called 'Quicksand',

which is a nihilist gothlike person,
so we aimed for biological goth.
I remember looking at Mexican death masks
but mostly talking about love,
to be honest.
As the last of the Mohicans
in post-Netflix Hollywood.
He brings together the timely
and timeless,
which is what cinema is all about.
The Golden Record
beats the caviar quilted flab bag
on any given day,
toting the ultimate message
in a bottle
to the paparazzi.
The Feynman followed.

Broken Nature,
the kingdoms of life.
In this era of global warming,
melanin is the new gold.
Philosophically,
practically,
ethically,
humanely,
social
and anthropologically
for doing such a thing?
Up until now,
our work has been culturally agnostic.
This project takes us further
into charged territories.
Biological building,
could it as structure
and skin,
varying its concentration
as a function
of a site-specific sun path diagram?
To transform the methodology
of building.
Today we have materials
that are translucent
and we have materials

that are load bearing
and she is hoping
we could reach the day
when we have materials
that could behave
in multiple ways.
Release light
and store energy.
It is such a grand ambition,
I don't think it will be fulfilled
in my lifetime,
I might be wrong.

Since she is a gifted artist,
what comes out
through whatever process
she uses are beautiful objects.
People are fascinated by these lovely objects.
From my perspective,
from a wish
that her grand ambitions
are fulfilled,
this is like a sideshow,
but it's a sideshow
that gets a lot of attention.

Arctic Circle

WORLD WILDLIFE

It is eating up the land…
you cannot do anything about it.

The sea washes down the coast
every year,
it is practically all ice–
permafrost–
and it is thawing.

June isn't really
June anymore.
The reindeer are becoming despondent,
the people who are taking the decisions,
they are living in the South
and they are living in towns;
they don't mark
the change of weather.
It is only people
who live in nature
and get resources
from nature who mark it.
One oil spill would be the end of us,
we've fished these waters for centuries,
as a whole it's a hard life;
we've survived in doing so.
We need a policy
for the Arctic that considers
the next 100 years,
not the next 10 years.

Country fund.
They're too mushy,
the next generation coming up
is not going to experience
what we did,
we can't pass the tradition on
as our ancestors passed on to us.
In the summer 40 years ago,
we had lots of icebergs,

you could land
your boat on them
and climb on them,
even in the summer;
now in the winter they are tiny.
The weather has changed.
Everyone knows it.
It's global warming.

Everything is falling apart,
the permafrost is unforgiving.
It is an example of how fragile it is
and how careful we should be,
if the permafrost melts.
This city will not collapse overnight.
There is time to adjust,
but it requires very serious investments
of labor
and money.

It was supposed to increase
over the next years,
up to 20 million tons of oil,
it's 20 million this year;
we can expect up to 100 million tons,
over the next 10 to 20 years,
to be transported through our area.

What has never happened
before is a big accident in the high seas
in the arctic,
in Norway,
they have at least 50 bases
of this kind.

People ought to not paint the arctic
in some sort of raving sense where
a spill is always serious.
In the Arctic it will naturally
take longer to clean up
because there is less wave action,
and breakdown is slower
in colder temperatures.

We're not prepared to deal
with the huge ships.
Emotionally huge ships,
emotionally
or in other ways;
it's how we do the business
that's more important.
There are more environmentally
friendly ways in which we can
do development
and still live a certain way,
with a way of life
and business
that can balance both.

The whale
and the supercomputer.
even if you support
oil development
and think it makes sense,
there's a point at which it
becomes West Texas
or the gulf of Mexico
and is not really the Arctic anymore.

Argentina

UNITED NATIONS

Abortion
Abortion in all
or most cases.
I have seen women take two,
eight,
twelve pills,
never 40.

What socorristas do
is deal with the right
to information
and information is legal.
The system is very crucial.

It changed me,
because from that moment
I was always living in conflict,
the pressures of society,
my Catholic family,
the law.
I knew it was bad
for my image
as a doctor
to do abortions,
I don't like being called
'Dr. Aborto,'
but I wouldn't change
what I do.

Health.
A state of complete physical,
mental
and social well-being
and not merely the absence
of disease
or infirmity.

There's a lot of hypocrisy,
doctors say they're against an abortion,
but when someone they know needs one,
they will ask another doctor to do it for them.

Armenian Genocide

IMMIGRATION

It hits very close to home,
when you hear that denial
and it's part of your family tree,
it's very personal.
All I have to do
is follow my family tree
to see it's interrupted by genocide.

Genocide.
Glendale has been my home for 25 years
and to know that an elected body
in my city
has acknowledged
an Armenian Genocide Remembrance Day
is very significant;
it brings relevance to it,
it is a victory–
if we can educate more students
and children
and faculty on what really happened.
My personal family is very small,
because of what the Ottoman Turks did.

Our wounds are still open.
1915.
In this world,
we aim for equality;
we march to appreciate the days
they didn't have.
Every day we walk,
we know they deserve to be in our shoes,
to live
and not die,
the generation who survived
the Genocide taught us to be strong.

Absolutely perfect.
My father's grandparents
were Genocide survivors.

I always heard their stories
when I was little.
There is no Armenian
in the world
who doesn't have a relative
that was affected by the genocide.
This is not a movie.
It's our reality.
It's pain
and it's hurt.

MILITARY

Army Recruitment

Golden Knights.
We're the goodwill ambassadors
for the army.
Why not use it
as a recruiting tool?
After the jumps we had
lots of kids came up
to us
and said
"*I didn't know
you could do that
in the army!*"
The only way kids think today
is by asking
"*What can you give me?*"
They came to realize
that freedom isn't force.

It got me to join,
we came to the air shows
to show taxpayers
what they are getting
for their money
and to inspire kids
who are interested in the Air Force.
When you have three hundred thousand
people out here hopefully
you'll inspire some of them.
All of the military
is having a hard time,
because the economy
is so bad;
this is shocking,
but true.

It peaked my interest in flying.
Seeing all the planes
really encourages you

and I'd like to jump
out of a plane one day.

It definitely works.
We talk to parents
who want to put their children
into the military.
We also talk to high school students
who are looking for something to do.

Art Collector

AMERICA'S NEW TRIUMPH

    The prices were scary,
    it was such a young audience
    I thought for a moment
    I'd wandered into
    'Gladiators'.
    It must be internet money.

    There were a lot of new,
    younger buyers,
    one first-time buyer
    bought a Warhol painting.
    Women in Tub,
    Two Women.
    Two Women.
    Loesungen I – IV.
    Skull 545–3.
    Boy.
    Gnaw.
    Sensation.
    Young British Artists.
    from the Saatchi collection.
    Golden Eye Table.
    Untitled Rorschach Series.
    Heady,
    but,
    what happens
    when the economy softens?

Art Museums

VENUES

Museums are in a transition moment,
what we're seeing is people
who are moving into the region
are excited about the arts.
A city reaches a certain critical size,
then you've got both the financial resources
and also the intellectual resources.
The community's good will,
to want to have a museum
and support it.

Many people have the extraordinary
desire to connect with works of art,
do not want a mall-like experience.
Every other sort of entertainment
for folks these days,
we have to kind of make it
as unobstructed
and comfortable
a thing as it can be.

Aryan Nations

UNITED NATIONS

Yes,
they've won a round.
They were able to steal
a man's property,
but we're going to be here
in this area…
and those who don't like it
will have to lump it.
Enjoy diversity,
the Aryan Nations is not dead!
Communist Jews
have not won
the war,
they've just won a battle!
What do you think,
when you put fifty years
of your life into something?
When you physically
work to build something.
Spend twenty-five years here,
it's hard to go
and yet I'm proud of that;
I've been able to stand
in the face of adversity.

Remember,
if you've ever worked for anything,
if you ever stood for anything,
you stand for it
all of your life.
They can take every material possession,
but there's one thing they can't
take from you
and that's your honor.

So reprehensible that it is repugnant to anyone
in a civilized society;
by any means shock
the conscience of the court.

Idaho.
The Human Rights State.
Everyone is beautiful.
Shalom.
We wanted to make sure
there was a visible opposition
to Richard Butler
and his fascist thoughts,
history has shown
that if you ignore fascism
it just gets stronger,
why the jury felt strong enough
to make the award against Butler.
He's going to be deconsecrating
the ground at the Aryan Nations.

Hail Victory!
I don't agree with the beliefs,
but I think people like that
should be left to believe
what they want.
Foolish,
shortsighted
and unrealistic.
There's plenty of blacks
in Spokane
about thirty miles west
of Coeur d'Alene,
but we don't have
the big gang activity
and there isn't
really any big racial tension.
Richard Butler is fine,
just fine.
We bought him a house,
we bought him a new car,
we put new clothes on his back,
and Morris Dees
can take a flying leap.
Morris Dees
doesn't have the last word
in North Idaho.

Asian Economy Crisis

ECONOMY

We've seen a definite slowdown
in orders in the Pacific Rim
develop over the past thirty days
as a result of the crisis
in Japan
and Korea;
it's had a ripple effect
all the way through
the value of the cattle
back to the rancher.
The Asian problem
is going to the drive...
probably the worst calendar
fourth-quarter earnings season
that we've seen in the past
three
or four years.

We're all nervous,
I think we're in
for about two years
of tough sledding for our sales
into Asia Pacific,
to the degree that the product
ends up here instead of Asia;
it will provide lower beef prices
for consumers than they otherwise
would have had.

In tough times,
you lose people,
friends disappear
and you just hope you make
the cut every year.
There were very few farmers that
will be generating any profit
at the prices we're talking about today
of seventy-two cents per pound
for San Joaquin valley cotton.

About seventy percent
of all our shipments go
outside the United States,
so economic disturbances
on the scale we're seeing
in the Pacific Rim
are of great concern,
this should have a good impact
for economies
like the United States,
which are quite sensitive
to energy prices,
even if it affects the big
oil producers a little bit
because of the drop in oil prices,
there will be a fifteen percent decrease
in the total energy bill.

When Mexico went down,
it was quite easy to direct
product to Taiwan,
but here you have a sequence of markets
that hurt…
I don't think
the farmers quite caught
up with the magnitude
of the problem.

Asian Games

SPORTS

This is our biggest delegation
to the Asian Games,
especially with many team sports.
We have a lot of young people
getting some good experience
in these type of events.
Everybody is focused
in sports now,
particularly this part of the world,
over the next 10 years
and we hope
we can have a lot of home support,
certainly the spirit is there.

With team sports,
it's not very often
that Hong Kong has a chance
to participate in such events,
but we are being encouraged
by the government.
There will be tremendous pressure
on the teams,
but I feel confident
if we can perform well,
it will lay down a marker
for Hong Kong
for future events.

The policy address
of the Hong Kong government
places the emphasis on team sports,
so that's why
we have all eight teams here;
both men
and women.
We are putting together
a five year plan
for the development of team sports

that will be beneficial
to our sporting future.

We don't know
how they will perform here.
The Olympic Games in Tokyo
means…

Astronauts

AMERICA'S NEW TRIUMPH

Space Programs
NASA

You have joined the elites
you are the best of us,
you carry on your shoulders
the hopes
and dreams
of the American people.

So what they want to see
is that you are well-rounded,
but that you've also chosen a path,
are passionate about it
and have excelled in that field,
whatever that field may be –
as long as it's a science,
Technology,
Engineering,
and Mathematics field.
To that end,
I've pursued my passion for
planetary geology
and studying Mars;
I've built a career around that
with the assumption
that if being an astronaut didn't happen,
I'd still be fulfilled
and enjoy planetary geology.

Robb's professionalism,
integrity,
intelligence
and work ethic are second to none,
this is so perfect.
They grow up so fast,
"#proud."

One of these folks behind us could
be the one that takes that
next iconic giant leap
and says the words
similar to what Neil Armstrong said
when he stepped onto the moon
and bring the entire world with them,
that what the future is for
these folks
and it's very,
very exciting
when you think about it.

Astronomy

NATURE

North Star.
This is going to go away,
into thinking that science
discovers lots of stuff
which later on
is always disapproved.
Not even wrong,
new leptoquark.
The public gets confused,
because science is supposed
to have hard rules,
but these hard rules
are applied by real people.
It's an important
part of science that
the public doesn't see.
Some correlations
are not meaningful,
I like to think
that there are mechanisms
behind the correlation,
that there's an explanation
that makes sense.
I almost view myself
as schizophrenic.
I get up in the morning
believing one thing,
then I read a paper
and then I believe something else.

Right
or wrong
I think you'd find
that the rejection rate
for scientific papers
is pretty low
sooner
or later,
anything can get published.

These people don't have
any particular reputation;
there are lots of good people
I haven't heard of.
I don't know
how the corkscrew theory
got published,
something that is so obviously
incompatible with the data
is going to be shot down pretty fast.
Still,
these things do get
through the cracks.
Often,
the truth of results
isn't clear,
but that is
in the nature of science.

When people are trying
to do very difficult things,
it's expected that
some results will fall
by the wayside.
If people were very conservative–
they always publish only
what they expected to find–
there could be a few new discoveries.
Astrophysics is a discipline
where the facts don't always agree
with each other,
so people use subjective judgment
to assemble a self-consistent world view.
You can sift through the things
that are out there to support
any kind of cockamamie argument.
Indication of Anisotropy
in Electromagnetic Propagation
over Cosmological Distances,
unrelenting promotion
by the two universities' press offices;
one of the most fundamental findings
about the universe in recent years.
It's not the mainstream thing,

but I'm trying to get some cosmologists
and particle physicists
worked up about it.
Cosmological principle
we've come one-hundred-eighty degrees,
there isn't a center,
there isn't any special direction.
Until last Tuesday,
one of the most difficult
questions in science,
is how do you know
when it's garbage?
When you require different
levels of proof depending
on whether you're looking for something,
if you see something
that you don't expect to see,
the standard of evidence is higher.
I don't think
the twist in space
is of a standard of evidence
that people are going to abandon
the cosmological principle.
People buy lottery tickets
with worse odds.
It's not a crank paper.
It's not a stupid thing
to look at.

Augusta

SPORTS

Golf
To kick the s***!
A rare example of kicking a man
when he is up.
A rare example
of kicking a man
when he is up.

Couldn't have hit that any better,
he's got a three-shot lead,
all the pressure is on him...
he's got that to deal with,
that to sleep on tonight,
'*I am leading,
I mean I guess so.*'
At the same time,
he's going for the career
grand slam,
you can see this either way.

The man recovered of the bite.
The dog it was that died.
I'm hoping one day
he'll talk about his past.
It would be a great cleansing process for him,
but I don't know if he will ever do that...
What happened at Georgia,
what happened at Augusta State,
what happened with his parents?
I wish he would get it off his chest,
because I think it would help him
become a better person.

Automated Teller Machine

ECONOMY

    ATM
    It's about having the choice,
    if you've lost your card
    or left home without your wallet,
    chances are
    you still have your smartphone
    in your hand.

    Skimming,
    we've put safeguards in place
    to protect our customers,
    knock on wood,
    people's jaws dropped;
    they thought it was magical.
    You just had to look at the machine
    and money would come out.
    We want to be ready
    when people no longer carry cards
    and leave their wallet at home,
    but that timeline is developing
    more slowly than perhaps we thought
    it would a few years ago.

    Think of things that don't have cards
    issued against them,
    like money market accounts
    or Venmo,
    unlocking cash access
    to those accounts would be a really big deal.
    It isn't something I would rule out.

Automatic Firearms

GOVERNMENT

Firearms Manufacturer
All of them,
the Benedict Arnold of the gun industry.
Someone who is not a police officer
can buy one made elsewhere,
but we can't do anything about that,
what we can do
is be a responsible firearms manufacturer
ourselves
and we believe we are.

Studied gun metallurgy,
gun mechanisms
and gun designs
came to regard the gun
as a uniquely engineered tool.
When you mention
you are in the gun business,
people looked shocked,
they infer that you have an utter disregard
for human life,
which is preposterous.
There's so much hostility,
so many people stimulated
to violence,
but to be talking about gun legislation
as a cure for this
is ridiculous.

To take a responsible position
to head off any further restrictions
that might even have banned
all semiautomatic firearms,
Ruger and His Guns.

You give people
who are truly anti-gun
an inch
and they'll take a mile,

as I am sure you can appreciate,
Mr. Ruger died many years ago
and folks who were around
and worked with him directly
are long gone.
Indeed,
none of the Ruger family
has been involved
in the day-to-day operations
of the business
for more than a decade,
as such,
there really isn't anyone who can speak
to his comments
or views.

I'm a big believer
in the Second Amendment,
I'm a gun owner
and take my son shooting,
I think it's completely reasonable
to make it more difficult
for those who do not have a legitimate right
to a firearm to obtain them.

You know,
the National Rifle Association
used to be very big supporters of mine,
institutionally;
they are not so much anymore.
I will say honestly,
a vast majority of Pennsylvanians
agree with my approach
on background checks,
so on balance,
I don't think it hurt me politically.

The way to move Congress
is to show where the people stand
on this issue
and you do that most effectively
through state ballots
and state legislation,

if the truth be known,
I see no real harm in the concept,
the trouble is,
where does it end?

Avocado

NATURE

Stumping.
There is a lot of anxiety
and angst out there,
water is not something
you can skimp on.
Plants either get what they need
or they die.

People need to know
that in Southern California,
water is a precious resource,
but they'd rather water their lawns
and cut off the farmer.

You pray it's not going to be the case,
but there are some
that are on the edge.

The tree would be hurt
more having water cut back
than if you cut it down
and shut the water off,
where do I go
with a tree
that's as high as that beam?
What about trees this high,
maybe 3 years old?

Some of them said,
'*I had a broken pipe,
if push comes to shove,
we can shut the meter off.*'

I think I'm waiting until the last minute,
you have these trees
you've been raising for 40 years
and now I'm going to wipe
both the crop
and the trees.

As long as they have enough water
to put on their lawn
and wash their dishes,
they're happy.

SOCIETY

Baby

B

*"I've never lost hope,
I believe
that every parent
has the obligation
to fight
for their children,
to struggle
on their behalf."*

It's very sad for me
to see Ignacio
in the state he's in.
I asked God to cure him,
to alleviate him,
to give him health.
Everything in our lives has changed,
I'm always nervous about them,
always vigilant with them,
he's getting very heavy,
the day is going
to arrive when
I won't be able to carry him.
Some days,
when he just cries and cries
and we don't know what
is hurting him,
I just sit down beside him
and I cry too.
I do not speak English,
so there is nothing
that I could have said to her.

I worry all the time:
what is going to happen
with my boy?
The boy who beat my son
he is in the right place now,
with doctors
who will take care of him,
I hope that someday,
he will forget
what he's done
and lead a normal life.
My wife
and I talk about this a lot.
We end up crying,
I've never lost hope,
I believe

that every parent
has the obligation
to fight
for their children,
to struggle
on their behalf.
His brain is at rest,
it just doesn't grow
like we would like for it to.

It's global,
the problem that we all,
as parents,
develop expectations for our kids,
having these hopes
and aspirations one day
and then the next day finding.

Bail Bond

JUSTICE

A Declaration of War.
We have the responsibility to stand against
the forces of tumult
and division.
Dog the Bounty of Hunter,
we must stand united
and strong,
willing to fight back
and wage war against
the special interests
who would destroy law
and order in this country
to advance their radical agenda.

I think the reason you're seeing such intensity
by the bail industry to undermine reform
in New Jersey is that it will have an effect
on the national landscape,
the industry is upset
about losing business in New Jersey,
but the bigger problem is:
if there's successful reform
in New Jersey,
it can be replicated elsewhere.

A modern-day scarlet letter.
Severe deprivations of liberty,
created a system
where African-Americans
in New Jersey,
disparate treatment.
The right to companionship
with her son.

Dangerous, fake reform.
People are not in jail,
because they're poor–
They're in jail,
because they broke the law.

Excessive bail.
A catastrophe,
it's enormously unjust
and it enormously costly
and now that it's being scrutinized by people
and the government,
I don't think the industry's efforts
to fight this movement will succeed.

Bail Bonds

JUSTICE

Criminal
It would put us out of business completely,
Junior.
King.
It's better to know me
and not need me
than to need me
and not know me.
We're a mom
and pop store–
a San Diego family business.

Pretrial risk assessment.
Validated risk assessment tool.
Low risk.
Medium risk.
I stand to lose a business
that I built from nothing,
'Am I sad?
I am very sad.
I am not sad for Wendy,
the bail bondwoman.
I'm sad for California,
because we're going to lose
our Eighth Amendment right
to bail.
I'm here to rescue you,
people are treated very badly
when they're arrested,
but just because you were arrested
doesn't mean you need to be treated
like a criminal.'

The law will put tens of thousands
of criminals back out on the streets,
I think it was irresponsible
of the legislature
to pass this bill.
It's very disheartening

that the governor did not stand up
to Senate Bill 10,
our job in California
is to make sure people are treated fairly,
not to protect one industry
over another.

I would be out of business
if my client didn't show up to court,
I employ 19 full-time investigators
that help make sure defendants go to court,
if someone misses court,
we don't put a warrant into the system.
We put them into custody...
We spend 2.1 million a year...
on recovery,
locating individuals.

I can see why people would think that,
King.
But there's a false narrative
spread by the people
who created this bill.
They act like people are languishing in jail,
because they can't afford to bail out.
Most people don't know this,
but bail bond companies
don't charge 10 percent anymore.
They can charge up to 10 percent,
but most of the time it's way under that.
There's a lot of negotiation
that goes on
depending on what they can afford.

Bankruptcy

DEBT

Our decision to initiate
a court-supervised restructuring
was a difficult,
but important step to address
our immediate liquidity issues,
the court process will allow us
to right-size our balance sheet
and reduce our debt.

Yield co, a subsidiary that buys projects
from its parent company
to fuel growth,
free up cash
and pay shareholders
a big dividend yield.

It doesn't work
to try to be the biggest
and the biggest market share
at the expense of profits,
you do have to have some focus on:

A.   Your strategic competencies
             and
A.   The bottom line.

One of Sun Edison's problems
was that they had no idea
what was going on
within its divisions,
because it had so many of them;
I certainly long ago lost count.
It was dabbling in wind,
it was talking about storage,
sending teams into new markets
all the time.
There's a lot of stuff there
that needs to be sorted out.
Cooperative award.

The simple reality
is that many of these companies
have been depending on financing,
especially federal financing
and its means they take risks
they normally would not take.

Intend to seek all legal remedies
available to it
in respect of such a willful breach.
I think what we found
is that management
was incredibly optimistic
as how to deal with
what they were pulling together
would pan out
and that optimism ran counter
to the market forces at large.

There are good projects here
that have signed contracts in place
and they have very reasonable returns
associated with them,
you have a number of other developers
and solar assess buyers
that will be interested in taking this on,
looking at these projects
and perhaps taking them off of Sun Edison's hands.
You can see some of its peers
like Sun Power
and First Solar are profitable businesses.
You can see that he industry itself
is growing both within the U.S.
and at a global level
and that the cost of solar
is falling as well.

Bankruptcy

ECONOMY

Paying back the debt is important,
because it shows fiscal prudence
and by repaying the debt early,
they are giving themselves
more operating flexibility
in the future,
but things seem
to be going smoothly,
they seem to be on target.
In the long term,
they have more to do
than just meet debts.
They have to operate the county.
They can't just hold up shop.
They have core responsibilities
in the community.
Very impressed.
What they've been doing
is a sign of fiscal discipline.

We have this black cloud of debt
hanging over the taxpayers
of Orange County
and repaying it
should be a top priority.
We are always getting requests
to spend money
on new programs,
but this board
has to learn to say no.
I think we have already addressed
bond defeasance early repayment
as a priority
and need to look at other areas.
There is a price you pay
when you don't keep up maintenance–
it ends up costing more.
When you talk about
building more jail beds,

it's an issue of community safety.
All the indicators are looking up.
The bankruptcy is being forgiven,
from what I can see,
Orange County's debt
was never really that high.
So they've gone from a county
with very little debt
to one somewhere in the middle.

Beach Explorer

AMERICA'S NEW TRIUMPH

Miocen Epoch Clams

I looked over and saw these clams,
then I realized
they were sitting inside rocks
in the tide pools.
The rocks were filled with lava flows.
I figured they have to be pretty old.
When he told me that the fossils
appeared to be Miocen Epoch Clams
and likely 17 million years old.

This the Miocen Epoch,
a period when the megalodon,
an extinct species
of a stockier version of the great white,
swam in the oceans,
this was the beginning of the whales
and primitive sea lions.
The megalodons would have been swimming
in water above these invertebrates.
These clams used to be at the bottom of the ocean.
Over time they washed up higher on shore
and died.

This creature would likely have crunched
the invertebrates using its cylinder-like tooth
from its upper
and lower mouth to crush them,
they would have lived here
more than 12 million years ago
and would have come over from Asia.

Geologists will note the location
and get a Global Position System reading
and through that get an idea
why these fossils are right here
and nowhere else along here –
by putting this on maps,

it puts together a history of the area.

It's exciting,
because the average person
doesn't walk across fossils
that are 17 million years old,
to hear how it all began
and how it's exposed now –
as a person who loves the ocean,
that's neat to see.

SOCIETY

The Beep

Leave your message after the beep.
There are moments of my day
where I think,
if I hear another beep,
I think I am going to shoot
the disease.

The sound was something
very remote,
very powerful
and very frightening;
after all,
it was a man made entity in space
over the United States.
The beep made it much more real.
For some reason,
Americans believe that the device needs
to shout at you–
hence the loud beep.
The French,
on the other hand,
believe that the user should not be distracted
from solving the problem,
that the device should indicate
the problem to the user
in a calm manner
and not get in the way
of solving the problem.

The time has come for the beep
to die an honorable death.

If you wanted to design an annoying sound,
you can't do much better than a beep,
beeping is cheap.

Beeps have become
like the little boy
who cried wolf,

they are often ignored
even when they might have been useful.
Having a computer that constantly
emits the identical sound
whether it is just happy to see you
or is on fire
and about to explode
is akin to having a housemate
that is similarly afflicted.
Human factors.
It's a pity people don't use chimes
and bells more often.
Uh-oh!
You've got mail!
Uh-oh!
So sue me!
D'oh!
Star Wars…

The downfall of the beep is only in fiction,
in the real world,
the beep is still thriving.
When people start designing devices
that demonstrate
subtle,
well designed sounds,
that are less intrusive
and more effective
than the beep,
the beep will be shamed…
in our
existence,
vibration was huge,
consumers just loved It.

Bankers are very sensitive
about not making mistakes,
so the beep gave the users
an immense amount of psychological stress;
if you use a beep to signal a problem,
people hate it,
because they feel socially responsible
for making a mistake.

Bees

NATURE

African
People were walking all over the bees,
driving over the bees,
they felt the dying bees
all over the ground.
That just makes no sense to me.

It's heartbreaking to hear
that with all the trouble of
trying to bring bees in the area
and they would go out
and just decimate the hive,
it just seems irresponsible.

Deathly allergic.
We don't take a chance
with public safety.
When you're trying to relocate
a beehive,
it takes more time
and you're increasing the risk
that someone may be stung.
Bees are not endangered.

Belarus

UNITED NATIONS

We had the skit where
I was Dr. Zubr
and I had a queue of
Lukashenkes coming to see me,
they were saying,
"*Doctor,
I don't know
what's wrong with me,
I constantly jail people.
I kill them.
I don't want to keep doing this,
but there's nothing I can do
to stop myself.
What's wrong with me?
What do I do?*"
I would reply back to them,
"*Well,
it's clear that you can no
longer govern the state,
you should step down;*"
after I diagnosed two patients,
I was just taken away.

The last dictatorship in Europe.
One of the notes
that the United States can play
is to speak clearly
about the need for Belarus to be free,
are plain banditry
disguised as democracy;
no amount of money
will be able to topple the existing
authorities in Belarus.
I want those who carry this money in sacks
and suitcases
through embassies to Belarus
to hear this message.

The big problem
is that 99% of the population
here are zombies.
Round the clock,
the broadcast media work
toward the common goal of turning people
into zombies.
I wouldn't be surprised if Lukasharks
come out on central television tomorrow
and announces he's gotten a scientific
report that walking on all fours
improves digestion.

Biologist

JUSTICE

When a car is found on the bridge
with the keys in the ignition,
our experiences have been
it's a suicide.
At the top of his generation,
I don't know what to say,
we're all at such a loss
no one knows what happened.

It's sad,
but every year we get five
or six jumpers who leave
their car on the bridge
and sometimes don't find a body
for months.
We still don't have any answers.

He was so upbeat
and successful,
I had seen him
on many occasions
and I had never seen
a dark side.
In variably,
he was very,
very solid.
He didn't have that edge
of mania
that some very upbeat people have
that makes you wonder
if they are capable of something like that.
Maybe there is an independent streak
that could have gotten him in trouble
when he was accosted,
he was highly,
highly original,
known for tackling problems
that seem beyond the bounds of possibility
to others,

Don was invariably friendly,
but also sort of critical,
like a scientist should be.

Was not overseeing,
advising,
consulting
or assisting in any way.
There's never been any evidence
that this is connected to terrorism,
it's not like anyone has called up
and said,
"*we've got the doctor
and he's going to make a bioterror weapon.*"
I told them it was a missing person case,
nothing else,
at least not now.

Black Friday

ECONOMY

Holiday Sale
Black Friday.
In-store specials,
obnoxiously good deals
on High School Musical 3 DVDs,
cashmere,
Cuisinart,
boots,
coats,
Black Friday never fails to attract people.

Door Busters.
The drop-off in traffic on Friday
seemed more marked to me
than it did in years past–
it could mean we're heading
toward a lukewarm Christmas.

Plain and simple,
it's all about electronics,
before we opened,
we already had 50 to 100
people waiting outside,
buy one,
get one free.

When things are great,
saving $200 may not be
with the effort,
but when you're struggling
to pay bills,
because of higher fuel
or food process the $200 savings
may mean whether you can buy
the Christmas presents
for your children or not.

Border Wall

IMMIGRATION

Up to 20.
Aesthetically pleasing to color,
for us,
that's called home-court advantage,
we were going to turn the wall
on its side,
if you will,
I have no interest
in designing
or building anything
that will further Trump's agenda.

I understand that project
is extremely polarizing,
some projects you don't like,
but you have to do your job
and sell the product.
In the world of supply,
you follow the large projects.

There are other things being built
that are more cost-effective
and just as good,
it's lightweight,
durable
and strong as hell,
it's what they need.

Bosch's City

VENUES

Forever link Bosch to Den Bosch,
we thought:
There's something more
than the paintings,
there's this intangible heritage,
another aspect of Bosch,
his time,
his city,
the market square,
his studio.
That's all holy ground.

Hieronymus Bosch:
Visions of Genius,
Bosch by Night,
Garden of Earthly Delights,
Jheronimus:
The Road to Heaven
and Hell,
brown cafe,
Jeroen Bosch,
1450 – 1516.

This order had a certain religious glamour
and there were more people
who wanted to be part of it,
so they started taking members
who weren't clergy –
dues-paying members,
but at the core they were
sworn brothers –
they were 'made men' –
and they belonged to the church's
hierarchy.
Sworn brother,
it didn't mean that he
was allowed by the church
to exorcise demons in people.
That was only done

by full priests,
just being called an exorcist,
for an artist who dealt
so heavily in demons,
is something that must've
meant a lot to him.
Garden of Earth Delights.
Bosch Experience,
Ascent of the Blessed.

Brazil

UNITED NATIONS

Presidential Race
It is necessary to consider
which of these two principles
must be sacrificed
in the name of an election
that is neutral
and not tainted by deceitful news,
sometimes the excessive concern
with freedom of expression
ends up violating
a more important principle–
the democratic principle.

It is our intention to infringe
on anyone's freedom of expression
or their right to voice an opinion,
the big question is
when does a personal opinion
become a lie
about a candidate
that is published
with the specific intent
of harming them
and in doing so
interfering with an election.

These laws are not adequate
to apply to the tactics of today,
the evolution of the internet
and communication,
makes it hard
to be relying on laws
from the 80's,
the 60's
and the 40's.

The elections in Brazil
are a priority for us
and we have been taking a series of steps

to make sure our platform
gives people a voice,
encourages civic engagement
and helps strengthen democracy.
We have made several product improvements
to reduce the reach of low quality content,
eliminate the economic incentives
behind most fake news
and prioritize content from trustworthy
and informative sources.

While there is always more to do,
we believe the actions
we are taking
will help prevent
the spread of blatantly misleading,
low quality
and downright false information,
we have already seen
troublesome initiatives
and a proliferation of laws
aiming at active monitoring
and regulating of online speech
and delegating fact-checking to authority.
In the American election,
freedom of expression
trumped over fake news,
here in our country may be exercised,
it can also be abused.

Brazil

UNITED NATIONS

Rio de Janeiro
It's all bars,
walls with broken glass on top.
If there are flowers,
they have thorns
for a defensive effect.
An isolated house
is poison on the market.
Security is the top priority,
the great challenge,
of every project.
You can't work freely.
Security defines everything.
We are going back to the Middle Ages.
We are history behind walls.

Armed response.
Lightning abductions.
I made a gentleman's agreement
with the robbers–
I told them I would help them
get anything they wanted
out of the apartment,
as fast as possible,
as long as they did not hurt
my wife
or my daughter.

Incompetence of the state.
Parallel states.
Violence is the fruit of hunger,
in that sense,
it is a hard place to raise kids,
it makes them distorted young people.
They never leave.
They grow up thinking
life is beaches,
shopping malls
and beautiful girls.

They don't know
the first thing
about getting around the city.

It is penitentiary existence,
the rich in Brazil
are prisoners of themselves…
I hope that,
in the future,
the 'Alpha villains' will realize
that it is better not live
in such an isolated manner.

A rising number of individuals
are sometimes criminals using heavy weapons,
so criminals are being hired to protect property,
because of this,
illegal security has become a public safety problem.
Today,
you have infrared devices,
cameras the size of a button,
but the big worry is well-trained men,
just as police are involved
with drug traffickers,
there is corruption
within security companies.
We have to guard the guards.
We have to work very hard
on recruitment,
psychological testing
and periodic checks on our people.

Brexit

UNITED NATIONS

European Union Citizens

Stop Brexit.
To say no to Brexit.
You have the chance to vote Labour
in the local council election
to send a clear message that you,
like us,
are against Brexit
and the lack of uncertainty
about the rights of Europeans Union citizens.

Fully supports.
Betrayal.
Britain is not leaving the European Union.
European Citizens –
your chance to say no to Brexit,
the vote on May 3rd
presents possibly the only opportunity
for you to influence the Brexit debate,
please take it.

Practical steps.
Campaign to stop Brexit.
Stop Brexit.
Hammersmith & Fulham Labour
has taken this independent stand,
because we believe it is the night thing to do.
Whatever happens next
will affect our country
and our continent for generations to come.
We are campaigning to stay in the European Union.

Our manifesto was quite clear
that we were going to implement the decision
of the referendum
in leaving the European Union.
That's the important electoral
decision results will have no influence

on it whatsoever.
Labour accepts the referendum result
and a Labour governement
will put the national interest first.

Mention the positives.
Opportunities of Brexit.
Maneuvers.
Deserves the full support
of her ministers,
Leavers
and Remainders alike.

Boris Johnson
and Philip Hammond…
must understand
that the surest route
to a bad deal,
is to go on behaving
as they are.
They must stop their games now,
because the stakes for Britain are too high.

The negotiations are structured
within the European Union
so of course
the council has delegated a mandate
to the commission,
the commission
has appointed Michael Barnier,
but the decision will always
be taken by leaders.

Divorce bill.
Goodwill gestures are not enough–
it is doubtful
that European Union member states
would consider that offer
£ 20 billion to be sufficient
progress on its own.

The Prime Minister
does not need to set out
the exact solution tomorrow,

but she can set out the Government's parameters.
These details are important,
but they are inherently technical.
That,
together with the Treasury's reluctance
to even mention the positives
of leaving the European Union,
such as the Brexit dividend,
is why the Government
has not talked positively
often enough about the opportunities
of Brexit.

For our industry,
this really is crunch time,
many firms are already moving parts
of their operations out
of the United Kingdom
and Europe.
When they're gone,
it's hard to see them coming back.
The states grew as closely as possible,
it's too late to plug the exits,
people are already moving–
it's now a case of slowing it down;
in an ideal world
it would be brilliant
if people could press the pause button,
but we've gone beyond that.

Buddhist Chanting

FAITH

I feel it just makes me
a better human being,
more human,
it enables me to understand
the suffering of others
and reach out to others.
It is a philosophy,
a way of life.

Searching for some meaning.
I felt there was a vacuum
in my life,
the chanting has helped
it stops you from thinking
about only yourself;
it makes one think of others first.
The chanting is not invasive
and runs parallel
to what we practice as Hindus,
it opens a doorway
to another stream of happiness
into one's life.

Hindu chanting is linked
to religious ritual,
Buddhist chanting is a free space
where you chant
and are not tied down
to other aspects of religiosity.

Nam-Myoho Renge-Kyo,
you feel invigorated.
It's a great feeling,
if I didn't chant,
if I went back home
with all the heaviness of this
very challenging work…
I would not be able to survive,
I would have a compassion deficit.

Burgers

ECONOMY

Premium

McDonald's is so secure
in its own market
that now it's going after casual dining,
for four bucks,
that is hard to beat.

It may be the last affordable luxury,
it's an easy way to reward yourself
without feeling like you're blowing the bank.

You should be flashing a warning light
before you order this,
because if you do order it,
be prepared to share it.

It gets folks to spend more money
without raising prices.
It's intended to satisfy burger lovers.
Far exceeded our expectations,
if it continues as it does right now,
we'll keep selling it.
This is a game-change for us,
it pushes the ceiling on what we've offered,
but there's very little consumer pushback,
we're catching casual dining customers
trading down.

A premium burger
is any burger
that a restaurant can convince
you is somehow better than average.
I doubt that the average consumer
understands that Angus is a breed of cattle;
people will buy it,
because food chains are very good marketers.
They can make Angus

sound like it has a chorus of angels
behind it.
Premium.
Beauty is in the hand
of the beholder,
it's good to be at the top
of the food chain.

Premium burger.
High-quality.
Angus.
Sirloin.
If McDonald's does it right,
it's good for the industry,
but if they do it wrong,
it's bad for the industry.
If they doubled their price,
we'd probably still pay it,
but if they want to change who they are,
well,
that's up to them.

Business Plan

ECONOMY

I am the owner,
employee,
accountant,
driver
and cleaning up crew.

She drastically underestimated
the amount of money
it was going to take.
Has excellent technical skills,
it's one of her major strengths,
she went into this
without really having a business plan.

This really does work,
it's not just textbook stuff.
Instead of immediately trying
to make the leap of Peachtree
or Quicken,
a very simple way to keep track of her time
and money,
price administration
is the single most important item
a small business person needs
to focus on.
Friends
and family are the largest source
of equity for a start-up business.

There are a lot of places
to get loans if you have a business plan
and good credit,
this all comes back to the business plan
and the need to analyze the budget
to see where she really needs to be,
you can't survive for long undercapitalized.

Butterflies

WORLD WILDLIFE

Blue
Look at the seams.
This one is ready to pop.
Go!
Go!
Go!
You can do it!
Go!
Pop.
Hatching,
Shake it off,
this is the part that
makes me so freaking nervous.
We can't fly
and if he can't fly,
he can't mate
and if you're not pretty,
you get rejected.

Do what you gotta do,
defying gravity,
wicked.
Don't look down,
it's renewed my faith
in the resilient nature
of this species,
that said,
we've given it a lot
of help along the way.

Rescuing butterflies
kind of rescue me,
I have never seen someone
watch it
and say,
"Oh,
that's nice,"
they just light up.

When you watch a living thing
struggling for its survival,
it's automatically the underdog,
and you just start cheering it on.

Butterflies

WORLD WILDLIFE

Monarch
Stampede.
This year we will have great numbers
of monarchs.
Each butterfly has to get to Mexico,
and there are three
or four generations
removed from the butterflies
that moved north
in the Spring,
the real question
is how does a butterfly in Maine
know where it is,
as opposed to a butterfly
in Minnesota?
How do they sense
in an approximate way where they are?
They use a sun compass–
they,
in effect,
have a physiological mechanism
that can track the position of the sun
and they use this as a guidance system,
but that can't be the entire mechanism
by which they get to Mexico.

Cambodians

IMMIGRATION

Americans

People would come here
and forget all about their grief
and just relax
and remember the things
that made them happy.
It was a place of healing,
killing fields,
sometimes it's like the sky
was too high for them,
but we are still trying
to get to the top.

People know us as victims,
but we want our people
to be proud again,
we've talked about it enough
let's talk about something else.
I shouldn't have stood in the way
of what my people wanted
we lost half the nation.
You cannot even fathom
the sorrow of the people.
That's why this name,
the killing fields,
must be remembered,
the killing fields was five years.
We have a 3,000 year-old culture.
We were kings.
We made some of the greatest wonders
of the world;
Made in Cambodia.

Nothing is going to happen
in Cambodia Town
until the younger generation steps up,
the vision to see your culture grow.
The vision of Cambodian strong!!!

All Khmers,
please remember the roots
of our great country,
I hear baby cry
and I watch them grow.
They'll learn much more
than I'll ever know
and I think to myself,
what a wonderful world.

Campaign Finance Reform

GOVERNMENT

Open-Door Policy

Legalized corruption.
Illusory.
Super PACs.
The bottom line
is we have very serious problems
with the functioning
of our democracy
caused by the unstrained flow
of influence-seeking money
into the elective,
the amounts are unprecedented
and provide an extraordinary advantage
to the very rich,
when you are dealing
with huge amounts of money–
and when there are no laws
to contain them–
they overwhelm the process
in a way that small sums can't.

Abuse of entrusted power
for private gain.
The corruption in the United States
does not stem from officeholders–
putting money in their pockets,
this is systemic corruption
of the process itself.
When you are dealing with billions
and billions of dollars,
much of that focused
on buying influence,
it overwhelms the system
and it is much harder to defend against
and maintain representation
for ordinary Americans.

All politicians are corrupt.
Strongly reflect the preferences
of the most affluent,
but bear virtually no relationship
to the preferences of poor
and middle-income Americans.

Some argue
that there is no casual relationship,
but as numerous former congressmen
have testified,
that is not the case,
huge amounts of money
are not being given
for charitable purposes,
but to obtain benefits.

There are indirect ways
of buying favors
which work in more subtle ways.
You are influenced
by the people around you–
who you spend time with,
who you have dinner with.

Canada UNITED NATIONS

Aurora, Ontario I thought people passing
by couldn't see it
and the developers
wouldn't see it,
so it didn't bother
my conscience too much.
Using a dryer
may have made sense
30 years ago
when energy was cheap
and we weren't aware
of global warming;
it doesn't anymore.
Right to dry.
I can see why
people would want to do it
for the environment,
but the houses here
are so close together,
you don't really want to look
at your neighbor's laundry.

If we can't change
simple stuff like this,
we'll never handle the big things,
we need to do for the planet.
Barrier to conservation.
People say,
'*Oh,*
Phyllis,
you want to turn women
back into the laundry lady?'
It's about the environment.
Restrictive covenants.
The people who moved here
wanted convenience
and a suburban paradise–
sheets
and clothes hanging out
symbolized a less sufficient time.

I'm not worried,
these days the people
who are skulking around
aren't the ones drying
their clothes outside,
but the ones who oppose it.

A clothesline
is not a solar panel
or a Prius–
it's something that
everyone can afford.

Similar
as drying clothes on clotheslines
or clothes racks.

When it comes to drying clothes,
we find that our consumers
are very busy
and are looking
for the fastest dry time.
Of course,
line drying is the more energy–
efficient option,
provided the weather is good,
but it is not convenient
or time efficient.

We spend a lot of money
on architecture and design–
we tell builders
which windows they may use–
so this is a long list of protections
that evolve to protect homeowners,
to keep things looking
nice for everyone,
this is the right time.
I think many developers
would gladly delete it–
but some people
will not like the fact
that they're seeing
their neighbor's underwear.

Canada

UNITED NATIONS

Moose Jaw, Saskatchewan

Atlantic city.
You'd marry anyone
to get out of Moose Jaw,
Saskatchewan.
The Friendly City.
It was a revelation,
the Canadian self-image
is that we have a bland history
that the American West
was violent
and colorful,
while in Canada
it was peaceful
and bland.
Once the tunnel thing exploded,
people went,
'*Wow*!'
and instead of calling Moose Jaw
'*the Friendly City*,'
it became '*Little Chicago*.'

'*Uncle Al*.'
Uncle Al is a big draw,
people are jumping
on the bandwagon.

Research tourism.
I call tourism the shake
of the new millennium,
the last thing I need
is to be the guy
who kicks this thing.

BETTER FUTURE | 111

Cancer Researcher

AMERICA'S NEW TRIUMPH

Everyone asks me,
why haven't you found
a cure for cancer.
I tell them,
you don't understand
that we're just now finding out
all these new things
related to cancer.
We're entering a whole new phase
of cancer research.
We really didn't understand
how cancer worked,
but now we think we do.
My goal is to be able
to tell a sixty-year-old man
with prostatic cancer
that he can do something
to slow down the growth
of that tumor
so it won't impact
his lifespan for thirty years.
If we can slow down
the growth of prostate cancer,
which already is a slow-growing tumor,
that would be tantamount
to a cure for men
who are in their sixties
and seventies;
it may be that programmed cell death
can be altered
by the nutrients around the cells.

Sparks.
P-53 gene that blocks
programmed cell death
when it becomes mutated,
is kind of the last ditch
emergency brake
a cell has,

if a cell recognizes that
it's going to turn into a cancer,
it then turns on the P-53 gene
and commits hara-kiri.
If you mutate P-53,
you deprive the cell
of even that last refuge.
This raises the possibility
that former smokers
are responding favorably
and it certainly raises
an even stronger possibility
that they are responding
differently than current smokers.
I used to think that
I wouldn't see any cures for cancer
in my lifetime,
but now I do.
Actual genetic cures,
it hasn't quite happened yet,
but I believe it probably will happen
over the next couple of decades,
which means it might be next year
or it might be twenty years from now;
It won't be longer than that.

Cancer Treatment

SOCIETY

You never get used to the size
and scope.
Cancer.
Making cancer history.
I thought they were going
to save him.
A chance to live longer.
You get your hopes up,
and then you are dropped
off the edge of a cliff,

I'm starting to hear more
and more that we are better
than I think we really are.
We have a lot of patients
who spend their families into bankruptcy
getting a hyped therapy
that many know is worthless;
game changer.
I thought we were going to have
a treatment where we'd at least
have a good block
of quality time.

We continue to see great strides
in identifying the generic mutations
and related factors
that can drive the seemingly random formation
at abnormal cells in cancer.
Cure cancer in two years,
eliminating suffering
and death
due to cancer.
We're offering what we have,
but making it appear that it's
more than what it is,
there is a disconnect
between what researchers think
is statistically significant

and what is really significant for patients,
patients hear 'progress,'
and they think that means
they're going to be cured.
We use national media to help educate
cancer patients
and their families about the latest
diagnostic tools
and treatment options...
All of our advertising undergoes
meticulous review for clinical accuracy
as well as legal approval to ensure
we tell our story in an informative
and responsible manner,
in compliance with federal guidelines.

A chance to live longer.
A chance for a longer life.
It's true.
Your heart sinks
when you see those ads,
makes you wonder if they're
going down the same path
that we did.
At the time of patient follow-up,
time of follow-up.

It's not false;
it's just incomplete,
they don't give patient's
or the patient's family enough information
to make a reasonable decision.
The physician is the ultimate decider
on treatment,
they made false
and unsubstantiated claims
in advertisement
and promoting their cancer treatments.
Genomic testing.
Precision cancer treatment.

Cannabis

SOCIETY

U.S. Food and Drug Administration (FDA)

An aide came to reception
and asked,
'*Where's the pot guy?*'
He seemed to be looking for someone
in a tie-dyed shirt
with a joint stuck behind his ear.
Pot.
Weed.
Cannabis.

People are taking a more sophisticated approach
to using cannabis,
especially in using the right dosing,
we don't want people to think of it as negative.
It had always called cannabis
either weed
or pot,
with the occasional 'grass'
or 'dope'
thrown in for variety
or to sound cool.

Baby Boomers.
Generation Xers.
Pot,
weed,
grass.
Merry Munchie Meal,
munchie.
People in our industry
and activists don't like the word 'pot',
because it doesn't focus
on the medicinal value of the plant,
which is what's important;
we don't like the word 'marijuana',
either.

You hear newscasters
referring to the dispensaries
as pop shops.
You don't hear the same newscasters
referring to a liquor store
as a booze shop
or an alcoholic's store;
language constantly changes.
It's the social process that can cause disruption.
The word 'gay'
used to have a much different meaning
than it generally does today.
People get accustomed to words.
Then the words go out of date.
They can be disruptive.
Disruptive.
Marijuana Menace.

I had to refrain myself
to use 'cannabis'
or 'medical marijuana'
in my new professional capacity,
as I quickly learned,
that industry
almost universally preferred those
over the names I was used to.
My dad was born in 1949
and he still refers to cannabis as pot,
even if I asked him not to.
I accept it.

Capital Punishment

GOVERNMENT

The rise in executions
last year is profoundly disturbing,
not for the last 25 years
have so many people been put to death
by the states around the world.
In 2015,
governments continued relentlessly
to deprive people of their lives
on the false premise
that the death penalty would make us safer.

Limitations in Amnesty International's ability
to corroborate data in a number of countries,
continued to use the death penalty
in ways that contravene international law
and standards;
including on people with mental
and intellectual disabilities.

Career Change

LABOR

Nineteen years,
nineteen years,
one job
and one company.
I was let go
about three months shy
of my 20th work anniversary.
It was my first job out of school,
I never really put together a resume
or even thought about looking
for another job,
because I really liked what I did
and the people I worked with;
I just assumed those reasons—
and the fact that I was good at my job—
were enough to stay there.

We worked on it
our next two meetings
and I went back
and really looked at what I did
in my former job
and mimicked everything out of it
that I could,
I am the perfect liaison
between your client
and your company,
the essential facilitator
who works with your sales,
production,
delivery
and maintenance teams
to ensure 100 percent customer satisfaction,
resulting in increased sales
and revenue,
with 18 years' experience.
I consistently helped customers
achieve their goals.

I was a casualty of consolidation,
there were people in another office
doing what I did
and they were doing it
for much less money.
I realized there were a lot of things
I didn't necessarily like
at my former job,
but I put up with them,
because I liked my situation,
I guess you call that complacency.

In large corporations,
all the good feelings in the world
can't make up for a loss of revenue
or overspending in a certain area,
if you look deep enough,
every employee-retention decision
that doesn't directly relate to performance
comes down to dollars.

My first resume was a bust,
because it was all about my experience
and what I had accomplished;
luckily,
my severance included five sessions
with a career coach
and the first thing she did
was to tell me that my resume
was total crap.
She told me–
and rightfully so,
I had to admit
after being initially shocked–
that my resume was like a historic document,
nothing about the future,
exactly,
I just-assumed my resume
was supposed to sum up
all of my experience,
but when all that experience
comes from one company,
it can come across as a history lesson.

Backing up a statement
about your proficiency
with actual numbers
is always a good idea,
tell me your customers love you
and I think,
*'Are you going to tell me
they hate you?'*
show me the amount of money
that customer love
helped produce instead.
That's how you get my attention.
Not money
employers are concerned with loyalty
these days,
because they know
they'll lose people
to the highest bidder,
but they still place a value
in employees who will stick it out
for a few years,
it's costly to train employees,
so bringing in someone with a resume
that includes six jobs
in five years is a risk.
Hiring someone who sees the value
in a long-term work relationship
can help companies with stability.
There's an expectation
that startups hire the best
and the brightest,
but with those hirings
comes another expectation–
that they'll move on
to the next startup with a year.

Career Connections

LABOR

I didn't go to camp as each child,
this is my adult version.
Camp counselors.
A few years ago
I met somebody
who ended up being a good friend.
He was a speaker,
we hung out,
bonded over beer
and stayed in touch ever since.

Instead of sitting in a hotel
at a conference in Las Vegas,
this seems different.
It's laid back,
you still learn something,
you get great speakers
and people's guards are down more,
it could last an extra day
or so with that many good speakers.
I always take something
out of each session
and it's also about the fun side of it,
like a 'Gong Show.'
Getting into that child side
of your personality
and letting loose
instead of being uptight business people.

You get to know these people
in a way that's so different
from a traditional conference,
we create
'sand boxes'
for the entrepreneurs
and thought-leaders–
grow yourself,
grow your business,
make a difference

in the world
and have fun.

Based on what you bring
to the campfire,
we'll be doing things
to break people out
of their comfort zones.
Easter eggs.
Built for Growth.
Sure,
you'll suffer day bit of withdrawal,
but if you merely change
your location
and remain in the thick of the battle
via your iPhone,
you have missed the point.
Principles of Transformational Leadership.

It's primarily about pulling away
from the highly scheduled
and stressful day-to-day.
The moment I went to camp,
I had a new set of friends.
We started a monthly breakfast
before work to keep each other accountable
for goals
and projects,
professional
or personal interests,
do we like the same activities?
Do we have a shared experience
with tug of war?
If you can start a relationship
from genuine fundamentals,
it's so much easier creating a business relationship
out of that rather than
'Oh, he works in X,
he can probably help me.'

Castle Doctrine

JUSTICE

I'm not going to let them
get away with this,
"*move and you're dead*".
I shot the burglar.
Castle doctrine.

Property is not worth killing
someone over.
Why is he still a free man?
Joe (Mr. Horn) didn't have
to kill these people;
Mr. Horn became the judge,
the jury
and the executioner.

Joe (Horn) gets a Texas '*attaboy*'
from me,
justice was served,
law
or not.
Urban Cowboy.
Castle doctrine.

Joe (Horn) has never
been anything,
but a gentle person.
He's not the type of master
that they are making him out to be,
castle doctrine.
He's not drunk at a bar somewhere,
he's a guy who intercedes
in a situation next door;
if a jury believes he was standing
in the shoes of the owner,
that might affect their decision.

This is not an individual
who stepped outside
and gunned down

two pedestrians on the sidewalk,
in a situation
where there is some uncertainty
about which side of the law
someone was on.
The best thing to do is assemble
all of the information
and present it to the grand jury.

Catalina Island Conservancy

NATURE

It's like the rising of the phoenix;
we're not looking to kill them all,
as some might tell you,
but we need to reduce the population
so that we can manage better.
Seed banks,
kick-started.
That's why we were in an emergency state,
because we had the potential
of losing 13% of the habitat,
including some really rare
plant associations.
Very tasty for the deer.

Nuclear devastation.
Killing is not the answer,
it's sickening,
it's horrible
and it's sad,
because tourists
and locals alike are very fond of these deer.

Catholic Churches

FAITH

Predatory Priests
Hand yourself over
to human justice
and prepare for divine justice,
hush up
or not take seriously any case.

They perform abominable acts,
yet continue to exercise their ministry,
as if nothing had happened.
They have no fear of God
or his judgment,
but only of being found out
and unmasked.
Their boundless amiability,
impeccable activity
and angelic faces,
they shamelessly conceal
a vicious wolf ready
to devour innocent souls.
Slander.

FAITH

Mother Teresa

Saint of the gutters.
She was the symbol of perfect love.
The poorest people–
people who others
would not even look at–
always had a place to go.

When she was here,
the poorest came to receive
and the rich came to give,
everybody loved Mother Teresa
and she loved them.

With Mother Teresa gone,
we wonder
if we will still be able to eat,
when we heard that she died,
we all started to cry.

Our beloved Mother Teresa
went home to Jesus.
For the sake of sorrow,
have mercy on us.
India has gained,
because Mother Teresa is in heaven;
she will be praying
in a very special way.
We have lost
the mother of India.

She has touched so many lives here.

Mother Teresa is a beautiful image
of our invisible God.
The Holy Father said to her,
"You must know that
I and the church
and the world love you,"

"He said he loves me."
and she got back on the phone
and said
"Holy Father,
I love you,
too
and I love the whole world."

At that point,
there was not a dry eye
in the room.

I personally hold to the fact
that the woman is a saint
of the church,
a saint of God.

It was a beautiful experience,
because the people
just really responded to her,
it really affected them,
you could see it in their eyes.

What a visit that was,
I think it's almost a sign
of contradiction for our time,
she's world famous,
world traveled,
yet completely devoted
to the sick
and dying.
What an example.
As far as I'm concerned,
she went straight up.

I still think
it's kind of amazing
in the sense
that out of all the photographs
that have been taken
of this person,
mine ended up being chosen.
I think it's the highlight
of my life as a photographer.

Catholicism

FAITH

New Catholic Church

Look at all you have accomplished
in 10 years,
you have done it here,
the Gospel's about living love,
our God
and each other.
You are on the right road
and the Lord is walking with you;
Never forget it.

It's a big day
for our diocese,
it is beautiful,
this is their church
we built this for them.

We love you father Tom.

Commonly known as Mother Teresa,
the religious sister
and missionary was born
in what is now Macedonia.
She eventually moved to Ireland
and then to India,
where she spent most of her life
a charismatic figure,
she drew widespread attention,
because of her prolife appeals,
her service to the poor,
her vows of poverty
and obedience.

Catholicism

FAITH

Saint Padre Pio
My heart is crying.
Whenever we had problems
or we felt sad,
we turned to Padre Pio.
He changed my life.

I pray to Padre Pio.
I don't ask for money
or anything like that,
but for love,
family unity
and peace.

He always had so many people
around him,
he'd look at you
with this steady gaze,
a stare
and you'd get scared,
because you knew,
he knew everything
you had done.

The faithful feel anguish
and astonishment
about what has happened
and many faithful are offended.
Hands Off Padre Pio!
Tampering with the dead.

Today we venerate his body,
inaugurating a period
of particularly intense pilgrimage.
The presence of Padre Pio's body
invited us above all to one memory,
all the good that he achieved
among us.

FAITH

World Youth Day
It wasn't too bad.
Actually it didn't really have an impact
on me;
I think he's still learning
how to address young people.
As we were saying yesterday,
half a year ago
he was just running around Rome
and now he's pope.
So he's still learning
and that's all right.

Benedetto!

Is there,
not Benedict himself.
Milestones.
There were Twelve Apostles
and each of them had her.

It is good that day.
In many cultures,
Sunday is a free day
and it is often combined
with Saturday
so as to constitute
a weekend
of free time;
yet this free time is empty
if God is not present.
Sometimes our initial impression
is that having to include time for Mass
on a Sunday is rather inconvenient,
but if you make the effort,
you will realize
that this is what gives a proper
focus to your free time.

It is pushed too far,
religion becomes almost
a consumer product,
religion constructed
on a *'do-it-yourself'* basis
cannot ultimately help us.

It was very impressive for me
to see that this was primarily
a listening pope.
My own opinion
is that condoms are a way to be safe,
because AIDS makes problems
in Africa,
but with time,
maybe the position
of the pope will change.

Relativism—
what do you mean by that?
We try not to judge others.

Center for Disease Control and Prevention (CDC)

HEALTHCARE

HIV/AIDS

We have the technology,
we have the expertise,
to prevent HIV
and allow those
who unfortunately contract it
to live healthy
and productive lives,
but the funding is never enough
and the stigma in the South
is still a debilitating factor;
especially for people of color.

Trump's war on the Affordable Care Act–
his policies that would make it harder
for people to get on
or to stay on Medicaid,
work against the first step
in controlling the epidemic,
if you look at the map of HIV rates
and pull up another map
of Medicaid expansion states,
guess what?
many of the states
that didn't extend Medicaid
or that put work requirements into place
are the states that are struggling with HIV.
Hot spots,
if we don't expand Medicaid
in our Southern states,
it's going to be very difficult
to eradicate HIV,
HIV is an epidemic
that is entrenched in poverty
and inequality,
you can't separate the inequalities–
the racism,

the homophobia,
the transphobia–
from this epidemic.
It drives the epidemic.

We can do everything we can
to have the services that they need,
but the funding is never enough,
people have to make all kinds of choices:
'*Should I pay my rent
or should I take my meds?*'
'*Do I spend $2.50 to travel to the clinic
or do I buy a sandwich?*'
We are already stretching beyond our seams.
People who inject drugs–
that's where the emerging challenge is,
but the South lags behind.

We're still not talking about sex in Mississippi,
we're not talking about it in the Legislative,
we're not talking about it in the schools
and we're not talking about it in the church,
in order to talk about HIV,
you have to talk about sex.

Central American Migrant

IMMIGRATION

These are our people,
we want to do what we can
for them.
The caravan is not going to lose
its unity,
we are going to insist
and insist
and insist until we are able to enter,
if God allows.
La Lista.
The List was born.
As long as we're not in Honduras,
there's no problem.
We feel very relaxed waiting.

If we had work
and a proper government in Honduras,
we couldn't have had to embark
on this difficult trip
and live outdoors,
this ambassador
and all the other politicos
from Honduras
should be in jail!
They stole all the money!
We live in a regular house in Honduras,
but the branches here
help keep the place cool
in the day
and warm in the evening.

I'm glad to find better condition,
but I can't go to the other side.
I can't go back to there,
I ask for asylum.
I went up to the border
and asked to come into
the United States,

but they said '*No!*'
Maybe I'll apply for asylum here,
just so I can find another shelter,
but there's no way
I'm going back to Honduras.

Crisis.
Short-term solution.
There is no agreement
of any sort between the future
Mexican federal government
and the United States,
since the first caravan arrived,
about 3,500 have applied
for asylum in Mexico.
People are scared.
Scared that there will be repercussions
from the people of Tijuana,
there was a rumor
that they were going to evict us.
A lot of people are asking to go home.

Violent behavior
of a group of migrants.
They tried to enter the United States
with violence
and that had a very strong effect
on Tijuana,
the port of entry
is of utmost importance
for the economy of the city
to do its job
so that these migrants
are in compliance
with our immigration laws.
Be immediate subject
to the corresponding deportation process.
Until their claims
are individually approved
in court,
stay in Mexico,
catch
and release.

Our very strong policy
is Catch
and Detain,
No Releasing into the United States.
Safe third country.

IMMIGRATION

Chain Migration

Chain migration.
I can confirm that Mrs. Trump's parents
were both lawfully admitted
to the United States
as permanent residents.
The family,
as they are not part of the administration,
has asked that their privacy be respected;
so I will not comment further
on this matter.
Chain migration.

That would be the logical way to do it,
the preferred way to do it
and possibly the only way to do it
under the facts that I know,
extraordinary ability.
Extraordinary-ability.

I came here for my career,
I did so well,
I moved here.
It never crossed my mind
to stay here without papers.
That is just the person you are.
You follow the rules.
You follow the law.

China

UNITED NATIONS

Beijing
Bad news.
Troublemakers,
I was told not to go to Beijing
during the 17th Party Congress,
how can a powerful party
be so scared of an individual?
What a funny idea
is that a professor can't go to Beijing.
Personally,
I've never seen any democracy
within the party.

Harmonious society,
scientific development—
programs focused on helping
the underprivileged,
are slated to join the ranks
of Mao Tse-Tung's thoughts.
Deng Xiaping's theories
and Jiang Zemin's doctrine
of the Three Representatives.
Princelings.

Democracy with Chinese Characteristics.
Right now they can live with political
gridlocks and economic growth,
what happens when the music stops?
... it's going to be interesting to see
the train wreck when it happens.

Most delegates have a fundamental
understanding of how the party
expects them to vote,
highly dangerous,
harmony society.
How to manage inequality,
even if you can't reduce it,
will be an important theme.

Lower medical costs,
easier entrance procedures for students—
these sorts of priorities will
take time to implement,
but I think the overall
direction is right.

Right now I think
China is far,
far away from its goal
of a harmonious society,
which in mind would mean
really listening
and explaining
their policies to ordinary people.
Personally,
I don't care too much
about this conference,
over the years
I've seen too many
and their decisions have
such a minimal impact
on the average person.

ChinaUNITED NATIONS

UNITED NATIONS

Hong Kong

Hong Kong
must have the world's
most spoiled commuters.
This escalator
is the most famous in the world
that tourists from different countries
come just to ride it.
Engineers came
from Singapore to study it.
Conveyor.
The Jetsons.
In the morning;
everyone is rushing for work,
everyone walks down the escalators
or sometimes dashes down
the escalators.
Only the elderly
and the tourists stand still
for the ride.

Riding the escalator
is like watching a movie,
you can observe people
on the streets
or through their windows
arguing,
making dinner
or even making love.
Chinese box
and Chungking Express—
the escalator helps our business a lot,
by bringing in thousands of customers
every day;
that we don't need to advertise.
Most of our customers are local,
so we try to be neighborly!
We shut our front doors at six
and we have to stop

serving alcohol at eleven;
a door bitch.
Oh,
yes,
we get along with our neighbor just fine,
but sometimes
the fellows who load the trucks
across the streets are a bit troublesome—
sitting on my steps
and drinking their bevies.
I have to go
out there
and say,
"you're not blocking
my window,
are you,
handsome boys?"
Hell money.
I don't mind
different kinds of people
and I didn't mind competition.
People around here work hard,
Western
and Chinese.
Auntie!
The rents go up,
then our prices go up.
Things get too expensive
and people move out.
Only,
but some of the restaurants
pay seven thousand dollars.
I'll tell you a secret.
The nuns
are one of the biggest landlords
in this neighborhood.
The nuns are wealthy.

The neighborhood
used to be quite a quiet place,
it used to be a street
of nuns
and temples.
Now it has become more complex.

China

UNITED NATIONS

> Hong Kong
> *Sin-British Agreement on H.K. was signed in 1984*

Sources: Albert Chang   (Outspoken Radio Talk show host)
          Chi-Ying Tsui   (Computer Engineer)
          Evelyn Iritani   (Times Writer)
          Maggie Farley   (Times Writer)
          Poon Kweai-Ping   (Police Inspector)
          Rone Tempeit   (Times Writer)
          Steve Stroud   (L.A. Times Photoj)
          Vincent Le, Dr.   (Chief of Ophthalmology at HK's Queen Mary Hospital)

It didn't really sink in
when it happened,
then I was out yesterday
and walked by this tiny shop
in my neighborhood
where the Chinese national anthem
was being played.
Suddenly,
I realized this really is a part
of China.
No more
'God Save the Queen.'

The new government
didn't want to allow
Democratic Party leader
Martin Lee to speak.
I suddenly realized:
if it were up to me
to stop him,
I don't know if I could do it.
I believe in the freedom of speech.
Before at Government House
there was a crown on the gate.

Now,
there's a new red Chinese seal
and a Chinese flag
on the flagpole,
it really feels
like you're entering a place
in China
and it feels very strange.

I looked on the stage
and saw
Chinese President Jiang Zemin
standing there,
I thought,
*'Oh my God,
what have we done?'*
Sure,
we prepared for 13 years,
but sometimes
even when you know
things are going to happen,
you are not prepared for the shock.
Teacup in a tempest.
They felt the British have left
a great city
to an uncertain future.

China

UNITED NATIONS

>   Open Door Policy
> Reform and Opening-Up Policy

Breathtaking.
Continue to be very important
in China,
at that time,
the people all wore Mao suits
and rode on bicycles,
my impression at that time,
even before 1978,
was that life was very simple
in China.
When the great day
starting in 1978–
two years after that visit–
occurred,
I was not surprises
that China would indeed have a great speed
of development
after the Party Congress of 1978,
emancipate the mind,
seek truth from facts
and united as one
in looking to the future,
breathtaking,
breathtaking.

One of the greatest accomplishments
of China is that it has seen
the biggest poverty alleviation
in human history,
because 700 million Chinese
have gradually shaken off poverty
since the 1970's up to today.
Innovation-driven growth,
development of high speed railways,
e-commerce,
mobile payment

and other advances
such as bike-sharing
facilitated by mobile payment.

China's door of opening-up
will not be closed
and will open wider,
it is a strategic decision
made by China
based on its need for development,
as well as a concrete action
taken by China
to move economic globalization forward
in a way that benefits people
across the world.

I would describe the importance
of the initiative
by using the language
of computers–
the software
and the hardware.
The software of the relations
of China with other countries
would be the trade
and investment agreements,
like the free trade agreement
between the Association
of Southeast Asian Nations
and China,
because those agreements
continue the framework
for trade
and investment to thrive,
but you also need hardware–
the modern infrastructure–
that is where the belt
and road comes in.

At the end of that day,
the government is the body of a country,
but the people are the heart of a country,
so people-to-people exchanges
are like what I was doing

for the Association
of Southeast Asian Nations.
I found that was the natural way
to develop ties between our two countries
and our people.
Collaborator,
donor
and market.

China

UNITED NATIONS

Republic of China
Instead of doing their job,
some comrades spend
their working hours discussing
issues such as who
will be made the next party secretary
or the next mayor.
Paramount leader,
this party congress,
will give a green light
to ownership—
you in the West
call it privatization—
of stale industries.
That means
that some state assets
will be sold to
non-state companies
or private owners.
This is a breakthrough
that will make the party
congress more meaningful,
more important,
than many of those in the past...

This is the start of the evolution
of the private economy.
Up to the past,
the government has not prohibited
this type of ownership,
but with this party's congress,
it hadn't approved it either.

Socialist has the public ownership
of any means of production.
The basis of a socialist
economic system
of the People's Republic of China
is a socialist public ownership

of the means of production,
namely ownership by the whole people
and collective ownership
by the working people.
The biggest issue,
will be how we define
public ownership
and common welfare.
Trans-century significance.
Power,
money
and beautiful women.
These are the primary stages of socialism.

People have had a saying
for a while,
they say:
"the primary stage
is a basket.
You can put whatever
you want into it."

Chip Cards

ECONOMY

Hanging out to dry.
At a certain point,
we're going to have to switch,
because we're looking
at no support
if there's any fraud,
we could afford a $3 coffee,
but it would be nice to mitigate
the risk with the bikes.

From the merchant's perspective,
it seems like optimism
has gone down a little.

This is the biggest change
in the payments industry
in the past 40 years.
We know the process
wasn't going to happen overnight
and so far we're pleased
with how it's going.

Deadline.
They say it's safer,
I don't know how,
but as long as it works,
I don't care.
It can be unreliable.
I don't care
if it's the go to chip only.
If that's the way it goes,
that's the way it goes.

Christianity

FAITH

Churches
Concordant of Agreement
some believe
that we're in the midst of a time
when an ecumenical window is open.
There is a sense of the moment
and the possibilities that now
are before us.
The major ecumenical event
for this century,
not only for the Episcopal Church
but for all the churches.
In the best of all possible worlds,
the dream still exists
for many of us of one holy,
Catholic
and apostolic church,
but I don't think
many of us understand
anymore that this means a church
that is monolithic
and uniform—
a church
that holds the apostolic faith
at its center
and still maintains
its unique gifts
and graces.

Brand loyalty
people don't join churches anymore.
People join people.
If a Presbyterian family
moves two states away
and comes to another town
and the Presbyterian church
there doesn't feel like the one
they came from,
but the Methodist

or Episcopal church does,
then they will join the Methodist
or Episcopal church.

To me
it's very difficult to control emotions.
I'm very grateful for this day.
Now after a generation
and a half we've gotten to a point
where we get to make some decisions
about what we've been talking about.
I know in my heart
that Our Lord wants
our witness to be in the world
and that it would be much more unified.
I think that opportunity
may be nearer
than we think.

A Mighty Fortress
is our God.
Today we have the opportunity
to make history
and make one small step
toward once again
becoming one Christian church.
This is the closest opportunity
we have had since the Reformation.
I'm a Christian first,
then a Southern Baptist.

A moment of Grace.
Pick
and choose
when you start looking closely
at the gradation of differences.
It becomes so silly that
man has put these rules in place.
A lot of it has to do
with people blowing things
out of proportion.
I think it's really important
for us to keep focused:
it's one God

and we basically
have the same beliefs.
In a given area,
congregation of Episcopalians,
Presbyterians
and others may find
more theological affinity
than between two Presbyterian
or two Episcopalian churches.
There is so much variation
within most of mainline denominations
that you sort of find your theological affinity
where you find it.

ChristianityFAITH

FAITH

Eulogy

The most hunted person
in the modern age.
Sing openly.
Astounding,
he's blown his top,
having blood on their hands.
Duty
and tradition.
Blood family.
She talked endlessly
of getting away from England,
mainly because of the treatment
she received at the hands of the newspapers.
I don't think
she ever understood why
her genuinely good intentions
were sneered at by the media;
why there appeared to be
a permanent quest of betrayal
to bring her down,
it is buffing.
My own
and only explanation
is that genuine goodness
is threatening to those
at the opposite end
of the moral spectrum.

Her royal highness.
She needed no royal title
to continue to generate her
particular brand of magic.
There is a temptation
to rush to canonize your memory,
there is no need to do so.
You stand tall enough
as a human being of unique quality

not to need to be seen as a saint.
She was,
in the end,
the most hunted person
of the modern age.

She would want us today
to pledge ourselves
to protect her beloved boys,
William and Harry,
from a similar fate.
I do this here,
Diana,
on your behalf.
We will not allow them
to suffer the anguish
that would regularly
drive you to a fearful despair.

Hypocritical
and evil.
I pledge that we,
your blood family,
will do all that we can
to continue the imaginative
and loving way
in what you were tearing
these two exceptional young men,
so that their souls
are not simply immersed by duty
and tradition,
but can sing openly
as you planned.
We fully respect the heritage
into which they have both been born
and will always respect
and encourage them
in their royal role,
but we like you,
recognize the need for them
to experience as many different
aspects of life as possible;
to arm them spiritually

and emotionally for the years ahead.
I know
you would have expected
nothing less from us.

Christianity

FAITH

>Protestants

I fundamentally did not change
what I believe,
but I changed brands.
Never took a hold of me,
a maze of people and titles.

Even if they came,
there was a tendency to lose them
in the second
and third generation.

We are very much a liturgicical assembly.
We have some of the ancient structures.
We don't use the resource of television,
radio
and the internet,
as well as,
many others.
These losses
would have been even more pronounced
were it not for the offspring
impact of immigration.

The presumption of protestant framework
for understanding the American
character is now a thing of the past.
We are an increasingly pluralistic society
and we,
Protestants,
now have to think
much about how we can contribute
to the common good;
as simply just one more wife
in the American choir,
we should not jump
too quickly to the conclusion
that secluarism has taken over.

There is much spirituality
out there among the unaffiliated.
We find this is to be an exciting challenge.
Traditional patterns of worship...
so they work for something
that the whole family can commit to;
is that treating religion
as a mere '*commodity*'?
Hardly.
It is struggled to find resources
that will help us deal
with some of the most profound
and intimate issues of our lives.

Early on,
Europeans came to America
at least in part so that they could enjoy
religious freedom.
Thus,
they adopted the principle
of the separation of church
and state.
So,
technically one would not say
that this was ever a Protestant Union,
rather this was a nation made
up primarily of individuals
who propose to be Protestant.

You might sort of think
of family problems,
but both at the level
of having children
and raising children.
Everybody in the country is losing members'
everybody is gaining members,
it is a very competitive marketplace
and if your rest on your laurels,
you're going to be history.

Christianity

FAITH

Sermon

Having an iPod is a guaranteed way
to get the sermon
if you're going to be out of town.

God casting.
I can't possibly have a conversation
with everyone each Sunday,
but this builds toward a digital discipleship.
Were orthodox in belief,
but unorthodox in practice.
Basically,
every church can have its own radio show;
if you really believe in the message
you're preaching,
you want as many people as possible to listen.
Spiritual multitasking.

Podcasts provide a way for people
who are very busy these days
to get their religion on the fly;
but for most people,
this will be a supplement,
not a substitute.
Rachel's choice.
Star Wars.

I don't force people to take my view,
Podcasts for us
have been a resurrection of radio,
it's the connection to a new generation.

Christianity

FAITH

>Xn

My faith teaches me to forgive.
I forgive all those who testified against me,
I leave these people to God.

I call out to those in the United States.
It is a shame,
you are trading
a strategic nationality
for a priest.
Acting in a parallel
and coordinated fashion.
To divide
and separate Christianization.

Fire.
Meteor.
One scene I witnessed
was 25 Turkish University students
taking an oath
by putting their right hands
over their hearts,
accompanied by the Star-Spangled Banner.

We even went to Turkish grade school,
because my parents
wanted us to learn the language
and feel comfortable in the culture.
To me,
it was home–
my family,
school
and friends were in Turkey.
I look at myself as a patriot for America,
but I didn't come
to represent Americans,
I came as a representative of God.
He has no interest

in Turkish politics,
he never gets involved
with anything besides religion.

Cigarettes

SOCIETY

    Teenagers

More people,
die every year from smoking
than murder,
AIDS,
suicide,
drugs,
car crashes
and alcohol–
combined.
Cigarette companies
intentionally designed to create
and sustain addiction.

Corrective statements.
It's both an important victory
and a frustrating one,
have spent millions of dollars
and a decade of time
resisting a court order
that simply requires them
to publish truthful facts
about their products
and their behavior,
here's the truth.

Fully complying with its obligations
under the court order.
To make money with little,
if any,
regard for individual illness
and suffering,
soaring health costs
or the integrity of the legal system.
Historically used to promulgate
false smoking
and health messages.

I certainly don't think
that what we have finally ended up with
is really in the spirit
of the original ruling,
the original ruling
was so that the American public
would understand
that they had been deceived
through multiple means
about whether smoking caused disease,
whether smoking killed people,
whether secondhand smoke caused disease,
whether nicotine was addictive.
The only reason they're finally printing
and broadcasting all of this
is because they were forced to do so
by a judge that found them guilty
of racketeering,
otherwise,
this would still be going on.

We told Congress under oath
that we believed nicotine
is not addictive.
We told you that smoking
is not an addiction
and all it takes to quit
is will power.
Here's the truth:
smoking is very addictive
and it's not easy to quit.
We manipulated cigarettes
to make them more addictive.
Forced public confessions.
Shame
and humiliate them.
Manipulation of cigarette design
and composition
to ensure optimum nicotine delivery.

Adverse health effects
of exposure to secondhand smoke.
Secondhand smoke causes lung cancer
and coronary heart disease

in adults who do not smoke.
Smoking kills,
on average,
1,200 Americans every day.

Circuit Breaker

SOCIETY

Classic Gadget blog,
core audience.
Feel neglected
when we're talking about Netflix.
We started out,
a few years ago,
building media brands on websites,
because that's where we thought the growth was
and we were right about that,
people started concentrating
around a few specific apps.
We invest based on where we see potential.
It's a high demand category.

We're going to be playing
the News Feed game
like everyone else,
from distributing perspective,
we're probably going to be changing,
like every 48 hours.

Climate Change

NATURE

Advance God's Kingdom
That is a recipe for the complete
dismantling thing
of our informed democracy,
war on science.
The issue of climate change isn't
about what you know,
it's about who you are.

A human being cannot grasp something
as a fact if it in any way
undermines their identity
and that is an immutable human foible.
These things have always been there,
but not at scale.
20th century version of the American dream
and the trust in government
to produce it was fully mythologized.
There was an usually high level
of trust that came out of World War II,
before the turn
towards a more cynical view
of the institution
and media –
after Vietnam
and Watergate,
he complicated things,
he really is an us –
versus them figure.
People aren't thinking
about the arguments.
They're thinking about
what side they're on.

Vaccines cause autism.
Motivated reasoning,
you have a basic psychological tendency
to perpetuate your own beliefs,
to really…

discount anything that runs
against your own prior views.
Backfire effect.

Science is about the biased
search for truth.
Being a scientist only means
that when I have an intuition
and see if I'm right.
A very,
very smart mentor
told me once,
'I don't trust anyone
who hasn't at least
changed their mind
once in their career.'

Coders

ECONOMY

They want foodies who code,
all companies are becoming technology-based
to some degree,
this is especially true in the hospitality industry.
If you're really into technology,
there's a revolution happening
in hospitality;
you can drive,
innovate
and take ownership.

We're developing our own in-house talent
to innovate,
test new ideas
and learn from them,
they have to hustle.
The casino employees,
chefs,
all the experts in each area,
so they can work together.

A digital transformation journey,
mobile use in India is going through the roof,
our population is young
and we need to meet them on the platform
they are using.
We need data scientists
to make of what is going on
so we can compete against online travel agents
like Expedia
and maximize revenues.

Sentiment report.
These are definitely jobs
that we thought we couldn't automate
five years ago
that we are automating now
using technologies
like natural language processing

and voice recognition,
a lot of the motivation is cost driven.
So if companies can get away
with using a technology
they will do it more
and more.
The travel brands should strive
to understand how the experiences
they provide make travelers feel.

High tech has become the norm,
hotels need to embrace it
and manage it,
but not forget
why they are there.
Sometimes,
there's no substitute for a real person
who delivers their expertise.

College Campus

COMMUNITY

       United States

A bad shot with a rifle
is better than a good shot
with a handgun.
The reality
is that these are not always handgun situations,
we can't tell a university,
realistically,
what's acceptable in their community–
that's up to them–
but we recognize the struggle
that every community faces,
because many of these shooters
come to the scene with a long gun.

I actually don't feel as safe,
you're seeing across the United States
this militarization
of many college campuses.

Color Blind

HEALTHCARE

        Enchroma Glasses

It looks a lot different
than I thought,
I always thought
it was just red.

Everything looks the same,
but everything looks a lot more there,
the pink surprises me.
It's very,
very pink.
The green does,
too,
and the red.

Holy cow, that red car!
I think I'm more excited
than he is,
I don't think he knows
what he's missing.
It bothers me
that there is a whole dimension
that he can't see.
I'm curious to see
how he sees things.

What we're hoping to do
today is give color
to those who need it.

I'm looking forward to it.
I'm trying to see
how everybody else
sees the world.
Usually this looks brown,
wow,
everything is a lot more intense.
Everything is a lot brighter.
It's going to take time
getting used to this.

Columbia

UNITED NATIONS

    Santa Fe de Ralit

These are some of the biggest,
most ruthless drug dealers in the world,
period.
They are essentially negotiating
with a much more organized,
much more dangerous
Pablo Escobar,
because these guys
actually have some clout
and much more organizational skills
than the rebels;
they are deadly.
They are politically very able,
which the rebels are not
and they are more popular
in certain areas,
they pale in comparison.

The leaders of these groups
are under the impression
that they can keep pressing
the state for additional concessions
to ensure that after they pass
some sort of bureaucratic procedure
they will continue doing business
as usual in Columbia,
in terms of trafficking,
enjoying their wealth
and eliciting assets they control.
He openly expressed
that these groups should demoralize,
even if it meant paying
a few years of jail time
or confinement.

We are the de-fact state
in all areas we occupy–

in health,
in education,
in roadwork,
everything that the state should offer,
we are the law here.
This is the most secure place
in the world,
we're illegal,
but we're legitimate.
Would you like me to put you
in a cage?
Neither would my pet jaguar.
We are not defected;
we are strong.

Concentration Camps

IMMIGRATION

We are here today
to protest
the repetition of history,
'you need to move right now!
What you don't understand?
It's English: Get Out!'

Is a false equivalency.
What happened then
is not what is happening now,
every country now knows
if you come into our country with a child,
you will be released.
It is our responsibility
to ensure the security
and safety of all the children
coming into our country
and I have confidence
that will be done properly at Fort Sill.

We need to be the allies
for vulnerable communities today
that Japanese Americans didn't house
in 1942,
it's our responsibility to help,
we are calling these camps what they are,
because they fit squarely
in an academic consensus
and definition.

Concentration camps.
They are the same kind of situation.
Why aren't they identified
as the same thing?
America's Concentration Camps:
Remembering the Japanese American Experience.

To call them anything else
is to mitigate the enormity

of the travesty—
a concentration camp is a place
where people are imprisoned
not because of any crime
they have committed,
but simply because of who they are,
we all have the responsibility
to stand up for justice.

Coroner

AMERICA'S NEW TRIUMPH

    Shut up—
    Leave me alone.

    Somebody,
    somewhere knows who she is,
    if anybody is a John/Jane Doe
    for more than 5 days,
    I start looking into it.
    Sometimes it just takes time.

    I didn't want to be around
    sick people all the time–
    the mystery of death,
    why
    and how people die.
    Apparently,
    the fingerprints hadn't
    been available before.
    Arizona–
    there was all sorts of identifying
    pieces of evidence on her,
    but we have just never been
    able to get her identified.

    It's frustrating.
    Mostly it boils down to persistence
    and not being
    willing to give up.
    I can't imagine
    how families must feel.
    I think it's important
    to help them
    get some closure.

    I make it a point
    to carry my house key
    with my business card
    and phone number,
    in case I drop dead

or get hit by a car.
I would hate
to be a John Doe.

I think he did a great job…
A lot of it was on his own time,
at home on his own computer.
Some comfort
and an end to suffering.
That's just incredibly great.

He is doing good work
and is very well thought of.

SOCIETY

Corporate Slaves

Idols

Idols…
To sell dreams.
No dating.
It's unheard of in the West
for the agencies to control their personal lives.
It's possible
comparable to the situation
in the 1940's
in the United States
when film studios
had huge control
over their movie stars,
but even then,
they may have been encouraged
not to date
or marry,
but there was less coercion.

They are very concerned
about how their talents are perceived,
in past because of several infamous scandals
in the 1990's,
if you go to the agency,
every young trainee
will give you a very polite bow
and there are notices
with the company rules
on the wall
to remind them how to behave.
Korea puts strong emphasis
on humanity,
but it can come across
as too extreme outside the country.

Corporate slaves.
Journalists who work for mainstream
Japanese media

clearly understand
what they're allowed to
and not allowed to
write so they operate on self-censorship.

Broken from the inside.
The life of fame
was never meant for me.
What else can I say?
Just tell me I've done well.
That this is enough.
That I've worked hard.
Even if you can't smile
don't fault me on my way.

Jonghun,
who loved music more than anyone…
Forever,
he will be remembered.

Court Interpreters

JUSTICE

Zero tolerance.
During the months of June
and July
our District Court
has experienced an influx
of cases requiring interpreters
of languages of India
and Nepal:
Punjabi,
Urdu,
Hindi,
Guajarati,
Bengali
and Nepali.
We have also had cases
requiring interpreters
of languages that have not been heard
in our District before,
such as Ashanti Twi from Ghana,
Mixteco language of Mexico–
urgently seeking contract interpreters.
These clients are in custody
and unable to communicate
with their attorneys.

I have been 100 percent busier
at this present time
as compared to 2017,
Operation Streamline.
I can tell you,
having a conversation over the phone
with an interpreter
is completely impractical,
there's no speaker option
on the phone,
no simultaneous translation.
You are essentially playing hot potato
with the receiver.
I think that the quality of the interpreter

or accuracy of the interpretation
is affected tremendously.

He's already spent nine days,
10 days in custody,
it seems a miscarriage of justice
to let this case go forward,
possible
and pending litigation.
Some of the concepts
of the United States criminal system
can't be directly translated.
The denial of an interpreter,
who can interpret defense counsel's advice,
questions
and information to the accused
is essential to the vindication
of the Sixth Amendment right to counsel,
without the ability to communicate,
the physical presence
of an appointed attorney
is nothing more than window dressing.

Craft Spirits

SOCIETY

Craft Spirits
distilling across the country
and here in San Diego–
probably even more so–
is absolutely on the same trajectory
as craft beer,
you can drink a lot of beer,
you are not going to drink spirits
the same way.

The target audience is similar,
we are betting that people
who like craft beer
will want to drink crafts spirits.

No harm,
no foul,
every single distillery
in San Diego reached out
and was willing to help out
in every way
that we needed.
Every single one
either texted
or called said,
'*Hey,
if you need anything,
don't hesitate to reach out.*'
He was talking about
the Brewers Guild
and how it helped
the entire industry.

We use food-grade corn
and brewer's barley,
both are higher end
than usual.
We want to make sure
we use natural ingredients,

by bringing out the real ingredients,
the true ingredients,
it completely changes the flavor.

The tasting room here pays our rent,
distributors don't want to pick you up
if you don't have existing accounts
and you can't get accounts
if you don't have a distributor.
30 under 30.

That extra buck eighty a bottle
is helping people expand.
At this point,
we don't make enough volume
to keep up.
We are fortunate to have
and grateful to have,
the rich foundation
that craft beer established here
in San Diego.
San Diegans love craft beer culture,
they love local products,
they are very loyal–
and this is a whole new frontier
for those people.

To the skin off

Creation

NATURE

This is a big toe,
the instep,
the heel.
It's about thirteen inches long,
but the people were probably
much bigger back then.

'*Back then*'
are of supreme
and final authority.
In faith,
life
and of every living thing,
of all flesh.
You shall bring forth
two of every sort
into the ark.

'*Neat.*'
'*Prove.*'
'*Anti-science.*'
Perhaps the most radical incarnation
of anti-science thought.
Well,
Carl Sagan knows the truth
about the creation now.
Of old you laid the foundation
of the Earth
and the heavens
are the work of your hand
they will perish,
but you will endure;
yes they will grow old
like a garment.

Next week,
we will get you
sedimentary rock
and Noah's flood.
I wonder
if we'll become extinct.

Cricket

SPORTS

Let's go,
gentlemen!
The peer pressure on them
is not to play,
to be hoodlums,
to just kick it.
I tell them
you can play cricket
or you can go kick it,
but you can't do both.
Already,
man,
you are respected
and well-known,
gentlemen,
there is no reason why
that can't happen.
I'm telling you
guys you are going to be,
you are going to be…
bigger than Oprah!

I laughed when
I first heard about them,
it's odd enough to think
of Americans playing cricket,
but Compton playing cricket!

The team is a fantastic idea,
you have to learn a lot
of patience
and discipline to play cricket…
and that would help
any young man.

I grew up in Compton,
I grew up in this neighborhood,
I was young
and I was a gang banger,

but my son,
he's not a gang banger;
he's no cholo,
he's out playing cricket
and I'm so proud of him.

It has showed me so much,
it shows me how
to have respect
and how to be responsible.
A lot of people put Compton down,
but we do want to accomplish
something in life,
I missed cricket a lot,
I'm trying to change
for the good.

We say baseball is sissy,
because you have to use
a glove to catch a ball.
Cricket can be a challenge,
two teams play on a round
or oval field,
using flat,
wooden bats to swat small,
leather-encased balls.
Instead of pitchers,
there are bowlers.
Instead of bases,
there are two sets of
wooden stakes called wickets,
topped with pegs called bails.
The bowler tries to strike out
a batsman by throwing a ball
past him and knocking a bail
off a wicket.
The batsman tries to scare
by hitting the ball,
allowing him
and a teammate
waiting at a matching wicket
to scare runs.
They'd tell me,
"*Hey,*

that sounds cool…"

They think we're famous.
They're the best fielders
we've ever seen,
they could be ripping good.

JUSTICE

West Coast

3Babiez.
What happens who disrespect this group of individuals?
You end up with a bullet in your head.
Original gangster.

He was perceived as a snitch,
he shouldn't have been running his mouth.
Yea West Coast
is getting on the stand
tomorrow
against the homies.

The West Coast Crips
did not approve of the 3-Babiez,
it's like to government jumps
to conclusions
and fits a story to fit around them.

Cryptocurrency

SOCIETY

Digital Currency

Wild West.
Days of cryptocurrencies.
Capturing risk
and enabling innovation.
3 Pillars in regulation:
Consumer protection,
anti-money laundering
and financial stability.

We're at that time now
where we need more clarity
and rules
and we need more certainty.
It's a good time to start revisiting
that 'wait and see' approach
taken by regulators,
a leader manages the risks
around crypto-assets.
Hallmarks of a bubble.

Regulation creates the guardrails
on the highway that allows
new entrants to come in,
particularly institutional investors,
an infectious disease.

SPORTS

Cross-Country Medalist

    Winter Olympics 2018

I'm just so happy
that we can finally get this monkey
off our back,
it was fun to show the world
that we were able to do it.
Slingshot past.

An emotional moment for everybody,
it was a long time coming,
as everybody knows.
When I first started,
we were excited if we got a top 30.
We're going to see it grow now,
for sure,
kids are going to see this.
This will create a pretty significant effect.

I envisioned a gold in there somewhere,
I always believed deep down
it was possible.
But to save it for my last Olympic race?
It's crazy.
It's the best ending
I could of asked for,
but this is the one we dreamed about
and it's the last one.

I can say I'm very,
very happy for Jessie
and Kikkan today,
I also think that's very important
for our sport.
I'm very,
very happy for them.
They are so worth this gold medal.
Watching Kikkan do her leg so well
and getting us into a position

where we were going to get a medal,
I was like,
'Well,
ok,
we're going to try to make it
a gold one then.
We have nothing to lose.'
I just had a lot of belief going
into that last lap.

It's quite cool to see
and for sure,
it's quite good for the sport.
It's amazing.
Congratulations.
It was a nail-biter
all the way up to the finish line.
When Jessie crossed,
I looked over at the score-board
and saw United States No. 1
and just let out a big scream
and ran over
and tackled Jess.
She said,
'Oh my gosh,
did we just win the Olympics?'
And I said,
'Yeeeeeaaaaaahhhh!'

Currency

DEBT

> American

She's deserving of it,
what she has done
and what she went through
no other person has done the same,
she was the woman who changed the outcome
of the United States
and I am very proud of her.

I'm very,
very pleased
and happy for Harriet Tubman
and her family;
her descendants.
She had to be a very remarkable lady.

The show has certainly caught
people's imaginations
and I think it's a great thing,
what we've been doing on the currency
and what they've been doing on the show
were really quite complementary.
We want people to pay attention
to the whole bill,
$5,
$10
and $20 bills.

Currency

ECONOMY

U.S. Coins

The Kennedy assassination
was a traumatic shock,
people felt we had to do something
right away.
The coins really were commemorative,
used to remember.

Money isn't just money,
money is also a ubiquitous
mass medium,
so if you want to get any kind of message
across in a big way,
putting it on the money
is a great way to do it.

Unifying principle.
In God We Trust.
Most reputable U.S. History courses
would no longer tell you
that it's because of a few great men
that this country
became what it is,
people would tell you about the importance
of social movements,
of culture transformation.

Cyberattacks

ECONOMY

We need to prepare
for that digital disaster,
we need a system to identify,
isolate
and respond to cyberattacks
at the speed of light.

Direct the national response.
We'll not empower
a government shutdown
or takeover of the internet
and any suggestion
on otherwise is misleading
and false.
Securing our national
cyber-infrastructure from attack.

The government needs
to get its own cybersecurity house
in order first,
before it tries to tell the private factor
what to do.
Tough questions to the president
and that isn't comforting,
because some presidents
will answer those questions
in troubling ways.

Botnets.
It's not like the Internet
has an on-off switch
somewhere you can press.
People want to know
if they are one
of the 10 percent
of the computers that are infected–
they just don't know what to do.
Most people just hope
they're one of the other nine.

Defense Reform

MILITARY

We need a balanced inventory
of joint capabilities
that are going to allow us
to deter
and defeat
potential adversaries
across the full range
of military operations.
We don't have the luxury
of choosing between
a force that can fight
the Islamic state
of Iraq
and Levant
and the one
that has a modern
nuclear enterprise,
robust cyber capabilities,
robust space capabilities
and robust conventional
and special operations capabilities.

The current inventory,
from my perspective,
doesn't have the kind of depth
that I would like it to have
and getting the balance right
in addressing the lack of depth
in the areas like ballistic missile defense,
intelligence,
surveillance
and certain logistics enablers,
frankly,
I think
is going to be probably
one of the biggest challenges,
during my tenure.
Although,
the Bipartisan Budget Act

is going to get us through fiscal year 2017
we still have $100 billion
of sequestration
looming over us
and a bow wave
of modernization requirements,
all of that
will kind of come together.
At the same time,
we're trying to get out.

At the same time,
we're trying to get out
of a fairly significant readiness,
managing that
over the next few years,
I think,
will be a significant challenge
and we need some significant changes.
We have supported
and supporting relationships
and that has all worked well
for decades,
but if you think about it,
the secretary of defense,
if the decider
and is the integrator
in the department
and he is the lower level
at which integration–
actually full integration–
takes place
amongst the combatant commanders.

As an aside,
I don't find
the current phasing
construct for operational plans
particularly useful right now,
I call it competition
with a military dimension
short of a phase 3
or traditional conflict,
but the activities

that they're taking
with regard to employment
of cyber unconventional capability,
space capabilities
and information operations
are absolutely not associated
with what we could call phase zero shaping,
the high likelihood
that any future conflict
will be transregional,
multi-domain
and multifunctional.

Today,
if you think about a conflict
with North Korea,
you have to quickly factor in
not only ballistic missiles,
but also intercontinental ballistic missiles,
cyber capabilities
and space capabilities;
in addition to,
the traditional conventional threat
that we confronted on the peninsula.
If I talked about a Korea scenario
right now,
I can quickly talk about:
the Pacific Command,
Northern Command
or
Strategy Command
...and that's if nothing else
is going on in the world
at the same time.

Deferred Action for Childhood Arrivals (DACA)

IMMIGRATION

The Deferred Action
for Childhood Arrivals (DACA)
program works,
this is giving me a light
to where my roots are.
It grounds me.
I feel like I cannot make the decision
about my life,
because it could go either way,
it's difficult to live in that uncertainty
every day.
Dreamers.
Seeing the children working,
trying to make a living,
it makes me feel privileged,
I understand why my family
made the decision to come
to the United States.

I think that mostly sucks,
the opportunities that were given to me
were not given to him.
I know we had the same potential.
I never thought
I would see her doing
what she's doing,
what resonates most
is to embrace the fact
that I am from both,
I am binational,
I am bicultural.
Last USA exit

If Trump decides to end DACA,
it will be one of the ugliest
and cruelest decisions
ever made by a president.
In our modern history,
if DACA is ended in this way,

it will be a humanitarian
and economic disaster,
this is a crisis manufactured
by Republicans
and it can only be solved by Republicans.
President of the United States
has the power to keep DACA in place,
Republicans suicide.
Ending DACA now gives chance
to restore Rule of Law.
Delaying a Republican leadership
can push Amnesty
is Republican suicide.

Chance to restore
Rule of Law.
Dreamers.
Very,
very hard decision.
We love the Dreamers.
With heart.
Human element.
Dreamers.

250 of my Apple coworkers
are Dreamers.
I stand with them.
They deserve our respect
as equals
and a solution rooted
in American values,
Dreamers.
Great heart.
Employment Authorization Documents,
also known as work permits,
are generally valid
they expire
or the government demands
they be returned,
deserve our respect as equals,
American values.

ENVIRONMENT

Deodorants

You can see
these really rapid decreases
in tailpipe emissions,
it just made sense
to start looking at other sources
and seeing
whether they could be growing
in relative importance.
It's stored in an airtight tank,
it's burned for energy
and it's converted
mostly to carbon dioxide,
but these volatile organic compounds
that you use in everyday products–
even though it may just be a teaspoon
or a squirt
or a spray–
the majority of those kinds of compounds
will ultimately end up in the atmosphere
where they can react
and contribute
to both harmful ozone formation
and small-particle formation.
Use as little of the product
as you can.

Dinosaurs

NATURE

Jurassic Park.
It's really a significant discovery
and it will be even more fantastic
when they find more of it.
Most crustaceous rocks are marine
in character during this time,
there are very few terrestrial deports.
There are some in Argentina.
There are probably some
that are nearly equivalent
in China
and Eastern Russia,
but there's nothing
I'm aware of that has shown
as complete material as what we have.

It's the first Terrain beds
in North America
that have ever produced
dinosaur skeletons.
It's going to be a charming dinosaur.
In a lot of ways,
it's going to look like
a baby triceratops,
except a more primitive one.
Our animal looks to be
a lot more primitive
than that one,
but not much older;
we're not naming the new species
for Christopher.

Jurassic Park.
This is the most complete
individual skeleton that one
of these guys has ever found.

I became so overwhelmed
with emotions
that I literally
had to put it down
for fear of dropping it.

Disaster

NATURE

Disastrous personality.
Call on God,
but now away from the rock.
There was karaoke music,
Everybody was laughing
and singing.
In just one second,
everything went from a loud,
happy,
wonderful moment
to total silence.
Every brain,
I guess,
was working like a computer
trying to analyze what had happened.
I started to react very differently
from normal.
I started to say,
"*O.K.*
there is option one,
or option two.
Decide.
Act."

I didn't say,
"*OK.*
The boat is sinking."
I didn't even think
about other perspectives.
I just pictured my very small world.

Some people didn't seem to realize
what had happened.
They were just sitting there,
I kept saying to myself,
'*Why didn't they try to get out of here?*'
"*Get out!*"
"*Get out!*"
"*Go!*"

Dogs

COMMUNITY

If she could,
I think Emily
would bring every dog here home
with her.
Meet the Breeds.
She's not afraid of the big dogs
at all,
I think she's gone right up to every dog
in here.

Dogs are part of the family.
This event gives people
a chance to come out
and see some purebred dogs
and to see which dog
might fit their environment.
Dogs are a long term deal–
you have to make sure
you get the right one.

They're non-shedding
and they're highly intelligent,
they can be a couch potato,
if that's what a person wants
or they'll get out
and run with you.
They're well-tempered dogs.

She's not a people dog,
I think she wants to get out
and run,
too.
Chase some rabbits.
It's nice to be here,
because people get more interaction
with the dogs
than what they would get at a dog show.

Dominican Republic

UNITED NATIONS

What will we do
that will benefit our country?
What Peña wanted,
we will fulfill.
We want to confront
the corruption
and lack of planning.
My strength is in finance,
management
and the reorganizing
of public affairs.
I expect to be an institutional president
who will not go outside
of the legal framework;
I will properly
manage the finances of the country.

Mejia made a mistake
by proclaiming himself
the winner so early,
now their people
have been drinking all day
and they are beyond his control.

Unconscionable.
The government process
of privatization was necessary,
but it affected hundreds
of families who were not able
to find a place
in the economy.

Here is an economy
that under Lionel Fernandez grew
to be an example
for Lahn;
so why did the government's candidate
not rise higher?

When Daniele spoke,
people weren't intrigued by him.

The rich say that there is economic growth,
but the only thing growing
are their pockets.
The people wanted a real
government to bring them work,
not just superficial words.
The women have seen
how there has been an inflation
in the kitchen
and in caring for their children.
We dealt with that
and we saw
we were on the precipice.
If you do not have enough
to feed your children,
there is nothing you can change,
but you can change
the government.

Dow Jones

ECONOMY

Stocks have soared this year,
lifted by the strong winds
of improving global growth,
optimism about pro-growth
U.S. policies
and still-low interest rates,
Dow 25k is not much of a stretch
from current levels,
we could hit that mark
by the end of the year.

It's good news,
the most recent market move
has been fueled
by a growing sense
that economic activity
will broaden.

Who knows?
if tax reform finds
economic activity,
the market can churn higher
as long as inflation remains at bay.

The week has again been characterized
by a continued bid
for the impoverished
and neglected corners
of the market.

Drinking and Driving

SOCIETY

Teenagers

L'amour,
Love.
They were always looking for fun,
making spur of the moment decisions.
I wanted to be just like them,
everyone did.

I loved Natasha more
than any one of her friends
did
or ever will.

Marian will never be the same
and will never have a
whole heart again,
it will always be half missing.
Marian had problems,
and because of Natasha
she fixed them.
For Marian to turn things around
and to face what she did,
that is remarkable.

Natasha was her world.
She should stop
and realize that none
of this will be easy
for her.

I will always love
Natasha
and Marian…
they were like sisters
in every aspect of the word.
A great loss has happened
and I think time will help,
but love is a great healer.

So all we can really do now
is love one another,
because that is what I believe
Natasha would want.

It's just a very tragic case,
I hope for the families
to receive the justice they deserve.

I think people will understand better
of what my father is trying
to do in time.

I think Natasha would like
to see her friends being saved,
I'll always be grieving for her
If there is something
that we can do that's positive,
it makes the process
more enduring.

Save a Natasha.
In the first few days in the shock
of losing Natasha,
there was an idea
that her death
was not going to be
completely insignificant.
Love in that moment
is having the strength
to be popular.

Every time I get into a fight,
having to take someone's key
or to tell them
that they aren't going to drive,
I do it for Natasha.
I do it to save her.
In hope of telling her,
one day,
when I get to heaven,
that her death did have reason.

If we achieve something…

There would be a party
that didn't happen,
an accident
that didn't happen.

Drones

GOVERNMENT

Delivery drones are absolutely viable,
but these are a lot of technical handles
that have to be crossed,
we are very much in the prototype stage.

There remain numerous reasons
why drones are not a feasible,
form of delivery technology
at this time,
we're testing
a range of vehicle capabilities,
we won't launch PrimeAir
until we are able to demonstrate
safe operations.
A sea change
is going to be required
in how these vehicles are designed
and manufactured;
in order to support moving
from a hobbyist flying on the weekend
in a park
to a 24/7 delivery service
flying over your highways.

The technology is challenging,
but totally doable,
people underestimate
the technical difficulties,
it takes time
and effort to make something
the public doesn't have to think twice about.

Drug Cocktails

SOCIETY

Brokeback Mountains,
when most people think about poisonings,
they tend to think of little kids,
but the highest drug poisoning rates
are in people 45 to 54 years of age.

We're seeing more
and more problems
with people mixing medications,
because they don't take the time
to find out if they interact,
then sometimes they add alcohol,
which can cause respiratory depression.
You mix enough sedative type drugs,
whether they're over-the-counter
or prescription with alcohol
and that's a recipe for disaster.

Now the most common cause of death
in our jurisdiction
has to do with mixed prescription
drug overdoses.
They're taking multiple medications
that in
and of themselves
wouldn't prove fatal,
but in combination do.
That's typical around the country.
Twenty years ago,
we'd have to look for alcohol
and one other drug
and now we typically have to do five
to seven drugs…
find out not only that they're there,
but how much is present.
We're taking a close look
at those cases
to make sure they're able
to metabolize the drug.

Earthquake

NATURE

"*We need chainsaws,
shears to cut iron bars
and jacks to remove
beams; everything,
we need everything.*"

She's alive!
There are people
under the rubble,
the town isn't here anymore.
Show their best side
in difficult moments,
we must continue to work
and to dig through the debris
in order to save human lives
and give hope
to all those involved in the area.

Moment of pain.
Hearing the major of Amatrice
say that the town no longer exists
and learning that there are children
among the dead,
I am deeply saddened.

Distraught.
We flew to Amatrice
from Rome in a helicopter,
so I saw it from the air,
there are a lot of historical buildings
that are destroyed.
It's really bad.

We came to the piazza
and it looked like '*Dante's Inferno*',
people crying for help,
help.
We need chainsaws,
shears to cut iron bars
and jacks to remove beams;
everything,
we need everything.
Out of dead sleep,
the building was shaking
pretty good,

it was so strong,
it seemed the bed was walking
across the room
by itself
with us on it.

Earthquake

NATURE

       Chengdu, China

At least 60
or 70 elders lived there,
as well as children.
How did they survive that?
While others were crying out
for help.
We also need medical workers
to save the injured here.

Traffic jams.
No running water.
Power outages.
Everyone is sitting on the streets.
Patients had to be evacuated
out of the hospitals,
sitting outside
and waiting.

It was really frightening to be
on the 26th floor
and you had to hold on
to something
or you'd fall over.
It shook for so long
and so violently
that you wondered
how long the building
would be able
to withstand all of this.

East Timor

UNITED NATIONS

    Dili City

I have finished two levels of Portuguese;
however, I still don't speak it fluently,
just basic Portuguese.

The ability to speak Portuguese
since the 1990's,
shows that a shift in the language
has taken place.
The changes from what I see
are taking place quite rapidly.

This is a political decision
and I have to implement it,
like it
or not,
I have no choice.
As a judge I have to implement
the law.

We have to rethink
about our language policies.
I see no problem
with a nation having four official
languages;
we can give the people the option
to choose two of them
as compulsory languages.

E-Commerce

ECONOMY

It's sad,
the business is not there.
Fair representation
of a current Sears shopping experience.

We are fighting like hell,
Store Closing Sale.
Nothing Held Back.

It's Black Friday,
people are shopping elsewhere,
but we are choosing to be here,
Store Closing.
My dad explained to me
that Sears was like Walmart
before Walmart arrived,
there is so much history
and tradition;
it's a piece of Americans...
I hope it survives,
but I don't know if they can.

Westchester Slim Cashmere Pine.
I took my grandson
to this mall recently
and he asked me
'Nana,
why are the stores closing?'
It's depressing.

Ecuador

UNITED NATIONS

Quito

The reality is people are not happy.
We wanted to get the president out,
but we wanted a new president
with new ideas.
This is just the same old
political parties taking back over.

I'm no politician,
I'm a simple doctor.

He has a new Cabinet,
but it's under how much
support he has
and there are doubts
about his legitimacy,
especially abroad.

Egypt

UNITED NATIONS

Terrorist Attack

The scene was horrific,
the bodies were scattered
on the ground
outside the mosque.
I hope God punishes them for this.
Horrible
and cowardly.
The ban.
I can't believe they attacked a mosque,
my children were there;
my children were there.

We are swamped,
we don't know what to say.
This is insane.
I wish I never stopped to pray,
I'm not even a Sufi.
I was just there by accident.

Sorcery
and soothsaying.
Eradicate.
Disease,
criminal explosions violate
all heavenly commandments
and human values.
It is a grave challenge
to Muslims worldwide.

Electromagnetic Fields (EMFs)

NATURE

    Power Lines

Sources: National Academy of Sciences
             (Acute Iymphoblastic Leukemia)
             Elector Magnetic Fields

Turning Point.
Based on our results,
is this likely
to be an important cause
of childhood leukemia?
The answer is no.

Extraordinarily,
well-done
study.
A strong statement
about the lack
of association.

This study carries
a very substantial amount
of weight
saying it's less likely.
Undermined.
The best one
to date,
the most careful
and complete.

It is being played
as an absolutely
negative study,
but I don't think
the data published
in the journal
supports
that contention,
equivocal.

The many inconclusive
and inconsistent
studies
have generated worry
and fear
and have given peace
to no one;
that there is no convincing evidence
that high-voltage power lines
are a health hazard
of a cause of cancer.

Elephants

WORLD WILDLIFE

On May 1st
there will no longer
be a policy;
a moratorium
on the culling of elephants.
We will allow culling
in certain parts
of South Africa,
but there is no mention
of wholesale slaughter.

We didn't support culling
in any shape
or form;
culling elephants is not going
to be popular…
certainly people will take
that into account
when making decisions
about where they're going
to take their holidays.
It has to be subject
to very serious checks
and balances.

Cruel
and morally reprehensive.
The latest research has proved
that elephants have a sense
of self awareness,
placing them in a unique category
with great apes,
dolphins
and humans;
as much as we are,
then it becomes murder?

It's not something anybody
welcomes at all,

but we also have to look at
the broader conservation…
management issues,
the option of doing nothing
does not evict.
We have immense sympathy
for wildlife managers
in South Africa.
They can't just walk away
and ignore it.

England

UNITED NATIONS

Hyde

He betrayed their trust in a way
and to an extent
that I believe is unparalleled in history.
Real cause.
Deeply shocking though it is,
the bare statement
that shipman (Harold) has killed
over two hundred patients
and it doesn't fully reflect the enormity
of his crimes.
As a general draftier,
shipman (Harold's) *non violent* killing
seems almost more incredible
than the violent deaths
of which we hear.
The way in which shipman (Harold) could kill,
face the relatives
and walk away unsuspected
would have been dismissed
and faithful
it had been described
in a work of fiction.

Deeply disturbing.
The true number of victims
is far greater
and cannot be counted;
as I include the victims' thousands
of relatives,
friends
and neighbors
who have lost a loved one
or a friend
before his
or her time;
in circumstances
that will leave their mark

for war.
It is possible that he was addicted
to killing.

Yes,
buzz.
When my mum died,
he put his hand
on my right shoulder
and said,
"*I think I'll stay here
a while in case she wakes up
so she doesn't scare people.*"
I didn't think anything of it
at the time,
but I do now.

One of the most evil men
in history.
I do not think
I have met anybody
who said they hate him.
It's just difficult to understand
and try to work out.
I can't reconcile the doctor.
I know who came to look after
my sister
and who delivered my daughter.
To the doctor I know now,
who has caused the betrayal
of trust that has
affected us all,
the eternal question
we live with
in Hyde, England is,
why did he do it?

Well,
I don't believe
in keeping them going.

When I saw the first newspaper
story saying,
"*Hyde Doctor Under Investigation,*"

I remember saying,
*"Never in a month of Sundays
is there any way that man could
have done what they are saying."*

Epilepsy

SOCIETY

Funny,
happy girl.
Scarlett was a beautiful soul,
who lived life to the fullest.
She was always so full of love
and laughter
and brightened up the lives
of everyone–
one in a million
who can never be replaced.
Sorely missed
every second of every day,
Scarlett was hilarious
and full of witty banter.

Scarlett lived life on her terms
and was loved unconditionally.
Family
and friends are devastated
by her loss.
Scarlett will be eternally loved
and missed.

Scarlett was by all accounts
a lively,
much-loved
and full of life
21-year-old lady.
She enjoyed going out
and having a drink
and dancing
as you do
when you are young.
If one good thing
can come from this tragedy,
it is a lesson can be learnt
from this death.
Think twice
before you partake

in large amounts of alcohol
and cocaine.
Your risk is so much greater
if you have epilepsy.

Equality

LABOR

Equality now!
I have a Dream,
that all men are created equal.
Normalcy–
Never Again,
Jobs and freedom,
it was King's dream–
not his march,
Largely forgotten.
It's almost didn't happen.

In '65 or '66,
most people would not have said
it was the most powerful speech ever.
One of those things that we look to,
when we want to know
what America means.

Five score years ago…
Came as a joyous daybreak
to end the long night,
the Negro still is not free,
Bad check,
far from historic, clubfooted,
set pieces.

I say to you today my friends,
even though we face
the difficulty of today
and tomorrow,
I still have a dream.
It is a dream that one day this nation
will rise up
and live out the true meaning
of its creed:
"We hold these truths

to be self-evident,
that all men
are created equal.

I have a dream
that someday on the red hills of Georgia,
the sons of former slaves
and the sons of former slave owners
will be able to sit down together
at the table of brotherhood.
… in Alabama,
little black boys
and little black girls
will be about two join hands
with little white boys
and little white girls
as sisters
and brothers.

I have a dream today
from some higher place.
Free at last,
free at last,
thank God Almighty–
we are free at last!
I am personally the victim
of deferred dreams…
but in spite of that,
I close today by saying
I still have a dream,
because you know you can't give up life.
If you lose hope,
somehow you lose the vitality
that keeps life moving,
you lose that courage to be,
the quality that helps you go on
in spite of it all
and so today I still have a dream.
Content of character,
brotherhood will be more
than a few words at the end
of a prayer,
one-day justice will roll down like water
and righteously like a mighty stream.

He's off.
He's on his own now.
He's inspired,
tell them about the dream,
Martin!
Leader,
you swept today.
He's damn good.
Like some sort of jazz musician,
it's spontaneous parts
of the speech that people remember.

DEBT

Equifax

Credit Bureaus

Data breaches are on the rise,
be prepared. Big Three.
We don't really have a choice
to opt out of the credit report system;
we spend a lot of money
trying to protect our customers
and then we give that data to others,
we value our customers
and have been in close communication
with them,
car.
Automobile leap.

It was run a little more like a sports team,
you immediately had to get out there
and perform
and if you didn't perform,
you were cut.
The Merchant's Guide.

The Federal Bureau of Investigation
is constantly in our files,
it's been a nearly 10-year investment,
but now it's paying off
for Equifax,
they have something their rivals don't.
We have been blessed
in our history to never
have a major breach,
trust
and stewards of data.
If you're not ahead of security risk,
you're behind it.

Haunt.
The demand will not satiate
their hatred for Experian,

we could turn our response
into a good Public Relations approval
if done right,
this situation has caused us all to pause,
anytime someone is not securing member data
to the same degree that we do
and we expect,
we will take action on that relationship accordingly
I am unaware of a way to just stop,
from any individual lender perspective
and not cause consumer harm.

Euro

ECONOMY

We have moved against the grain
of European opinion for centuries.
It's been happening for over
a long period of time
and we mustn't be afraid of it.
Lost their enthusiasm.

No,
an upset in Denmark
could be the next shock
that triggers euro selling.
Euro,
no our economy
hasn't been so healthy
in our lifetime.
The benefits of being outside
outweigh the benefits
of being inside.

This is an area
where there has been no sign
of any losses.
Globally,
our share of foreign investments
is falling.
These jobs could be affected
by everything that could weaken
our trading links with the euro-zone;
it's all semantics,
if you are the person
whose job is threatened.

The assumption is that
we will be in at some stage,
so there's no need to take
short-term measures
or to start rethinking strategic
considerations.
Then,

that begins
to make people nervous;
is a fact of life for us.

Is a fact of life for us.
We have the worst
of both worlds.
The question of losing the pound
is an inevitability,
it's a question of when
rather than if.
Don't do what I do
when I get to the office
every morning:
check the price of the euro;
it's very time consuming.

Europe

UNITED NATIONS

Politics
Open Door Policy

We have the biggest newsroom
in this town,
Brussels, Belgium
and this was the hit
on our community.

Bias as always.
We were on sites,
pushing that button every day,
it had a multiplier effect
and that did not go down well.
We don't want to just write about politics,
but about these different actors
are doing the things they do.

We didn't really know
how many readers inside
the 'Brussels bubble'
there could be,
tens of thousands,
we produce a kind of news
for insiders that gives them
the juice that they can use.

Daily Show.
Everyone reads it,
it has really become the thing
that starts the daily conversation here.
It means you're spinning a lot of plates.

Some of the coverage is a bit superficial
and doesn't always get to the heart
of the matter,
peep–
show journalism.
Political is firing on all cylinders

to get people talking
about them
and they are succeeding.
It's too sensationalistic,
too into hyping up
small stores.

We are making them famous.
We're making them
relevant,
even when we are being critical,
we are feeling the stories
that make them human
and even sort of interesting.
The news has been very helpful
in making everyone see
that Europe is not done
and it's not boring,
it's a work in progress.

European Central Bank

ECONOMY

The unabated growth momentum.
At the moment,
I would not be so worried,
the longer this expansive monetary policy lasts,
the greater the chance
of overvaluations
and the risk
that there could be intense price corrections.

It's not something
we are concerned about.
Stands ready.
The eurozone is doing pretty well,
we're not there yet.
The success
of a relaxed monetary course
is apparent not at the beginning,
but when it ends.

European UnionUnited Nations

UNITED NATIONS

        Brexit
I feel,
like many others
of the 48 percent,
abandoned
and leaderless,
now it's gone the way
I don't want,
so I'm not going to accept
the result.
I don't give up
on any of the values
that made me want to remain,
based on a progressive partnership.

Cliff edge.
No deal Brexit,
Sir.
Do we discuss Marcel Proust?
No.
Do we occasionally go to Arsenal together?
Yes.
If you go to the pub with me
you will see him in his element:
down-to-Earth,
grounded,
connected to those around him,
suave
and uber-ambitions.
Simpering media reports
highlighted his smart suits,
floppy hair
and chiseled good looks,
indeed,
actor Colin Firth
was said to have based his performance
as Mark Darcy on Starmer.

He will seek out a decent position
to take those
with a range of different positions
can be associated with,
even where there are extreme polarities
of view,
in the end,
if you want to implement
the progressive set of policies,
then you need a strong economy
in order to do so,
the last thing you want
is to be different
to everybody else,
now it's fantastic that people just say 'Keir'
and most people know who they are talking about.

I think he is trying to be a bridge
between essentially irreconcilable positions,
Labour's position is ducking,
diving
and triangulation,
a cliff edge
with a long diving board
than the Tory one.
Everybody has been urging me
to jump one way
or the other
and I have refused,
at every twist
and turn.

Evangelist

FAITH

Crusades,
the Reverend.
America's pastor,
I have a feeling of identification
with this country,
almost more than any place
I have ever seen,
make a decision for Christ.
I know the church will triumph,
I know we are going to win.

Thou hast permitted Richard Nixon
to lead us at this momentous hour
of our history.
I wonder whether I might have exaggerated
his spirituality in my own mind,
they're the ones putting out
the pornographic stuff,
this stranglehold has got to be broken
or the country's going down the drain.

I don't ever recall
having those feelings
about any group,
especially the Jews
and I don't have them now.
My remarks did not reflect
my love for the Jewish people.

Instant redemption.
Above all,
go to church.
Hour of Decision,
My Answer,
Youth for Christ.
Calling Youth to Christ.
Canvas Cathedral.
Puff Graham,

have a word for prayer.
I don't suppose it could do any harm.

Many people who have not agreed
with Dr. King can admire him
for his nonviolent policies
and in the eyes of the world
he has become
one of the greatest Americans,
this nation will not be defeated,
most of my life has already been lived,
I'll be glad when the moment comes
when the Lord calls me to heaven.
I get tired down here sometimes.

When I heard he had gone home,
I burst into tears,
it was like he was a family member,
someone who changed your life.
It's not that I wasn't a believer before,
but you couldn't be around him,
even from a distance,
without seeing the reality of his faith.
Authentic
and Humble.
The huge transformation in individual lives.

SOCIETY

F

*"The digital space
can't keep operating
like the Wild Wild West
at the expense
of our privacy."*

Facebook

Privacy DataPrivacy Law
DataPrivacy Law

Shadow profile.
Bad actors.
In general,
we collect data on people
who are not signed up for Facebook
for security purposes.
Collected for growth reasons
as well.
When a user signs up
for Facebook the first time…
their entire friend network
will essentially already be there.

You've said everyone
controls their data,
but you're collecting data
on people
that are not
even Facebook users,
who have never signed
a consent
or a privacy agreement.
Consumer's should have the right
to keep their information
private.
The digital space
can't keep operating
like the Wild Wild West
at the expense
of our privacy.

Shadow profile.
I don't want to regulate
Facebook
half to death,
but these are things

that need to be changed.
Our bill will help
protect Americans' online
data fingerprint.

Globally tragic,
astounding ridiculous mistake.
We cannot have a society in which,
if two people wish to communicate,
the only way that can happen
is if it's financed by a third person
who wishes to manipulate them.

Falun Gong

FAITH

The show is 5,000 years' worth of culture
in one night.
The colors are amazing,
the message is very lyrical
and clear.
The Falun Gong has a very well organized,
managed
and elaborate program
of public relations
and Shen Yun is part of that;
people want to know more
about the Falun Gong.

For 5,000 years
divine culture flourished
in the land of China.
Humanity's treasure was nearly lost,
but through breathtaking music
and dance,
Shen Yun is bringing back
this glorious culture.
Traditional Chinese spiritual practice
has been very demonized,
we were taught that Buddhism
was stupid,
so a lot of Chinese students
came to the United States
and realized they were brainwashed.
In the United States
they saw something authentic.
They were able to read freely
and they started to appreciate
spiritual guidance,
truth fullness,
compassion
and tolerance.

Shen Yun
is not a cultural performance at all,

but a political tool
of 'Falun Gong'
to preach cult messages,
spread anti-China propaganda,
increase its own influence
and raise fund.
It blasphemies
and distorts the Chinese culture
and deceives,
fools
and poisons the audience.
Master Li.

The only resistant we've seen
has been from the Chinese Communist
Party Consulate,
in the beginning
they would call the theaters
and tell them not to let Shen Yun perform.

I left home when I was 13,
I didn't see my parents for seven years.
I would get persecuted
if I came back;
I had no idea when I left,
I was really clueless.

Federal Air Marshals

GOVERNMENT

Department of Homeland

What you're seeing are symptoms
of gross management;
you can't let people who bring shame
on the agency just sail.
If the public knew
just how little punishment,
if any,
these individuals have received,
they would be outraged.

I was the easiest one to blame
because I was flying with him,
it was the whole cover-up
and protection of this guy
that should be the cause for the alarm.
There's nobody
who's overseeing
what they do,
they don't want
to answer to anybody;
they retaliate against those
who disagree
with them.
As soon as the marshals they hired
started seeing the place
wasn't going to run well,
they got demoralized
and left.

Do not reflect the commitment
and professionalism of the thousands
of federal air marshals
that protect our skies every day.
The anonymity of our air marshals
is very important to our mission,
that's the primary reason
we don't divulge details of investigations.

As far as I'm concerned,
all situations were handled appropriately,
there are some people
who came disgruntled
and probably still are disgruntled.
The job of an air marshal requires
an enormously high degree
of professionalism
and needs to be done right.
You want to have a high level
of confidence in your air marshal.

He didn't ask if
I was OK.
He said,
"Don't call the police.
I'm a cop.
We don't need
to call anybody."
He could have killed me,
and all he got
was a slap on the wrist.
That blows me away.
Extreme Drive Under Influence.

We don't reduce
many Drive Under Influence cases
down to reckless driving,
there has to be a good reason
for us to do that.
We responded to assist
Federal air marshals
In an internal investigation,
we determined it was
an accidental discharge
and that it wasn't criminal.

They couldn't produce the evidence
that I was legally drunk.
I disclosed it in my hiring process,
they were just looking to can
certain people
and not others,
it cost me my career.

He came back to his seat
like everything was ok,
so I assumed everything was ok,
reckless disregard for the safety
of others.
Everyone makes mistakes,
Murphy (Mark),
Federal Air Marshals Service.
Oversleeping
and missing time…
Federal Air Marshal getting lost
from his team in airport
etc.

Federal Clemency

GOVERNMENT

U.S. DEPARTMENT OF JUSTICE

The number of cases
that are not being acted on
is skyrocketing.
There have been times in history
when there have been just many applications,
but not this huge gap.

The processing
and evaluation of these cases
take significant time
and in many cases,
several years.
The department is aware of the staffing
needs to process the increase
in clemency positions
and is working to address this.
The department will continue to evaluate
the staffing needs of the office
routinely sending
clemency recommendations
to the White House.
The timing of the clemency grants
and denials is the president's
constitutional prerogative.

We wither encourage
nor discourage
clemency recommendations
and do not interfere in the process.
Clemency decisions are made
on a case by case basis.

Hardcore.
Valedictorian.
Naïve.
I thought that something
rational could be done,

I don't have a bottomless pit
to get the best lawyers
in Washington.
Even if I did,
I am not sure
that would help
Instead of just pardoning a turkey,
we would like the president
to also commute the sentences
of some human beings.

Now is the perfect community
for John to be given the choice
to provide the positive benefits to society
through his considerable musical talents.

This is not just a call
for (Bush) to get with the holiday spirit;
it may also be a call
for a new Attorney General to recognize
that his job
is also to be attentive
to the more common injustice that,
sadly,
we can get numb to.

Federal Government Shutdown

MILITARY

        United States
Steady as she goes–
hold the line.
I know our nation can count on you.
We will continue to execute daily operations
around the world–
ships
and submarines will remain at sea,
our aircraft will continue to fly
and our war fighters will continue
to pursue terrorists throughout the Middle East,
Africa
and South Asia,
while training for reservists
must be curtailed,
active forces will stay at the posts
adapting their training to achieve
the least negative impact
on our readiness to fight.
The command remains
mostly unaffected,
because our war fighting mission,
holding our military hostage
over their desire
to have unchecked illegal immigration.

I want to make sure that tonight
we send a clear signal
that we don't want one moment to pass
with there being any uncertainty
of any soldier anywhere in the world
that they will be paid
for the valiant work
they do for our national security.

Republicans have shut down the government
despite having control of the House,
the Senate
and the White House,

running the government month-by-month
causes longstanding harm to people
and our National Security,
this is no way to run
the greatest country on earth.
This could have all be resolved
If Republican leadership would allow a vote
on either one of the two bipartisan compromises
to find a fix for Dreamers.

Schumer shutdown,
we do some crazy things in Washington,
but this is utter madness,
Senate Democrats shut down this government
and now Senate Democrats need to open
this government back up.
Democrats are far more concerned
with Illegal Immigrants
than they are with our great Military
or Safety at our dangerous Southern Border,
they could have easily made a deal,
but decided to play shut down politics instead.

MILITARY

Filipino WWII Veterans

We have been waiting for this
for the last 60 years;
You can imagine how ecstatic we are.

The Filipino veterans
of World War II fought bravely
under the U.S military commands,
helping us win the war.
I commend my colleagues for
supporting those veterans
who stood with us.
This bill has a provision of honor.

I see this as a matter of honor,
I know some of my younger colleagues
might see this as expensive.
About 1 million Filipinos
were killed in defense of our country.
This bill restores their benefits…
how long can that last?
I appeal to the Senate.
Budget neutral,
these people were the key
to the Pacific,
without them,
we would have seen war
for another few years.
They gave us the time
to survive.

Not to be deemed to be
or to have been.
I'm not sure anyone can
say we didn't do our share,
is quite frankly
about our veterans today.
I hope this is the last time
while I'm here that…

the veteran's committee
brings a bill to the floor
that does not have bipartisan
support.

Financial Programs

FINANCE

          Digital Apps
Referee.
Finance for Normal People.
When it comes to diet
or exercise,
you have to muster self-control
every time you are hungry,
face a steak
or dessert
and every time
you have to get out of a warm bed
to go to the gym;
with financial resolutions,
you can set up a 401(k)
or Individual Retirement Account
and have payments
go into it automatically.

Automation is a way
of making a decision once
and having permanently overcome
that inertia,
if this,
then that rules that link
with digital apps
and move a set amount
of money into savings
based on certain conditions.

Do something–
take a walk
or sit down
and write it out–
where you put your perception
of reality
in front of you,
we are so constantly switching attention
and distracting ourselves,
especially from painful things

and we don't even know
we're doing it.

I've been spending time with executives
at some of the highest-performing
technology firms
on the planet
and this is the recurring theme,
set your goals
and choose the right ones.

JUSTICE

First Amendment

The first amendment provides
extremely broad protection,
but it does not permit
unbridled exploitive speech.
At the expense of Mr. Dustin Hoffman
and his distinguished career.

Dustin stood up for his rights,
and he was vindicated.
This is a victory for all celebrities.

Grand Illusions.
Tootsie.
Dustin Hoffman isn't a drag
in a butter colored silk gown
by Richard Tyler
and Ralph Lauren heels.
The right to use plaintiff's name
and likeness
is an extremely valuable commodity
and privilege.
Not only,
because of Mr. Hoffman's stature
as an actor,
but,
because he doesn't knowingly permit
commercial use of his identity.
Made absolutely no effort.
Tootsie.

First Lady

AMERICA'S NEW TRIUMPH

We loved her,
she was such an icon;
first lady
and wife.
Their love story,
was inspiring…
he wouldn't have been anything
without her by his side.
I loved how devoted
he was to her,
how much he knew
he owed to her.
He had a good wife
and he trusted her
for council
and she supported him
throughout everything in his life.
She truly cared
about her husband.
She was a very important first lady
and she was the second in command president;
not technically,
but she was his conscience.

Lying in repose
represented the best of America;
it's a tribute to the bygone era,
back when both parties
would be along with gratitude,
for your expression of sympathy
in honoring the life
of Nancy Davis Reagan.
She wasn't subservient in any way
and yet she still had that honor,
that respect
and that love for her husband.
Young people today
need to learn from history

and know how to be wives
that God wants you do be.

No cards,
no gifts for her
only the bus!
We're collecting them here revered.
Pass this on
"*just say no!*"
This is history,
I know it's not what they'd rather do
right now,
but they'll remember it
we welcome the public to come up
and pay their respects.
The president would have wanted her
to be honored this way.
The Reagan Foundation
is touched by this out pouring of support,
they're very honored,
it was just nice to be a part of history.

I'm here to pay my respect to Nancy Reagan,
the greatest first lady ever,
she was very loyal to her husband,
protective
and she was a great attendant
to President Reagan.
It was very,
very emotional.
I really sort of broke down,
I hope she is with her better half.

Nancy Reagan represented
what a first lady should be.
It's sad,
it's a generation that's going
it's a legacy that's ending.
She was a great role model
and their whole love story
just got to me,
I'd never seen
nor heard of a couple
being so much in love

as those two.
Defined by their love for each other...
without her,
I don't feel
he could have been president.
Her determination
was so ferocious
even God
might not have the guts
to argue with her.

Flight Schedule

SOCIETY

          Airlines
There may be trouble ahead,
let's face the music
and dance.
Flight numbers used to be an art,
believe it
or not.

Most people think…
10,000 is a lot for any given day,
it's not.
We're running out of numbers!
Southwest explains in a post,
'The Science Behind the Numbers'
to start with,
the numero uno industry wide rule
is that no flight number
can contain more than four digits,
meaning we only have up to flight 9999
to work with.

No airline can use five digit flight numbers!
While this has been debated
in the industry for years,
the level of effort to make the change
from four to five digits
would be huge
and even the level of technology change
to add alpha characters
to publish five numbers
would be gargantuan…
although it would be fun
to 'name' flights–
'Now boarding,
Southwest Airlines flight
FRED to Los Angeles.

Heavier-than-air flying machines
are impossible.

Now the only thing
that seems impossible
is finding numbers
to designate where's the time
to just face the music
and dance.

Flu Vaccination

COMMUNITY

Swine flu
and delay in vaccination
prolongs the time when a child
is susceptible.
The schedule that has been recommended
is based on scientific data
and studies that have been performed
to look at how safe
and effective these vaccines
are when given in combination
and have no way to project
what could happen
if their child is not vaccinated.
One can look at 10 children
and can't tell which 2
will be hospitalized
with measles
or severe rotavirus.

We need to do a better job
of monitoring the false information.
We need better ways
of providing information
to parents
so they understand
that vaccines
need to be taken seriously.
Parents need to prepare
for their children's pediatrician
appointments,
with questions
and a better understanding
of what to expect.
It helps them focus
on what they need
to get out of the visit.
Keeping clear records is vital,
especially if you have more than one child
or a child with a serious health condition.

Families with children of different ages
often ask,
"as the children age,
what do I need to do,
why
and which immunizations
do they need?"
This tool helps answers
all of those questions
and more.

A big concern now
is the potential impact
of swine flu on pediatric patients;
it's a very substantial threat.
So, it is as important as ever
for people to be vaccinated,
against seasonal influenza;
it's good protection for kids
and it turns out to be a good way
to block transmission when influenza comes
into a town or neighborhood,
which is usually passed around by kids–
which is how an epidemic occurs.

It's a personal health record for the patient,
you can put in information about each child
and receive reminders
about when to do the next checkup
or what immunizations are due,
you have the information right at your fingertips.

Swine flu.
We know seasonal flu is a threat,
make clear to everybody
that ordinary people
just like themselves
and their loved ones
are at risk;
not only from catching the flu,
but from severe complications of the flu.
Yet, many people will refuse to vaccinate.
With excuses varying from
not wanting to bother,

because they don't think it's serious in kids,
which is wrong,
to not wanting their kids
to have that momentary pain from the shot,
which it doesn't hurt more than a mosquito bite
and the risk far outweighs a quick prick,
to whatever individual health…
the greater good,
should be the health of the family,
as well as that of the community.

HOUSING

Foreclosure Auction

    Source: DataQuick
                  Information Systems

We're a nervous wreck,
exceptional inventory clearance.
Incredible deals.
It feels like we got a good bargain.
We're tired of renting,
homes are going for a great price.
We should have bid a little more–
I think we would have got it,
we're a little disappointed.

Some people tend to look at auctions
as their first option
as opposed to three years ago.
Once,
twice,
third
and final opportunity…
Sold!
Wonderful.

They've got money tied up
in these houses
that's not generating anything
for them,
it's basically a dead loss.
People see these big signs
'*Sale 20% Off,*
50% Off.
Off What?'
We don't know
what the price of housing might be.
The real price right now
is whatever they can sell if for.
They do have pretty strong incentives
to sell.

It's more exciting
than the fantasy football draft,
the market's right,
it seems hard to pass up.
Flipping it in two to three years.
We're going to another auction
on Wednesday.

Foreign Spies

GOVERNMENT

    Dangerous Love,
    academic.
    Having a handsome,
    romantic
    and cultured foreign boyfriend
    is great!

    Darling,
    there shouldn't be any secrets
    between us.

    You are a state employee,
    yet your ability to keep secrets
    is concerning.
    You are suspect of violating
    our nation's laws.

    Green cards.
    Hostile foreign forces.
    Foreign.
    Dangerous Love.
    Mistakes commonly made
    by women drivers.
    Often while on their own
    women can't find places
    that they have visited
    many times before.

Founder's Brunch

ECONOMY

We are all out there,
far off in the future,
in a place where no one knows,
where the big wins are going to be,
we are all trying different things,
and we all learn from each other.

Space Camp.
Computers are the wave
of the brave.
There are two massage tables up there.

They remind you to think
without barriers
and to take big bites
out of life.

Founder's Brunch is important
for the same reason Silicon Valley
is important:
These are all subtle
network effects,
otherwise why wouldn't you start
a tech company in Fresno
where everything in cheaper?
The advantage to being in Silicon Valley
and the San Francisco area
is that so many other people are doing
the same thing.

It is fascinating how the valley has
gone from steaks
and Manhattans,
to quiche
and granola,
to sushi
and Chardonnay.
Each new generation reinvents it.

I always come away
with some new way
of looking at my business
or markets
or technology,
it's a comfortable environment
where we can vent a bit
with each other;
something we can't do
with our investors–
you have to keep your game face
on all the time when you're the CEO.
Except at Founder's Brunch.

Anti-networking,
I get zero value out
of the Silicon Valley event.
Founder's Brunch
is something I'm religious about.
I don't really get up
this early on Sunday,
but this gathering is very powerful.

Fox Cubs

WILDLIFE AID FOUNDATION

They are wild animals,
not pets.
Nasty commercial element.
Fox cubs for sale,
120 pounds lovely pets.

Disappeared.
Only charged to get real people,
not idiots that will take them
for money
and end up not looking after them.

After 37 years rescuing wildlife,
not much surprises me,
but I am gob smacked
that anyone would attempt to sell
fox cubs as pets.

Free Speech

JUSTICE

Free speech zone.
City officials had an emergency
meeting Wednesday
with the National Football League
and agreed to invoke
an overflow cause in the contract
that allows
the National Football League
to restrict free speech
activities in the stadium area.
Jew for Jesus members were told
they could pass out leaflets,
but only in a small zone that the city
set up that is so much removed,
they can't reach their intended audience.
The constitution gives people the right
to speak freely,
but it also gives them the right
to speak effectively.
You can't do that if you're
put off in a corner.

We believe the zone
meets the criteria,
there's a lot going on
in the parking lot—
private parties,
staging for the events,
tons of television trailers,
as the exclusive user
of the lot that day,
it's primarily
the National Football League
who has the right to say,
"*We're only going to allow
people with tickets
into the parking lot.*"
Squelching.
It's so that people

can get to the game.
The nature of the Super Bowl
could tend to attract
large numbers of people
who want to take an advantage
of the Super Bowl,
to promote their own cause.
A worldwide media event provides,
unfortunately,
a perfect opportunity for terrorism.
A crime of violence.
The more people
there are in the parking lot,
the harder it is to make sure
they don't try to plant
a bomb
or something like that.

We're disheartened,
we feel it's within our First Amendment rights
to distribute Gospel literature
exactly outside the ticketed areas.
Sudden death in overtime.
Religious literature,
with a football theme.

Gas Prices

ECONOMY

I will pay for it,
but I might have to send a letter,
to somebody,
every time I fill this thing up.
It costs about fifty to sixty dollars,
every four days.
Corporate America today,
you work harder than
you've ever worked in your life,
yet,
they degrade you
and raise the prices.
I think,
the whole thing's a scam,
somebody is getting rich here.
It seems to jump in spurts,
the prices are way too high.
Need I say more?
It's ridiculous.
Every time a holiday
weekend
comes around,
prices go up,
sometimes up to
twenty cents
a gallon;
the gas companies
put the screws to us
every chance they get.

This is three times cheaper
than in Germany.

The people are very thankful
to have somebody full-serve
out in the middle of nowhere,
it's a penny business.
We make only a few cents
on every gallon,

every time prices go up,
customers say that we're toying around
to attach the customer;
actually,
the independent dealer
is taking the hit.

Prices have already peaked
in a lot of locations
and are headed down,
the period of dramatic
increases is over.

The wholesale price of gas
has actually been stealthily decreasing
since August,
yet we're seeing
an average price increase
of six
and eight cents per gallon
for regular unleaded since August 20th.
Our only conclusion from that
is that the oil companies
are using the high gas consumption
over the labor day weekend
to gouge consumers.

Gender

LABOR

There's quite a few people
going through that
in Silicon Valley right now,
it's exploding.
It's mostly young men,
younger than me.
It's a witch hunt,
Dangerous.
I'm sitting in a soundproof booth right now,
because I'm afraid someone will hear me.
When you're discussing gender issues,
it's almost religious,
the response.
It's almost zealotry.

The creep.
Decency pledge.
In just the last 48 hours,
I've spoken to a female tech executive
who was grabbed by a male
Chief Executive Officer
at a large event
and another female executive
who was asked to interview
at the venture fund,
because they
(feel like they need)
to hire a woman,
we should worry
about whether the women-in-tech
movement has gone too far
sometime after a couple of these
aren't regularly happening anymore.
It's become fashionable in Silicon Valley
for people like James,
a white man,
to be put into a category
of less desirable for promotion
and advancement,

we'll give you a bonus
if you're a hiring manager
and you hire 70% women
to this organization.
That's illegal.

Which aren't.
Contrarians,
diversity dogma.
Rarer than in most businesses.
There's a gun to the head.
There's a high awareness right now,
which is positive,
at the same time–
there's a fear.
The emperor is naked,
since someone said it,
now it's become sort of acceptable.
The whole idea that diversity
improves workplace output,
it's not scientifically decided
that that's true.

What Google did
was wake up sectors
of society that weren't into
these issues before,
The Myth of Male Power,
the less safe the environment is for men,
the more they will seek
little pods of safety
like the tech world.
When you're on a mission from God
to set the world straight,
it's easy to go too far,
there was no control over women
hiring women.
No eyebrows are going to rise
if a woman heads up fashion,
but we're talking about
women staffing positions–
things like autos–
where it cannot be explained
other than manipulation.

Charles Darwin himself
would be fired from Google
for his views on the sexes.
Dear @ Google,
stop teaching my girl
that her path to financial freedom
lies not in coding,
but in complaining to Human Relations.
A sea of brilliant women.
Figure out how to more fully empower them,
it's exhausting,
it's created divides
that I didn't anticipate.

General Motors

ECONOMY

We're aiming for a future
of zero crashes,
zero emissions
and zero congestion;
we need to accelerate acceptance
of electric vehicles.
General Motors is sending the message
to investors
that it is speeding toward
an autonomous electric future
that will include ride-sharing
and will be profitable,
getting to the point
where we can launch this technology
is the beginning of the journey.
It will rapidly improve
from the minute it is launched,
there will be a step
and massive learning curve
and the product will massively get better.

Biggest Internet of Thing.
Network ever,
software is the differentiated products,
meaning a company
is developing it
and if you're sufficiently advanced
may not be able to compete,
that's how you can create a gap
between AV ride-sharing
with it somehow.

Our vehicles encounter challenging
and often absurd situations
up to 46 times more often
than other places
that self-driving cars are tested
and while we're generally drawn
to tough problems,
we test in San Francisco only,
because cars at scale.

Generation Y

SOCIETY

Baby Boomers
It's really difficult
to be a Gen-Y now,
because this is the generation
that grew up to be optimistic.
They were told that they were bright.
They were told that they were the future.

Suddenly,
terrorism hits
and the economy falls.
Even if they did get a job,
they will not be promoted
to vice president,
like they had hoped.

Tonight show.
This is a generation
that likes to buy fancy sneakers,
they may not have as much saved
as they had hoped.
I do think
that they are an entitled generation.
A lot of parents say
*"If I am going to give them
a good place to live…."*

Midlife crisis.
The unique challenges of life
usually occurs
in your fifties.
A natural increase,
that means our sons
and daughters.
If there is a crisis,
the crisis is the home market.
The crisis is found on the echo
with the baby boomers,
the Y generation.

I think there is a lot
of evidence now that shows
the market has peaked.
It's hard for me to imagine
the prices dropping;
I think you'll see the note
of appreciation slowing down.

Germany

UNITED NATIONS

Have never had it better.
Poorest neighborhood in Germany.
I think it is tragic
that the Tafel Food Bank even exists,
that it needs to exist,
I don't know what the politicians think
is happening here
and what they are doing.

Superficial
and undifferentiated.
That is her mantra
and it is true for a large majority
of the people of Germany,
but the growing prosperity
of the majority
has come at the expense of many others.

Poverty
and Wealth are structurally connected
in this country,
as they are in the United States.
Part of society that has benefited
from the changes of the Agenda 2010
that the prime minister refers to repeatedly
and increasingly positively,
but if I look at other developments,
such as the precarious job situation,
1.2 million people who hold down jobs,
but still live below the poverty level–
the food banks have more than 1.5 million people
whom they are helping–
how an average family
has never had it so difficult
to find affordable housing
in Germany's large cities–
these are development
that Angela Merkel to block out.

Time for equality.
Time for Martin Schulz,
in the beginning,
he tried very hard to just sell the left-wing positions
and I think he was very successful.
People believe him
and they like the idea of turning left,
then came the Saarland elections
and he just did a flip-flop move.

They make some good points,
but considering what I do,
they are out of question,
sending them to six seminars
on how to apply for a job
will not increase their chance of getting a job,
we have the impression that the next government,
we are preparing for that.

What has been forgotten
is our generation of women,
those of us between 70 to 80
and started our families
with little
or nothing,
we were taught to make do
with what we had
and raise our children,
but now we find ourselves with nothing.

Ghost

FAITH

Imprisoned souls.
White light.
Actually,
I'm the last one people call
when they have something strange
going on in their home...
They've called the exterminator,
the electrician,
even the plumber,
then,
they'll call the minister,
yet,
the noises still continue.
So,
then,
they call me.
They're almost apologetic.
They think it's probably nothing.
I say,
"Go ahead
and tell me about it."

Anywhere that people hang out,
there are ghost hanging out there,
too.
I run into skeptics all the time,
I get hate mail.
My response is:
"There is no way
I can convince you,
but these things do exist."
Hundreds of people
have called me in the past thirty years,
because they thought
they had ghosts
in their homes
and they usually did.
It's a blessing to be able
to help people;

without them having any fear
of being judged that I'm going to look at them crazy.

The world's most psychic family,
I was at a dinner party once
and the last thing on my mind
was ghost.

People die the same way they live,
with friends,
loved ones
and colleagues,
in communities.
Theirs.
We were just overwhelmed
with what was there,
people kept talking about
the orderliness of it all,
people used what they had
learned in grade-school fire drills.
"Stay in line,
don't push,
we'll all get out."
People were quelling up!
It was just absolutely incredible.

Man,
there wasn't a sound in there.
Not a scream.
Nothing.
My thought was that,
I'm responsible for these people.
I think most of the employees
feel that way.
I was pushing people out the door,
kind of like cattle,
to show them where to go,
this is my party.
They were,
because of me
knowing where to go.
Keeping a clear head
was the most important thing,
because your brain–

at least mine–
just shut down.
When that happened,
you need to know
what to do next,
one thing you don't ever
want to do is to have
to think in a disaster.
Stop.
Be still.
Be silent.
Be calm.

When I went into the house
and there was one,
a man,
standing at the bottom of
the staircase smiling…
it's a curse,
it's a blessing to be able
to help people who
are afraid of what I do,
or don't believe it,
or think I am evil.
I'm sorry to hear that,
I guess you're getting it.
They just happen to be dead.

Imprisoned.
They are afraid to face God,
because of some things
they did in their life.
There is someone
they do not like
who has died
and they don't want
to run into them in heaven.
They think going to heaven
is going to be a real drag.

They feel a strong pull
of a loved one on this side,
so they stay,

thinking they are helping them
in their grieving process.

People are so afraid of ghosts
and they don't need to be.
People could get rid of them
by putting their foot down
and saying,
*"You're not welcome in my house.
I want you to go to the white light
and go home."*
You are the one with the body.

Just because a window curtain ripples
or there is a cold spot in a room
doesn't mean there is a ghost,
I would say it needs to be proven.
I could imagine that just about
all your ghosts are things
that could be something else
and they probably are
something else.
The sixth sense.
Ghost.
Always.

We enjoy this field of study,
because it provides physical evidence
of life after death
and that we should not fear death.
We work with many people
who are approaching death
and can give them comfort
about the life to come.

Glass Towers

VENUES

In this day
and age,
society wants to be more transparent,
look at the Internet,
where information is free
and available to everyone.

32 stories of cool blue luxury
in the heart of San Francisco.
I wanted a look that would be fluid
close to water.
San Francisco's urban form is
kind of sad-looking,
solids
and concrete
or stone.

The idea was to create a fragmented
crystal with striations that keep shifting,
it's more about the shape
of the building
than the color of the grass.

We were really tired
of being pre-cast concrete panels
with green-glass windows;
to get something
with its own integrated color
seemed like a nice change.
Curtain walls.
Contribute.

Blue.
Reluctance factor.
Blends.
Glass is changing rapidly,
because the demands
on the glass companies
are changing rapidly.

Sustainability is coming on
like a rocket ship.

Curtain walls,
contribute to the visual
unity of the city.
Highly reflective materials,
particularly mirrored
or highly reflective glass,
should not be used.

I can't say we've said
"Aha,
there's the perfect solution."
Our job is to take the collective view.
This city has such overwhelming masonry,
the balance won't be tripped
by the latest crop,
but we could be at a point
south of Market Street
where we encourage
the next set of guys
to come in with something
other than all-glass facades.

A diaphanous candle stick,
this is an art,
not a science,
we're trying to do our best
between all their compelling objectives.

Global Warming

NATURE

These are really exciting results,
nobody had ever actually done
a large-scale experiment
like they've done,
under the conditions
that they did it.
Carbon dioxide.
basalt core for solidified carbon dioxide,
like limestone,
permanently storing the carbon
in the rock.

We were surprised,
We didn't expect this.
We thought it would be a project
that would go on for decades.
May be 20 years from now,
We'd have an answer to the question.
But that it happened so fast
and in such a brief period of time,
that just blew us away.
This is really the start of this,
at the highest level,
which is sort of unusual
for research projects.

They look like salt
from a salt shaker…
on the surface of this gray
or black basaltic rock,
these result are so encouraging
that it's worth figuring out
some of the places
where that could be done,
and trying that out
on a larger
and longer scale.

Google, Incorporated

ECONOMY

Google has this aura
about them,
but now the shine
has waned;
whether deservedly
or not.
Google's position
is
and will remain
pretty formidable.
We have had some conversations,
again to think about
possibly buying more.
Even though there is still a lot of hype
around the company,
they can't necessarily guarantee
that that's going to always be there
to support their stocks.

This is Google's first rough patch,
that will test their quality
as a company.
An Owner's Manual
for Google Shareholders:
Google is not a conventional
company;
it has no intention to become one.

We'll have to see,
if this is the kind of market
where you act first,
then ask questions later.
When you begin to ask
the questions,
where you come to the conclusion
that is this still one of the best
business models in the world?

It suddenly changes
people's perceptions
of the company,
they wonder if the stock
is priced too high
or if the growth
is gone.
It can be hard for a company
to regain momentum
once their investors change
sentiment.

I think Google is going
Through a rough time
right now;
we are just waiting
for some good news
to come out,
before we start
rebuilding our position.

Google for Jobs

ECONOMY

The challenge of connecting job seekers
to better information on job availability
is like many search challenges
we've solved in the past,
right next door.
It's still early days,
but we've seen promising results.

We are happy to see
that 13 years after Indeed launched,
Google has woken up to the fact
that searching for jobs
is one of the most important searches
in anyone's life.
Increase the efficiency
of job matching,
it's something we see
in the search logs.
We see signs of our users
being frustrated
and being stressed
while they're doing job seeking queries.

Google's always looking
at new things it can do
with the skill set it has
and particularly ways it can get deeper
into search
and deeper into enterprises.
Jobs are a good fit
for both of those,
where it can provide
a custom
or deep search function
for job listings
on the 30 employers,
job boards
and staffing agencies.
This partnership with google helps

us accomplish that goal,
it has the potential to radically
improve discovery of the millions
of jobs on LinkedIn.

JUSTICE

Golden State Killer

DNA
New Technology

It's a lot harder to be a serial killer
or rapist now that it used to be—
they get identified sooner,
depending upon what D N A
or other forensics there are,
we can link them together sooner
than in the past
because of technology,
familial DNA.

The Night Stalker got away with a lot,
he could have been identified through DNA
if they had the same capacity,
because he was a convicted felon.

The DNA is the answer.
Collecting the sample
from the guy
is the ultimate. That's the proof.

Government Shutdown

FINANCE

            U.S. Debt
It's nerve-racking.
It sucks,
to be honest.
I want that budget for the wall,
I also have skin in the game.
I'm not getting paid
and I'm defending our borders.
We're going to do our job
like we're supposed to,
nothing changes,
except we don't get paid.
It costs billions of dollars
every time they do this,
not to mention the impact
on consumer confidence
every time they threaten to do this,
there are two things we don't want
or this time of year,
ice storms
and consumers worried
about whether they're going
to be getting their paychecks.

Business as usual.
As long as there are sufficient fees
to support operations,
the safety of human life
and the protection of property,
in previous shutdowns,
we have maintained personnel
to support the International Space Station
and its crew
and currently operating space missions,
such as satellites,
landers,
rovers,
to ensure they're safe
and secure.

There have been many negotiations
like this in the past
and we've looked back
at the way they've been covered
and it looks like people
were much more hysterical
about what might happen
that in retrospect
would have been logical,
portends a difficult set of negotiations
going into the debt ceiling,
which can be much more problematic
than a shutdown
for the faith
and credit
of the United States economy.

Border Patrol people.
I'm a builder
and I would have Mexico pay for it,
believe me.
Big,
fat beautiful door
right in the middle,
build a wall.
Build a wall.
Build a wall.
One way
or the other,
we are going to get a wall,
we are going to get a barrier.
In the White House,
working hard.
We are negotiating
with the Democrats
on desperately needed Border security,
gangs,
drugs,
human trafficking
and more.
But it could be a long stay.
Artistically designed steel slats.

We're still talking,

very far apart.
We have certainty,
we will end this
the first week in January.
Somethings broken
and we don't have the strength
to look in the mirror
and fix it,
the American people
are going to grow more
and more cynical.
They brought this about,
because they're under a lot of pressure–
we all know this–
from their far left
feel compelled to disagree
with the president,
pushed the pause button
until the president,
from whom we will need a signature
and Senate Democrats
from whom we will need votes,
reach an agreement.

All my beautiful working people
of the Federal Government,
come to any of my places
with your families
at the bar between 2-5pm
for a free sandwich,
everyday until back to work!
Because of one person
and one person alone–
President Trump.
We arrived at this moment,
because President Trump
has been on a destructive
two-week temper tantrum
demanding the American taxpayer
pony up
for an expensive
and ineffective border wall
that the President promised
Mexico would pay for.

Graffiti

JUSTICE

If somebody really likes
to '*bomb*',
they don't care.
They may be afraid
of the *Vandals Squad*.

Hall of fame.
Tagger.
They paint,
take a picture and go home,
they don't have to go
to the Empire State building.
That's enough for them,
because in this art form
you learn nothing lasts forever.

They'll come over
and film themselves
tagging the train,
then we'll arrest them
and use the videotape against them.
They usually intend to stay a day,
but they end up staying
a lot longer,
because they get caught up
in our Judicial process.

I believe when the phrase
'*quality of-life crimes*'
began to be used,
that was one of the turning points
for viewing graffiti as something
more than just scrawling
on a wall by a young person.

Crews.
Tag.
It's only been in the last
few months that we looked

at this new way
of putting a case together,
I think the courts are more ready
to take graffiti seriously…
so we're in a new mind set
to start looking at new ways
of precaution.

There are a lot of people who,
when they come, say,
*"Where are the trains
with the graffiti on them?"*
In a lot of people's minds,
that's what New York looks like.
They caught one
or two,
but they can't stop the other hundred
who are coming behind those kids,
for some kids,
it's their way of sticking
their hand out of a crowd
and saying,
"I exist."

Nicer crew.
Being from the Bronx,
I could paint a train here
and it would be my rolling gallery,
because it would ride
through Manhattan
and end up in Brooklyn
or Queens.
Then it would ride back
and everyone in New York
would see it.

Arrests are up
and incidents of graffiti are down.
The reason we really target
graffiti is,
because when you leave
graffiti in an area,
it creates an atmosphere

where people believe
they can engage
in criminal conduct
without fear of retribution.

Grandparents

PARENTS

My grandma
is the kingpin of
Torrance
and when she likes something,
everybody hears about it.

When I need a ride,
I just dial the telephone number
and press 1,
when I'm ready to come here,
I dial the number
and press 2
and they already know where I am.
It's already an ideal situation
for me…
being without a car,
it's a nice alternative.

Technology is really critical
for older people,
especially in terms of help
and assistance.
The number of older people
is increasing,
but care is declining.
That care can only be filled,
in a large part,
by technology.

That's a mistake,
aging in place,
shortly after grandma lost her vision,
she broke her leg.
I started looking into
how expensive a caretaker would be
to help with groceries,
odd jobs
and transportation.
The price seemed unreasonable.

I'm totally a child of the 21st century;
I would rather just use an app
to pay for the groceries
and pay the $6 delivery charge,
but of course grandma doesn't have access
to those things.
Now she does.

It's a great thing he's done
in a fairly niche view
of the need,
but he needs to carry it
a step forward.
There's so much opportunity
in this space
and there are not many people
focusing on it.

Great Britain

UNITED NATIONS

       Head of the Commonwealth

Vision,
duty
and steadfast service.
Sincere with.
Deeply touch.
In every possible way.

Strong consensus,
no small measure,
because of the vision,
duty
and steadfast service of Her Majesty
in nurturing the growth
of this remarkable family
of nations.

On behalf of all our citizens
I want to express the gratitude
for everything Her Majesty has done
and will continue to do,
His Royal Highness has been a proud supporter
of the Commonwealth for more than four decades
and has spoken passionately
about the organization's unique diversity.
It is fitting that he will one day continue
the work of his mother.

Green Zone

MILITARY

> American Special Operations

Until he says what the conditions are,
all that means is
we'll be there as long as we want,
for whatever reason we want
and they don't have to lie to do that,
because the conditions will never be good enough
to say we're absolutely not needed.

The transition decade,
I would guess the United States
has to plan on being inside Afghanistan
for a decade
or more
in order for there to be any type of resolution,
it's definitely past his term in office,
no two ways about it.

It seems America is not yet ready
to end the longest war in its history,
as Trump stated,
'Americans are weary
of the long war in Afghanistan.
We shall cast further worry into them
and force American officials
to accept realities.'
I think a lot of the discussions
when people talk about American presence
in Afghanistan,
the memory comes
of when they were actively involved
in combat
and bodies were coming back
to the United States.
That is no longer the case,
the majority of those soldiers are helping us
improve our logistics,
organizational capabilities,

putting systems in place
while yes,
there is an element of counterterrorism operations,
it's largely airstrikes supporting
the Afghan special forces.

Grenfell Tower

GOVERNMENT

A gross breach
of a relevant duty of care.
We don't blame the worker,
we want to get at the corporation
or those involved in making the decisions.

Value a human life in money,
publicity order,
a much larger company will take legal advice
before embarking on a new project,
all that goes through rigorous compliance.
Duty of care.
It will be a test case for the act.

Guantanamo Bay

MILITARY

    Relay some of the concerns
    they have
    and some of the issues
    that they wanted to raise
    and discuss with us;
    critical.
    Most of the issues
    are issues we've been dealing with.

    A general lack of organization.
    Who is in control?
    Who is accountable?
    What are the system-wide procedures?
    The point is,
    the International Committee
    of the Red Cross
    still have unanswered questions.

    There are some serious issues
    between us
    and the Red Cross
    about Guantanamo…
    but they have nothing to do
    with the kinds of abuses
    that we've been hearing about
    in Iraq;
    the impact of long-term detention.
    Enemy combatants.
    Some improvements in the conditions
    of detention
    and treatment
    of the prisoners.
    Objectionable.
    It's not as bad
    as the International Committee
    of the Red Cross's report.
    on Iraq.

Guatemala

UNITED NATIONS

    Genocide

A Christian should carry his bible
and his machine-gun,
subversion.
Guatemala has come out of the darkness
into the light.
State of siege,
moralize national life
from the top down.

Internal enemy.
Communism.

Gun Control

JUSTICE

It should not be minimized
how big a victory this was
for gun control advocates,
not only does it affirm
the constitutionality of restrictive
conceal-carry laws in California's
major cities,
it also makes it less likely
the Supreme Court will step in.
California has really been
pursuing a gun control agenda
more vigorously than any other state
in the nation.

The 2nd Amendment may
or may not protect
to some degree
a right of a member
of the general public
to carry a firearm in public,
if there is such a right,
it is only a right to carry
a firearm openly.
Good cause.
Since The 2nd Amendment
does not protect
in any degree the right to carry
concealed firearms in public,
any prohibition
or restriction a state may choose
to impose a concealed carry –
including a requirement of
'*good cause*',
however defined –
is necessarily allowed by
the Amendment.

A total ban on the right
of an ordinary citizen to carry

a firearm in public
for self-defense.
While states may choose
between different manners
of bearing arms for self-defense,
the right must be accommodated,
a major victory for public safety.
The decision is well within
the legal mainstream,
aligning the 9th circuit with courts
that have upheld
nearly identical laws
in New York,
New Jersey
and Connecticut,
it is just the latest judicial recognition
that common-sense gun laws
do not violate the 2nd Amendment.

Given the political inclinations
of the judges on this panel.
Avoided answering the critical
legal question of whether,
if concealed carry is prohibited,
some form of open carry
of firearms must be followed,
California law bans open carry,
so the constitutionality of that ban
will now have to be tested
Possibility.
Out of touch.
This decision will leave good people
defenseless,
as it completely ignores the fact
that law-abiding Californian's
who reside in Counties with
hostile sheriff's will now
have no means to carry a firearm
outside the home
for personal protection.

I generally think
that judges are like the rest of us
and many of us don't want to see

people carrying guns
into the Starbucks
when we are getting our morning Latte.
We did not relax our standards,
because we wanted to wait
for a final decision in that case,
vindicated..
In Yolo Country.
I think this is an effective policy
and it seems to have been working
effectively for years,
how many times have
you been attacked?
How many friends
do you have
who have been attacked?
I'm not talking
about the exception,
I have five daughters
and I can say
I would not honestly give a weapon
to anyone of my daughters.

JUSTICE

Gun Control Law

Should the commerce of arms
and ammunition be prohibited
in Brazil?
This is not Switzerland
or England
or even the United States;
this is the country that kills
with firearms more
than any place in the world.

We're experiencing an epidemic,
a plague
and radical steps are required
to control the spread
and irresponsible use of arms.
We're still ahead,
but our curve is dropping
and they are gaining.
They've been stronger
than I thought they would be
and their strategy
is much more efficient
than ours.

Voting now has become a protest
against everything that is going on,
as if we were the government.

Once bandits know with certainty
that law-abiding citizens
no longer have guns in their homes,
that they can go in without fear,
then God help the Brazilian family.
If approved,
this measure is not
going to affect criminals,
but will only prevent ordinary citizens
from defending themselves.
Criminals don't go to the store

to buy their guns,
they get them clandestinely
through networks of contraband;
which are only going to grow.
If yes wins,
90 percent of what gets turned in
will be useless old junk.
Disarmament is good for criminals.
Wake up Brazil
and vote no.
Middle-class voters are terrified,
because they don't see the investment
being made public security,
that makes us talk much harder.

Hackers

ECONOMY

H

"There's this idea among hackers of information wanting to be free and that you should have access to software tools."

If you try to derive me,
I will take it from you.
The company took two years
to design this program,
I broke into it
in three months.
We're taking advantage
of their weakness.
Pfft.
We can do it tomorrow;
you're asking for something
very cheap.
Two dollars,
you have to understand
how they make the software
in the first place...
Crackers destroy.
Hackers create.
When you're a professional hacker,
you are a distinguished type of person.
There's something sacred
in the world of hackers.
The way I know a hacker is real
is by his words.
In order to become a member,
hackers all over the world exchange
their information with each other;
there are lots of websites to do so–
If you don't give,
you don't get.
We focus on business applications.

We have not found
that there is a specific correlation
between the price
of a software piracy
in a market.
Counterfeiters fabricate products
and sell it for whatever

the market will bear...
just lowering prices does not
necessarily result in less piracy;
there is more to it than that;
I can understand how a hacker,
who is following hacker ethics,
could feel that way.
There's this idea
among hackers
of information
wanting to be free
and that you
should have access
to software tools.
This is the way they're fighting back
against America's aggression.
They say a lot of companies
are giving to Israel,
so it's even better to use pirated
software than licensed software
since you're taking money from Israel.

Haiti

UNITED NATIONS

Everything is going to be alright,
we are here to do one job
for one person,
Aristide.
He is the hope after God.
The one we believe in after God.
He is the one who can do something.

I trust in the elections in Haiti,
but I do not trust the elections
in the United States,
they do not know
how to hold good elections
in their own country.
Haiti is a professional in elections.
We know how to do elections.

We are not going to recognize
this election.
We are going to assemble all
of the sector of society
who argued with the election.
We are going to look for
the support of the Haitian majority
who abstained from the elections.

I want to be free;
I want liberty,
I am not free,
yet.
Nothing functions,
yet,
I want change.
Aristide is the only hope
to take us all out of this misery.

The questionable legitimacy
of his government is less important,
in a funny way,

than the belief of the international
community that Haiti is a waste of time,
he is up against a double problem.
He has promised too much
to the Haitian people
and he has disillusioned
the international community too much.

JUSTICE

Hate Crime Email

He just snapped,
he was a high achiever—
a student at Cal Poly Pomona
and he thought that others
were receiving the advantages
that he was denied to.
So he voted.
He didn't mean to harm anyone.
He wishes he could take it all back.

I hate your race.
I want you to die.
Kill all wet backs.
Come down
and kill,
but this message stunned me.
I felt very vulnerable.
I feared for my life.
I finally broke down into tears.
Looking over my shoulder.

We hope that this case sends
A message that you cannot
hide behind the perceived
anonymity of the Internet
in committing such crimes,
this office will vigorously
prosecute those that threaten
the integrity of our system
through attacks based on
race
or nationality.

Hate Groups

JUSTICE

An organization that–
based on official statements
or principles,
the statements of its leaders
or its activities–
has beliefs
or practices that attack
or malign an entire class of people,
typically for their immutable characteristics.
They demonize women
as an entire population,
it's the same kind of language
directed at demonizing all women
and trying to make women look
like a lesser form of humanity.

This has been a year
that has been increasing divisiveness
and bigotry,
particularly in the mainstream
of American life,
there has been a substantial emboldenment
of the radical right
and that is largely due to the actions
of President Trump,
who has tweeted out hate materials
and made light of the threat to our society
posed by hate groups,
have brought them into the political system
in a way that hasn't happened in decades.

Blame on both sides.
The president condemns hatred,
bigotry
and violence in all forms,
he will continue to fight for all Americans,
regardless of race,
religion,
gender

or background
and any suggestion otherwise
is wrong
and insulting.

Mainstream black activist groups,
such as Black Lives Matter,
that work to eliminate
systematic racism
in American society
and its institutions.

Healthcare

COMMUNITY

Social unrest.
An unpopular war.
The draft.
The sexual revolution.
Assassinations.
Drug experimentation.

I had heard about this clinic
that was seeing all these young people
who needed help;
it was free.
They had saved my life–
I was in Las Vegas
when I got sick
and no one would help me,
but when I got there,
they saw me,
then sent me over to Cedars-Sinai.
It's nice to go somewhere
and not feel like
you're being a bother.

Last year,
I didn't have any insurance
and I went there.
It was good,
safe
and clean.
I was surprised;
I had expected
something else.

I went to work for them,
immediately,
at the co-op.
Our philosophy,
was always one of being non-judgmental,
of treating patients
with a humanistic approach

and believing that people are entitled
to healthcare.
I felt that we were making a statement.

The clinic had to struggle hard
to be keep afloat;
it was terrible.
I was so taken
with what was happening there,
how poor they were.
There was never any money for rent.
The Sothers Brothers paid the rent
for a number of months.

We didn't get depressed,
though,
because we were making a difference,
but if we could just get a studio
to get back our fundraising events;
everything would become easier.
The clinic
fundraising staff
has argued
that those who have the capacity
to give have a moral obligation
to do so.
It was sad,
because we were so optimistic.
Finally,
we thought,
the rest of the world
is realizing that
everyone needs healthcare,
but the need now
is more than it ever was.

The clinic needs to double its work.
We really thought that
we might go out of business,
because healthcare
would be for everyone
and we wouldn't have
people lining up outside
around the block to see us.

This is a clinic
that doesn't like
to say no,
but sometimes
we have to.
The biggest misconception people
have of us is that they think
we're some kind of county facility.
Before,
we were providing
more of a Band-Aid approach
to healthcare.
Now,
we provide more extensive
medical care than ever before.
It's not that different
from a clinic where you pay.
It's easy to think
there will be some
outside solution
that will come down the road,
but the reality is that
that hasn't happened
and it isn't going to happen
in the near future.

In the early days,
the clinic leadership preferred
to twist the arms of the wealthy
instead of asking clients to pay fees
or accepting government subsidies
to care for the poor.
We were tempted many times
to charge for this
or that.
I'm glad
we didn't do that,
we didn't have to do that,
because instead
we built up a lot of community support
and Lenny,
the clinic director,
only accepted one-hundred dollars
a week;

if he even got paid at all.
I have to give credit to the board
for holding things together
at that time.
Throughout our history,
the board has gone through
so many long,
philosophical battles
about whether they should ever
take a government dollar
and if they did,
would they be selling out?
I have to say,
there's a part of me
that's apprehensive
about a partnership
with the county,
because of the bureaucracy.
We believe in a partnership–
of the government
and the private sector
working together,
but we,
also,
have to have the ability
to sustain things
when government funds are shaky,
but indigent care
is what we're all about.

The clinic is a microcosm for
where healthcare should go—
to care for the whole person.
The doctors here only
have to worry about the patients,
we are a very efficient
and compassionate mode
of healthcare delivery.
We use volunteers
in a very core,
fundamental way;
not to straighten out the papers
or put stamps on envelopes.
We use them

to check people in
and to help deliver patient care.
We ask for quite of a commitment
and our ability to see patients
is dependent on them.
We dearly appreciate them
for providing such good service.
The doctors
and all the staff
who work here are very kind.
We couldn't have survived without
the business people on our board,
the banking community,
or the doctors.
They are truly kindhearted people.

No one in the community thought
we were encouraging
drugs
and sex—
The big criticism
was that we did draft counseling.
We see the opportunity
to do new things
and it's difficult
to restrain ourselves.
The biggest challenge
to the clinic right now
is how to continue
and balance the needs
of the community,
which are very overwhelming,
with the resources
that we are able to bring
to the table.

The clinic really played
an important role as leaders
on access-to-care issues in California.
They have spoken out on behalf of populations
who sometimes don't vote
and who often don't have a primary doctor—
who can advocate on their behalf.
We are in an environment

where government desires,
very strongly,
to act back on the money
spent on healthcare.
That is happening at the federal,
state
and local levels.
As Los Angeles County limits
the number of individuals
who receive healthcare
through the general relief program.

Los Angeles County
has the largest concentration
of uninsured–
2.6 million
of any community
in the United States.
Without facilities
like Los Angeles Free,
that population
would be even more poorly served
and at risk
then they currently are.

The clinic has become
one of the premier providers
of primary healthcare
to the poor,
the elderly
and the uninsured.
They don't do it
for the money.
They do it,
because they have a mission:
that healthcare is a right,
not a privilege.
The clinic is important to
those of us
who are advocators
of healthcare reform.
The ones in the trenches,
delivering the care.
The inspiration for

and a model for
what the future needs to be,
but have always practiced
what they preach.
There are one thousand
and one
reasons not to be involved
in a partnership with the county,
but they know
there is a potential
healthcare crisis
in the county
and they wanted
to be part of the solution.
They had every reason
not to get involved
with the community–
It's a pain;
it's a bureaucracy.

Heart Attack

SOCIETY

How do you know
you are having a heart attack?
Nausea.
Shortness of breath.
Chest discomfort.
Mild chest pain.

How old?
Fifty.

Hey,
Lenny,
we got another one.

Mr. Bricks,
you are suffering
from a heart attack.

Are you sure?
Yes,
before
and after.

To be frank,
I'm embarrassed
for the American Academy of Pediatrics
today.
Treatment with medications in the absence
of any clear date?
I hope they're readying
for the public backlash.

What is the data that shows
this is helpful for preventing heart attacks?
How many heart attacks
are we hoping to prevent this way?
There's no data regarding that.
Among the vast majority of children,
this will not even be an issue,

we're talking about the potentiality
treating thousands and thousands
of children simply to possibly prevent
one heart attack.
That kind of risk benefit calculation
is entirely absent
from the American Association of Pediatrics'
policy.

When you have a kid
whose cholesterol looks like an overweight
55 years old;
what do you do?
The committee had to balance
the risks of not treating children
with powerful drugs,
about which there is limited
long-term data,
with the risks of not treating
children with unprecedented cardiovascular
disease risk factor.
My concern
is what this is saying about society
when we are so quick
to prescribe drugs
for these conditions
before having systematically attacked
the problem from the public
health perspective.

We extrapolate from the information
we have in adults,
decreasing cholesterol
and giving some of those drugs
decreases risk of heart disease
or death.
So there's really no reason to think
that would be any different in children.
Obviously all of us want kids
to truly take care of their health,
we want them to eat well.
You try the least invasive things
always first,
but at some point

if that's not helping enough,
you need to go to the next level.

It will open the door
for pharmaceutical companies
to heavily advertise
and promote their use
in 8-years-old,
when we don't yet know
the long-term effect on using
these drugs on pre-pubertal kids.

Heroin

COMMUNITY

People who are using heroin
are discovering it is,
in fact,
a lethal drug.
Heroin chic.
There is a downside to it,
snorting
and smoking
were something that people
could accept as less harmful.
You can get addicted
and it would
not be bad.
However,
a number of individuals
are realizing
this is not the case.

Once they're addicted to heroin,
they must have it every day.
Every day,
they constantly have
to figure out how to acquire money
for that heroin.

Speed.
Crank.
Crystal.
Ice.
We called them the methamphetamine plague,
because they spread like an epidemic
across the country.

HIV/AIDS

COMMUNITY

There is no difference whatsoever
between somebody who is HIV positive
and myself;
we should approach people
who are HIV positive.
We must give them love
and support
and not marginalize them.
Nothing threatens us more today
than HIV/AIDS,
at present,
the AIDS situation is trending
toward rapid increase
and will depend on which position
the leadership of the country takes.

Homo Florescence

SOCIETY

Among the outstanding discoveries
in paleoanthropology
for half a century,
I think it's a big jump.
What's exciting
about this is that it's so late,
telling us about the processes
and patterns of evolution in a way
that's deeply informative.

It's a wonderful demonstration
of apparently archaic' human
adapting to the special conditions
of Flores,
I wouldn't have supposed
that such small brained people
descended directly
from Homo Erectus would be capable
of producing these artifacts,
but the evidence is pretty compelling.

It is probably the most significant thing
that has happened in my professional time.

It's rare,
extremely rare,
to find a hitherto-unknown species
of humans living
in the recent geological past,
perhaps like far-flung
caducean lands have acted
as a series of independent
'Noah's arks,'
each with their own trademark
endemic dwarfs
and giants.

It challenges the whole idea
of what it is that makes us human.

Honeybees

COMMUNITY

Swarming.
My grandfather
and oldest brother
had about 50 hives
around Naperville
for 50 years,
honeybees are essential
for our agriculture….
I think it's a great hobby.

We do need bees in the area,
it's a matter of having a reasonable
number of them.
About one mouthful in three.
Diversity,
color
and flavor.
Everything a bee does
brings more green
to the environment,
it's like a flea on a bee,
if we lost our honeybees,
it would have a devastating effect
on our food chain,
it would totally change life
as we know it
on the planet.
It's a very real concern.

If you put too many hives
in a spot,
you're not going to get
as much honey,
it's kind of self-regulating.

They're not necessarily
just concentrating on the one neighbor's
yard next door,
they're going to fly out

in this three-mile radices
in search for nectar
and pollen
and water.

Definitely excessive,
we really do not want
to prohibit them entirely.
It does reduce the yields
on flowers
and fruits,
having bees is a good thing.

The Horse and Cow

MILITARY

Best sonar shock in the Navy
nuclear waste.
When I was first in the Navy,
all I heard from the old salts
on the deployments was
Horse and Cow,
Horse and Cow,
Horse and Cow,
Horse and Cow is famous.
It's a place where
you can cut loose,
hoist a few
and tell a few stories.

Blind Man's Stuff:
the untold story
of American Submarine Espionage.
There are a lot of sailor bars,
but only one real sub bar,
it's like 'Cheers'
for submariners.
Blind Man's Stuff.
*"Excuse me gentlemen,
are you submariners?"*
"Sorta."
"Kinda."
*"Depends on how
you define the word submariner."*
Dolphins.
Sometimes one of the old guys
Who'd remember the Cold War
would tell us stories,
that's why we love
coming to the Horse and Cow.
A lot of submariners only feel
comfortable with other submariners.

Boomers.
I'd rather have a sister

in the whorehouse
than a brother in a boomer.
It can get kind of wild in here
when the boats are just back
from a WesPac,
I am a businessman,
I have to diversify.

Homicide Free Year

JUSTICE

Violence Crimes

Source: National City, CA Police Department

It's the first year since 1963
that we haven't experienced a homicide.
I attribute it to the investment
that the mayor
and council made
four years ago
to community policing–
hiring more police officers
and formalizing partnerships
with community stakeholders.
Two Tears.

If you actually walk our street,
day
or night,
you can see the difference
and feel the improved safety
and security.
You'll see women
and seniors often exercising
in the parks
and children using our parks
and libraries.

There is still crime occurring
in our city
and that's why we need
to continue working
with our schools
and our youths.

I think with the support
of the mayor,
the city council
and the community's defeat

of Proposition M,
it will allow us to continue
with our strategic plan
of making the city
one of the safest in the county.

Housing

ECONOMY

We are growing
and if we didn't have enough housing
we are going to have what we have now.
The price of housing is going up
and up
and up.
You can say
that we are all built out,
but the truth
is there are more people
coming every day.

We are not saying
that long-term the Antelope Valley
is not going to grow,
it's just not all going to happen
in the next five years.
Our ability to prowl outward
is becoming constrained;
we can't sprawl our way out
of this problem.

That is a tough task to achieve
when you have built-out cities,
it's like predicting the stock market.
It's going to be a very thorny fight.

Housing Developers

HOUSING

Boy,
was I wrong,
they were vehemently opposed
to development.
There's not much supply
and you wonder why
it's not more.
The only answer is
we've been going more than a decade
where we haven't added much
to the supply
to the middle
or lower market
where it's so desperately needed.
From what I can tell,
it's true up
and down the coast.

When a developer comes along
and has got to the pay the fixes cost,
whether it's a starter
or luxury home,
he's going to pick
a luxury-home every time.
There are still issues
with impact fees–
they continue to escalate,
you don't need to scrap
all the fees
if you could just stop
some of the increases
at the margins.
They make a hell of a lot more
money than they pretend.

We got kind of pigeonholed
into the higher end,
it was not my business plan,
but the market looked at us

and we said we'll take the upper end
and KH Home can take the lower end.
We need more work,
quite honestly,
we've been looking at other markets
in Northern California
and looking again at Riverside.

There was a sea change
in the issue
with Governor Brown
finally acknowledging
that the housing crisis
is due to a housing shortage
and we're not going
to be able to subsidize
our way out of it;
we've got to build one way out of it.
If you deny 2,000 high-income families
the new housing they want,
guess what,
they are going to go down the street
and outbid
your cherished working class family
and take their housing units,
you can't win
by not building at the high end.

Housing Market

ECONOMY

Growing concern.
It's exploding,
so far the development
that we've done
has been embraced
by a continuing large population,
we have found
that the buildings
continue to fill up.
What they have discovered
is that it's a lot more fun
being social
than it is going home
at the end of the day,
closing the door
and watching television.

They are doing this
because they are having to compete
for a lot of the same talent
as the tech companies
and other employers
who are recruiting
at the same time,
they want to offer something
that's attractive
to their future employees.

Nodes,
nodes.
There is a larger impact
on the overall cost of housing
in the city,
while there's new housing stock
being created
on the high end
in particular
to respond to the demand,
overall what you are seeing

is that housing costs in the city
are going up very significantly.

It's the last place
we're ever going to buy–
we're here for keeps,
we are all in
on the condo
because the city has so much
to offer.

Humans and Dogs

NATURE

      Homo-Neanderthalensis

On the Origin of Species
simian peculiarities,
they were sapient people
that's probably the implication
of the last decade of results.

The Invacless:
How Human
and Their Dogs
Drove Neanderthals to Extinction,
Neanderthals had bigger brains,
sharper vision
and were better adapted
to the environment
than Homo-sapiens.

Plants
and animals
as Kudzu,
the zebra mussel
and giant African snails,
all of which
are the most invasive species
that have ever lived.

Fifty millennia
of Catastrophic Extinction
After Human Contact,
a global pattern of human arrival
followed by faunal collapse
and other ecological changes.

The unprecedented alliance
of Humans
with another top predator
wolf-dogs
many have been the final stress

that pushed Neanderthals
and many other species
down the slippery slope
toward extinction.

The white scleras
and open eyelids,
make the direction
of a person's gaze
highly visible
from a distance.

Human Dignity

SPORTS

I thought,
this is an opportunity to do something
that can make a difference.
This is not a charity;
it's not just about feeding people,
this is about social inclusion,
teaching people about food waste
and giving hope to people
who have lost all hope.

Human Trafficking

JUSTICE

How many of you believe
slavery is dead?
Well,
I'm going to tell you
that it's not.
It rears its ugly head
in the form of human trafficking.
Stop the trafficking!

It is the third most lucrative
International crime.
The first
being the trafficking of weapons,
the second,
drugs
and the third,
again,
is human trafficking.

Slavery is a universal crime.
If you take one child
and enslave that one child,
you enslave the whole world.

The U.S. actually has a leadership role
in fighting human trafficking.
We've actually engaged in education
of parents
and women to identify
a trained agent out there who is out
to capture a young child
and throw him/her into a life of slavery.
So we spend money,
millions of dollars abroad in counting
where this enslavement takes place.

Annually,
according to the United States government–
sponsored research completed in 2008,

approximately 800,000 people
are trafficked across national borders,
which doesn't include the millions trafficked
within their own countries:
the Attorney General's Annual report
to Congress on U.S government activities
to combat trafficking in prisons,
fiscal year of 2005.

Ever since 9.11,
trafficking has taken a difficult turn.
Traffickers used to bring
in all the victims directly
into the United States,
but ever since 9.11
with all the heightened security
throughout the United States,
they've been forced
to bring their victims into other countries;
generally Mexico and Canada,
because a lot of their security practices
at the airports have gone unchanged.
So that's why we're seeing
a tremendous increase of victims
of trafficking coming
into the San Diego border.

Hurricane

NATURE

Harvey
Unprecedented.
Beyond any experienced.
I think there's a chance
this could go down as the worst flooding
in United States history,
we're fearful we could be talking about this story
this time next week.
They're just adding fuel to the fire
of an already extremely catastrophic situation,
Federal Emergency Management Administration
is going to be there for years,
sir.
This disaster recovery–
this disaster is going to be a landmark event,
we're already pushing forward
recovery housing teams.
We're ready pushing forward forces
to be on the ground
to implement
National Flood Insurance Program policies,
as well as,
doing the inspections that we need.

As soon as that trip can be made
without causing disruption.
I don't need to tell anyone
this is a very,
very serious
and precedented storm,
we have several hundred structural flooding reports.
We expect that number to rise
pretty dramatically.
We can't wait for assets
to come from outside,
it's chest to shoulder deep
out there in certain areas.
"This event is unprecedented
and all impacts aren't unknown

and beyond anything experience,
follow orders from officials to ensure safety.
They now know the cavalry is coming,
our top priority is to protect human life.

If you are in a flooding situation,
stay calm,
do not panic,
do not go into the attic,
rescuers from the year cannot see you.
We've seen flooding before,
but never like this.
This is a whole new thing,
it's huge.
Staggering.
Worse than the worst-case scenario
for Houston.

You get in order to evacuate,
you are creating a nightmare.
It's so dangerous
that people would give themselves
the death penalty,
Sad–
breaks your heart for our city
and our state,
but it's Texas.
We'll get through it.
This could easily be
one of the worst flooding disasters
in U.S. history.
Landmark.
The problem is
that you've got these huge bands
of rain sweeping over the same areas again
and again,
the point we're trying to make now
is that this is just the beginning of the flood,
it's still too early
to say how it will turn out.
Super storm.
We're all shaking our heads,
watching the pictures,

years from now
people will remember that.

This disaster is going to be a landmark event,
work setting up
and gearing up
for The next couple of years.
Let's not lose our focus
on how bad this still is,
we're getting absolutely everything we need,
for having a White House
that is being very responsive,
very concerned about the people of Texas
and a tremendous help to us.
This event is nothing like Katrina,
this is completely different.
This is a storm
that the United States
has not seen yet,
I think we need
to set the expectation
that this is going to be going on
for a while,
not just the rain
and the flooding,
but the recovery effort
is going to be going on for weeks,
months,
probably even years.

Hurricane

NATURE

HarveyNatural Disaster

Natural Disaster

Catastrophic.
Unprecedented.
Local rainfall amounts of 50 inches
would exceed
any previous Texas rainfall record,
the breadth
and intensity of this rainfall
are beyond anything
experienced before.

This is a storm
that is testing the city
of Houston,
I know for a fact
that the city of Houston
will rise to the occasion.
So which neighborhood
would you have to evacuate?
You literally cannot put 6.5 million people
on the road!
If you think the situation right now is bad–
you give an order to evacuate,
you are creating a nightmare.

We requested boats–
all the things
that would normally happen
in a well-planned response
to an event like this–
but they can't get here,
we have always
been known as a community
where neighbors help neighbors,
to those of you who have boats
and high-water vehicles

that can be used in neighborhoods
to help move people
out of harm's way,
we need your help.
We need to get all these people
moved by dark.

There are many communities
inside the state of Texas
that are hurting.
State of the Union,
for years,
this disaster recovery–
this disaster–
is going to be a landmark event…
we're setting up
and gearing up
for the next couple of years.
At this time
it is unknown
if the subject passed away
from health conditions
or due to drowning.

It's bad
and it's not getting better
as the rain is still continuing;
all over,
the city is devastated.
Our residents
are still in extreme danger,
the storm came in from the sea
and now the flooding
is going to come down
from the inland areas.
There is flooding
all over the city,
please,
please,
please stay home.

I barely squeezed through
the first time,
my plan is to stay here

and let this water recede.
I called 911
like nine times,
but nobody came,
none of us can swim.

It breaks your heart
for our city
and our state,
but it's Texas.
We'll get through it.

Nearly 12 years ago,
Texas opened their doors
to the people of Louisiana
when Hurricane Katrina
devastated our state,
we will do nothing less
to support the people of Texas
in any way that we can
as they respond
and recover
from Hurricane Harvey.
This is what we do,
we're dedicated
to saving human life.

HurricaneCOMMUNITY

COMMUNITY

     Katrina

You have to have faith
that this was all for a reason,
we are not supposed to understand.
We are just supposed to believe.
We have been hit hard—
but we are going to make it,
we are going to survive.

A sense of hope,
that's all we have to give
each other right now.
Some of us don't have homes,
some of us don't have water,
electricity,
or food;
but all of us have a sense of God
inside of us,
to help us keep hope alive.
A mighty fortress in our God,
a bulwark never failing.
Thank you Jesus!
Amen.

People are resilient
immediately after a disaster,
but eventually,
little things–
like not having toilets that flush;
wear many people down.
Is God good?
Yeah!
Amen!

I think we're dead.
I want to pray for the soul
o' my mother who,
I found this morning

was drowned.

The proof of God
is that you are here
and not back there
and you are with people
who love you,
who will go to whatever lengths
they have to go to help you.

Get your lives back together.
I may have lost everything,
but I didn't lose my soul.

Why,
thank you for the lovely smile
and welcome to the great state
of Texas!

Hurricane

NATURE

Maria

People want to live here,
in too many cases,
we have not planned
for how to build
and live with the hazards we have,
so that when storms hit
we are not wiping people out financially
and putting people at extreme risk.
I am not someone who says
we should not grow
or build,
but we are continuing to build
in ways that are not sustainable.

Southwest Florida
has lost nearly half its wetlands,
there is no way to easily deal with all that water
if the land has become paved with rooftops
and parking lots
and roads.

When we cross this point
that the homes along the coast
are no longer valuable,
because they're really losing
their marketability?
We are certainly not there yet.
We are not even close to it.
This is the new normal,
if this wasn't a wake-up call,
if Houston wasn't a wake-up call,
I don't know what is.
We've basically been duct-taping
our infrastructure for years,
if you keep refusing to acknowledge
that climate change is real,
if you keep promising

an infrastructure bill
that never appears,
you're not much help to us.

We don't have the right
to satisfy our own appetites
to do anything we want,
I am hoping this re-commoditization of Florida
is short-lived
selling those big homes
that are closer
and closer to water
is more important than whatever
the aftereffect will be,
I think there's a lot of people
who don't want to look at the big picture.
They don't want to look past
what's going to affect them.

Today I ask how governments
will respond to this international crisis.
We ask the international community
to help us,
not because we want to out stretch
a begging bowl,
but because forces far beyond
our control have pushed us
to this dire situation, friendly nations
and organizations.
Widespread devastation,
mind-boggling.
Climate change
and its consequences
should not be a subject of speculation
or debate,
it's a truth which hits us
and which causes great uncertainty.
The small islands
have been saying
for so many years
in the climate change discussions
that this is possible.
It's no longer possible.
It's happened.

Hurricane

NATURE

Survivors

The first two days
we had almost nothing to eat,
the toilets were overflowing
and it was very bad here.
It's much better now –
three meals a day,
bottled water,
Port-a-Potties.

The death toll in New Orleans
was huge
and we can understand why
the focus would be there,
but plenty of people
are suffering here,
too.
The relief workers are very nice
and donated goods are increasing
all the time.
It's just that everyone
is stretched so thin.

Though they plan
and equip themselves
for something like this,
it's never enough,
we ought to know:
We lived in L.A.,
during the 1994 earthquake,
we were visiting New York,
on 9.11
and now we lived through this.
I told a friend
about all of that
and he said,
*"Do me a favor
and tell me*

where you're moving to next."

We're sleeping on the floor
in a second-story classroom
and haven't had so much as a fan
since we've been here.
My babies are burning up.
They said,
we should boil the water
before using it,
even for bathing,
but nobody does.
I'm starting to wonder
about the germs.

The sheetrock came tumbling down
and the bathroom came apart.

We wait out on the balcony
and jumped 12 feet to the ground,
we waded 30 feet through the wind
and the storm surge
to a concrete section
that looked like it would hold;
thank God it did.
We kept waiting
for some rescue person
to come by
and check on us,
nobody did;
finally,
we flagged down a cop
and they found a truck
and brought us here.

Everything we've got.
We found these waterlogged suitcases
at the motel,
cleaned them up
and packed in what we could.

We're sleeping outside
on this slab of concrete tonight–
it's too hot

and lose inside that school.
You would think the government
would have responded before this.
We lost our shelter,
our car everything.
We pay taxes,
same as everyone else.

Iceland

UNITED NATIONS

I

"As a matter of fact, when summer is finished— when it has been two months of nothing but brightness— then I'm waiting for the winter. It's more cozy."

Reykjavik

Depression?
I don't think
I have ever experienced
feeling depressed?
When you survey a ship
in the dark,
in fact,
you can't see as much
and it's cold;
plus it feels like the middle
of the night,
of course,
you get used to everything.

The monotony of horizon-less winter days.
It seems they can manage
and keep going in the wintertime;
they don't get slowed down
and don't become pathetic.
In many surveys,
Icelandic people came across
as happy people.
Everyone just puts on a brave face.
If you say
that you are sad,
then you are seen
as being weak.
It's a way of coping,
with gritted teeth.

Too in touch
with my emotions,
in London,
the climate was wonderful
compared to here,
I felt like I was living
in paradise.

It can be very romantic,
actually;
though,
I would like to live in Spain.
I'm not the outgoing type,
always doing stuff socially,
for we who live here,
it's always been like this.

As a matter of fact,
when summer
is finished–
when it has been
two months
of nothing
but brightness–
then I'm waiting
for the winter.
It's more cozy.
A lot of people just watch TV,
sleep
and work.
When you wake up
it's dark
and when you finish work
it's dark;
you never know what time it is.
I get very tired.
I'd like to go,
somewhere that's not Iceland,
although I think
I would always come back.

There are nice things
in the winter,
yesterday,
I was coming home from work
and I saw a creature
in a big world,
part of a great creation.
Just another shade of light.

You're nearer to your own soul,
you realize that you're there
for a purpose.
Sometimes people
say they get depressive,
but for me depression
is a very powerful creator.
You can be very happy
even when you're depressed.
Laughing people aren't necessarily happy
and a crying man is not necessarily sad.

Icy Weather

NATURE

        Beast from the East

"The Beast from the East."
The extreme weather
in the final week of the half
had a material impact
on our results,
but I am hugely encouraged
by the progress we are making
to transform Debenhams.

Disappointed Christmas.
We are holding share
in the difficult fashion market
and in other categories
such as furniture,
exciting partnerships have the potential
to transform our offer
to a grim sequence of declines.

Immigrant

IMMIGRATION

> Unauthorized

When I enlisted
in the Marines
I knew the risks.
It was something that could come up,
it was something that could come back
and hurt me,
I was just hoping
that I wasn't going to pay for that mistake
for the rest of my life.
Now I am able to finally go home
and live the life I feel like
I need to.

I think it's very unique,
as a matter of fact,
there's always this taboo
of people just coming to the United States
and taking advantage of the system;
I didn't want to be another Mexican
taking somebody's job.
I wanted to prove
that I was willing to do something
for this country,
that I deserved the right
to be in this country.
We don't choose
where we are born.

I could go to school,
but I couldn't get a job.
This was right after the economy,
in a really bad moment,
so there were no jobs to be had,
I couldn't live legally,
I couldn't live comfortably
it was very heartbreaking for me.

India

UNITED NATIONS

    Mumbai

Spoiled for choice.
Hyper market.
I've been shouting,
at her,
"*we have to go!*"

The reality
is that the Indian consumer
is exactly the same
as the consumers
of the rest of the world;
they're inspirational.
They have a need
for the nicer things;
particularly,
the younger generation.

A stopping expedition
for the Indian family
is a leisure pursuit right now,
there are not too many sports clubs
or parks.

We're not gonna see a lot
of retail casualties
over the next few years…
not everybody's going to get it right;
we're extremely conscious
that the competition is coming.

It's not like Europe
and America
where alternate jobs
are able to absorb people…
millions
and millions are engaged
in this occupation

and they will be thrown out.
Most of the people selling fruit
and vegetables are illiterate
or at best semi-literate.
While,
businesses such as,
Reliance,
won't take them in,
because they don't have
the qualifications.

Wal-Mart,
has probably made the smartest
moves it can
under the circumstances.
It's partnering with a partner
with a good record,
on getting things done in India,
which is key.
All the big retailers
should have plans to enter India,
whether they dive in right now
isn't necessarily wise...
there's probably an argument to say
*"Let's sit back
and see what mistakes
Wal-Mart makes
and see if we can learn
anything from them."*
India isn't going to follow
the same growth curve,
as China.
It might be slower,
but it's obviously on its way.

India

UNITED NATIONS

       Open-Door Policy

Goans' attitude
and openness
allowed the hippie culture to thrive;
Goa is not Goa,
it's India now.
Lots of Indian youngsters
have made bucket loads of money
and they just want to blow it,
it's a lot more yuppie now.

My parents weren't from this kind of culture,
if they came here,
they would be in full dress
and would be uncomfortable,
because people are in bathing suits
and drinking.
My parents never went on vacation
when I was a little boy,
my son is 2 years old
and this is his second time in Goa.
He's seen more of India than my parents.

Pure veg. scum of the earth.
Susegad,
sossegado,
Goa was a place to let your hair down,
to be who you want to be,
susegad.
Goans have a special culture of acceptance,
but lots of Indians are coming everywhere now,
bringing their social where now,
bringing their customs
from their conservative cities
and there's a lot of them.

The parate days are over,
yes,

there's been a clampdown,
in our countries,
we aren't so welcoming to foreigners,
we never would have let people live,
'susegad',
for this long.

ECONOMY

Initial Public Offering (IPO)

The Initial Public Offerings market
needs ice breakers–
instead it's getting quasi–
IPOs from early-stage biotech.
Our deal volume is so low to date
in the United States,
we have got to go back
to the recession
to see numbers this anemic
for the IPO market.
The fact that we didn't have any tech IPOs
in the first quarter
also says something.
Market conditions have improved,
since February 11,
which was the bottom;
that suggests investors
are getting more comfortable
with the existing set of IPOS
and would find some courage
to participate.

Despite the successes
of a handful of biotechnology companies
making Initial Public Offering,
the IPO window
for venture-backed companies,
in other sectors,
has been completely shut.
It tells you that the calculations
of the existing public biotech companies
have dropped 23 percent
from what they were a year ago
and that the new IPOs
are going to be priced
with that in mind,
in a market that is really nervous.

In the next three

or four weeks,
if things don't pick up,
then maybe 2016
isn't going to be a great year;
right now
it could easily change.
If you look at IPO statistics
and what is working,
biotech is it.
If anything is going to break
that closed window at the moment,
it is probably going to be biotechs.

Biotechs are often early-stage companies
with long lead times,
the market is a little more accepting
to do an IPO in choppy markets,
because you are not saying
"*hey,*
I am going to grow
a certain percentage
in the next two years."
You are testing a drug.
You are testing a concept,
that has some lead time.

Unicorns.
The fact that private valuations
are making these companies up,
so much,
it is not reality
of what the public markets will stomach,
especially in a down market;
I think many of them are going to be exiting
at far less valuation
than they were getting in 2014
and 2015.

Intangible Wedding Ceremony

SOCIETY

    Culture Heritage

Invited.
I learned the customs
from my grandmother
and my mother.
The tradition has been passed down
for generations,
I embrace every girl
who wants to take part in the event
and teach them
how to complete the ceremonies.

She likes taking photos very much,
so I applied for the free wedding photography
immediately after I got the news.

It was such a unique scene,
the photos we took will remind me–
when I'm getting old–
of the days when we were young
and happy.

Poor economic conditions.
Group wedding photos.
They arrived at 8 o'clock,
but our class started at 9.
I could feel their enthusiasm,
red roses represent passionate love
and the lily represents permanent love.

You are more stunning
than the flowers,
it's very touching.
We are accustomed
to an ordinary life.
There were no flowers
or a diamond ring,
but he made up for all of that day.

ECONOMY

Only the paranoid survive.
The mistake was,
when you grow with
great leadership
and great success,
your paranoia is focused
on the thing that is delivering that;
where computing is constantly shifting.

Intel has four main business lines–
personal computers,
mobile devices,
internet of things
and servers–
and it's hitting on one of them.
Now cost $10 billion,
at least
and the competition is catching up.

It's a much broader group.
People writing for machine's learning
and Artificial Intelligence,
networking chips,
how virtual reality feeds
into personal computers.
It's lengthened to 24
to 36 months,
the performance of the ecosystem
is much more than Gordon Moore's Law.

InterContinental Ballistic Missile

MILITARY

ICBM

They can simulate an ICBM warhead
on this kind of trajectory,
it's a kind of stepping stone.
It represents a substantial advance,
it clearly shares a common heritage.
There aren't really any interesting targets.
Demonstrating technologies
and systems to be used in future
International Continental Ballistic Missiles,
would allow North Korea
to conduct at least some
of the testing necessary
to develop an operational ICBM –
particularly launching ICBMs,
particularly if it includes the same rocket engines
closer to an operational ICBM;
than had been previously estimated.

We think they've had enough
time to mate a nuclear weapon
to a missile,
CBS this morning.
So the threat is now.

Neighboring countries.
Under the worst.
Re-entry situation,
going really high,
give you a very fast
and very brutal re-entry.
You learn something
but not everything,
if they've got a system
with a new engine
and can scale that up,
they've got a pretty believable
path to an ICBM.

Hey,
we're on our way.
If you want to talk,
Now's the time to do it.

Internal Revenue Service (IRS)

ECONOMY

Taxpayer Service Organizations:
Like every taxpayer,
I am outraged by the reports of abuses
by the Internal Revenue Service.
Tonight I challenge the Senate:
As your first order of business,
you must pass our bipartisan package
of Internal Revenue Service Reforms–
now.
There are a lot of sleepy bureaucrats
who will be upset about this.
It makes a lot of sense
and it is consistent
with the new customer orientation
at the Internal Revenue Service.
We think it will work well,
with whatever legislation
we come up with;
we think they will be
complementary initiatives.

Assuming this comes about,
this is a radical change in the approach
to the service of doing business,
to give a broader
view it will drive
some of the functionalism out of service,
more of an opportunity to specialize with
those types of issues dealing with taxpayers.

Reinventing the government...
modernizing America's tax agency.
Understanding
and solving problems
from a taxpayer's point of view;
thus,
the national office becomes a much
smaller corporate headquarters.
Wage

and investment income
has often disconnected
from the other functions
and the organization as a whole,
this is why taxpayers may receive
a notice from the Internal Revenue Service,
but when the taxpayer calls
the toll-free number,
the customer service representative
is unable to help.

International Affairs

SOCIETY

Nationalism

Half-way between the invention of the iPad
and the discovery of fire.
Don't cry,
because it's over.
Smile,
because it happened.

Thirty years ago this November,
the Berlin Wall fell down,
America celebrated.
We also learned
that the world might become more,
rather than less dangerous
as a result.
In the years that followed,
that fear has been validated
by ethnic strife,
increased destructiveness
of international terror,
the spread of advanced weapons
of technology
and the emergence of leaders
whose slogans echo the silent song
of fascism.
Still, there are many in Washington
and around the country
who think of our country as an island.
They believe we are unaffected by events
across the far side of the sea
and that we can build walls
to keep problems at bay.
They refuse to accept
that America's interests are linked
to the security
and prosperity of our neighbors,
allies
and friends.

They do not understand
our global leadership carries with it
both tangible benefits
and enormous responsibilities.

We have long passed the time
in our history
when we could count on the Atlantic
and Pacific oceans
to guarantee our security–
we could protect our interests
by maintaining a few key relationships,
principally Europe
and that we could safely
take a reactive approach
to most events
in most places
most of the time.

While there are some communities
across the country
who may be able to avoid these realities,
San Diego is not one of them.
You are home
to some of the largest military installations
in the country,
with thousands of sailors
and Marines stationed here,
many of them preparing to deploy
on missions across the Pacific.

Your future
depends on the expansion of commerce
in fast-rising regions of the world
such as Asia
and yet that future is threatened
by the prospect of economic
and military conflict,
whether in the South China Sea
or the Strait of Hormuz.
You're also only a dozen miles
from our southern border,
where this is a humanitarian crisis
being made far worse

by the indifference
of this administration
to the desperate plight of migrants
from Central America.

Your generation faces a moment of choice.
Will we treat foreign policy
as a dog-eat-dog struggle
in which no one wins
except at another's cost?
or will we carry the banner
for international cooperation?
will we honor the principles
upon which our freedom is based?
or will we try to seal ourselves off
from the ailments of the world?

In Vitro Fertilization

SOCIETY

Same-Sex Couples

I'm excited
to put all this in his baby book.
The other partner has to adopt a child,
I've wanted to be a mother
since as long as I could remember,
those were the longest ten days
of our lives–
no one had ever done it,
so we didn't know if it was going to work,
we screamed,
when we found out
we were pregnant,
we were going to be mothers,
it didn't cross our minds
that we had done something
that no one else had done before.
It's a great way
to involve both people
in the relationship,
he's loud,
just like me;
we worried
that he wouldn't connect to me,
because he has Bliss' DNA,
now that he's here,
he's attached to my hip.
Everything I was worried about
went away.

It was so exciting
knowing that I was growing
my own biological child
inside of me,
we were very,
very blessed.

Iran

UNITED NATIONS

We believe that the conclusion
of this agreement can both allow
for confidence-building in respect
of Iran's nuclear program
and represents a significant development
in retaliations between Europe
and Iran.
It is essential now for the agreement
to be implemented in full.

A solid,
long-term agreement,
with lasting confidence
in the peaceful nature
of Iran's nuclear program.
We have seen a little bit of this program,
hopefully,
over the last 24 hours.
If the superstition is lifted,
the process is deemed to have broken
and we,
the Europeans,
will withdraw
and go to the Security Council.

All the declared nuclear material
in Iran has been accounted for
and therefore such material
is not diverted to prohibited activities.
The agency is however,
not in the position to conclude
that there are no undeclared
nuclear materials
or activities in Iran.

Objective guarantees
are exclusively for peaceful purposes.
Firm guarantees are on nuclear,
technology,

economic cooperation
and firm commitments
on security issues.
The manufacturing,
importation of gas centrifuges
and their components,
all tests
or production
of any uranium conversion installation.
Active support is a voluntary
confidence-building measure
and not a legal obligation.

Iran's right.
Iran will be a matter of months,
not years.
The reason Iran has given
so many concessions is,
because the Iranian team was weak,
this is the outcome
of our best diplomacy
a pearl in exchange
for a lollipop.
That's not true.

Iraq

UNITED NATIONS

UNITED STATES
    Pardon

Al Baghdadia T.V.

An ugly act...
it is too late to reverse
the big
and ugly act that I perpetrated.

Come in,
it is your home,
too.

So I ask for your pardon,
Excellency.

Nonsense.
Baseless.
I am suspicious that my brother
wrote that letter to Al-Maliki,
because I know my brother very well.
I demand the government stop this matter,
it's a fabrication.

The president harbors no hard feelings
about it
and the Iraqis have a process
that they'll follow,
but he did urge them not to overact,
because he was not bothered
by the incident.
Although,
it's not appropriate
for the people to throw shoes
at a press conference,
at any leader.

    What happened to me

was just an accident in the melee.
It not—
I'm not bothered by it.
It's not all that pretty,
but I'm not worried about it.

We would hope
that the fact of a United States president,
standing next to a freely elected
prime minister,
of Iraq,
who just happens to be Shea,
who is governing
in a multi-ethnic democracy...
in the heart of the Middle East,
is not overshadowed by one incident
like this.
The fact of the president making that visit
under those circumstances
will probably overshadow any memory
of this particular gentleman
and what he did.

Ireland

UNITED NATIONS

           Freezing WeatherStorm
                    Storm OpheliaCoastal areas will be the worst first.

The sudden downpour
could result in flash
and spot flooding
and cause rivers to rise
and river banks to burst.

The minister's U-turn is very welcome.
Farmers are not starving,
but we don't want to have them starved,
that's what we are trying to avoid.
People have nothing–
you can imagine if you have 100 cows
and you've nothing to feed them.
The problem is we've nearly six months of a winter,
we've not enough of foliage,
enough of fodder
and the grass isn't growing,
because of that cold breeze behind me.

You have to keep animals fed,
but you can't even let them out,
because the ground is going to be too wet again.
We've had one load today
of 30 bales
and we hope to have another few loads
over the next couple of days.
People were ordering the last couple of days
and it's working out at about two per person.
There's people looking for six,
seven,
eight bales,
but all we can do is be fair
to everyone
and give one
or two bales each.

Out,

we were lucky that we cut extra silage
last year
and we were actually going to sell
100 bales that we didn't sell,
so that kept us going until now.
We're milking 120 cows.
It's been a tough spring.
We have another three weeks
or so of silage
and we've cows grazing.

The response by the government
has been shocking.
They should've known fodder stores
were so low in the country
and have had a back-up plan.
Farmers have been let down.
It's a worry for me if it continues on,
I thought I was safe until now,
but the weather hasn't improved,
but we'll have enough.
I've been farming all my life,
we've seen bothers like this before
and we've always been alright.
Critical.
There was no let up on the weather
in the past three weeks.
My son has another week of fodder left,
he's one of the lucky ones,
I've enough fodder to do me another three weeks,
but the weather is affecting the whole thing.
We saved a lot of fodder,
but the stock are back in again
though the last days have done a lot of harm.
It's been very wet.
Things can change very quickly
at this time of year,
but it doesn't look it.

Israel

UNITED NATIONS

Political
and economic price.
Distorted,
delusional
and absurd,
part of the swan song
of the old world that is biased
against Israel.
But,
my friends,
we are entering a new era,
disgraceful anti-Israel maneuver.
Will make us much harder
to negotiate peace.
Too bad,
but we will get it done anyway!

If you can't show the American
people that international organizations
can be more responsible,
there is going to be a break,
I can't support funding a body
that singles out the only democracy
in the Middle East
who shares our values.
Particularly hostile to Israel.

The principle enemy
of the settlement block
and the Jerusalem neighborhoods
is Netanyahu himself,
the man who just a month ago
told us that the United States
and Europe,
are trying to calm us with conceit.

The time has come to transition
from withdrawals to sovereignty,

the resolution being considered…
should be vetoed.

The security relationship
between Israel
and our great ally
The United States is deep,
meaningfully
and unprecedented
in its scope
and contribution
to our strength,
that is how it has been
and that is how
it will continue to be.

It is neither the first
nor the last time a head of state
blurts out something that
shouldn't be said.
But this time
may be a bit worse
than the others,
it is not the end of the world,
relation between the United States
and Israel at all levels,
including intelligence,
are so important to each side,
including in the fight
against ISIS…
that I see no real chance
of a future bilateral collaboration
being damaged.

FAITH

J

*"Jehovah's Witnesses
want to be average,
normal people,
he seemed to want
to be a normal person."*

Jehovah's Witness

Prince.
He was accepted
as our brother,
he wasn't treated
as maybe
the world would treat him.
Mild spirit,
I look forward
to the time
we welcome him
back on the Earth.

I don't see it
really
as a conversation,
more,
you know,
it's a realization
it's like Morpheus
and Neo
in 'The Matrix.'

My first thought is,
'*Cool,
Cool,
Cool.
He wants to use my house
as a set.
I'm glad!
Demolish the whole thing!
Start over!*'
I said,
'*You know what?
You've walked
into a Jewish household
and that is not something
I'm interested in,*'
he believed the same thing
the rest of us believe.

I guess he was willing
to let the Bible be his authority.

God came to earth
and saw people sticking it wherever
and doing it with whatever
and he just cleared it all out.
He was, like, 'Enough!'

Jehovah's Witnesses
want to be average,
normal people,
he seemed to want
to be a normal person.
Pale and tired.
Loyally submitting
to theocratic order.
The Watch Tower.

Judaism

FAITH

Chabad-Lubavitch

I disagree with Chabad
about practically everything,
but I envy the selflessness
of their young men
and women who fan out
across the world
to serve Jewish communities
in distress.
We must footer among
our members the same sense
of motion
and spirit of service
to the Jewish people.
See Chabad
and Orthodoxy in general
as fidelity
to ways of the past
that many people
had broke with
and that weighs upon them.

The Jewish community
is becoming deeply dependent
on them for religious services,
ceremonies,
education
and social services;
it's a clear
and present danger to Judaism.
This is the dominant aspiration,
profoundly
and perhaps
permanently.
I feel very honored
and blessed,
that I'm placed
in the rabbi's army

to reach out to every Jew
no matter their level of observance;
it's been really miraculous.

When a Jewish person
alienates himself
from his people,
God forbid,
it is only,
because he is thirsty;
his soul thirsts
for the meaningful in life,
but the waters of the Torah
have eluded him.
So he wanders about
in foreign domains,
seeking to quench his thirst.
Only a Sheppard
who hastens not to judge
the runaway kid,
who is sensitive to the causes
of its desertion,
can mercifully lift it
into his arms
and bring it back home.

This one,
Moshiach is ready,
are you?
The Taliban.
It doesn't take an Einstein
to figure out the rabbi
is the Messiah;
nonsense.
In our area,
it's a non-existent issue,
where were we going to get
the biggest bang for the buck?
The track record of Chabad
in terms of bringing the light
of Judaism
and the warmth
of the Torah around the world

is unparalleled.
I was adamantly against going.
Judaism at its heart–
which it should be.

Judaism

FAITH

Reform

If someone had told me four years ago
that I'd be going to the temple
every Saturday,
I would have told them they were crazy,
but it really became a crucial part of my life.
Traditional-progressive I always thought
of spiritual things as sort of fuzzy,
of no use,
because there is no way
to make a living out of it.
What's the point
of it if you can't put it on your resume?
That sort of attitude.
Then for me,
it just came to a point
where the system
that I had grown up with
was not doing it for me;
I just needed to observe life
from a different perspective.

At the outset of the movement,
Jews really wanted to participate
in the modern society:
in the professions,
in land ownership,
in the universities
and we literally came out
of the ghetto...
We are not afraid to emphasize
our Judaic heritage.
There are many,
Reformed Jews
who don't want
to keep being Kosher
and we don't want to be told
how to approach God.

If we try to dictate,
we may forget who we are.
The challenge now
is not to reform Judaism–
it's to reform Jews.
My hope
is that the new sets of principles
will be discussed
and will encourage people
in bringing more rituals
into their lives–
which can obliterate
much of the ordinariness of life
in the late twentieth century society.
Like the rest of the country
Jews are seeking something
more,
in our lives.

We can no longer make a career
out of fighting our enemies
and we have to ask ourselves
the question,
together with the rest of America:
"*is a big Audi
and a swimming pool enough?*"
The answer is,
it isn't enough;
not when our people
are dying,
and our people
are suffering.
People ask themselves,
"*What is my life about?*"
and the only way
they can deal
with that
is through tradition.

There is definitely a boom in spirituality
and ritual in the United States,
a greater emphasis on ritualism
and ritual.
In particular in Protestantism

and in other movements,
like Reform Judaism;
which forms very specific ideological
reasons that has discarded it.
People are newly
discovering an old truth:
Rituals are containers
that hold people together
and bind them to God.

Jordan

UNITED NATIONS

Events provide fresh opportunities.
Mew Palestinian leadership
can carry forward the vision of a viable.
Independent Palestine by delivery
on the reforms that statehood involves:
competent governance,
investments in public welfare,
fighting corruption,
tougher security against terrorism
and a real partnership at the peace tables.
Kept up the veneer of supporting
the Palestinian leader.

To some extent,
it was a personal thing;
they just couldn't get along
with Yasser Arafat.
Israel embodies such superiority,
from their position,
that it has no need
to make peace.

Puppet separatist authority.
Jordan's interested to see
an independent Palestinian stat.

KenyaUNITED NATIONS

UNITED NATIONS

K

*"We know
what we're doing,
we don't need
your advice."*

Lokwii
My mother was a very hard worker,
it was the toughest job
we had ever done,
but we had no choice,
it was the only way
to get the land to be plowed.

We kept waiting.
They told us,
"*Food is coming,
food is coming,*"
but we saw it
and it wasn't coming.
We know
what we're doing,
we don't need
your advice.

You really seem to know
what you're doing.
The hunger has taught you well.

They're still of the mode
that this should be an American product
we're using our tax dollars
to produce them.

They offered a very reasonable option,
they said we appreciate the project,
it's a good project,
but we don't want you
to bring in maize.

Kenya

UNITED NATIONS

       Overseas Piracy

1894.
British law
on Kenya's maritime regulations.
Int'l maritime
Org. standards

Fisherman.
I thought about my family.
My life,
it didn't make sense
that I would die like this,
in a foreign country.
I love the water,
everyone has his calling
and I guess this is mine.
The agent said
I wasn't working during that time,
so I would not be paid.

They don't pay me enough
to risk my life,
but I'm a sole breadwinner
with a hungry family,
what's my choice?
If I tell the owner I won't go,
he'll just go hire someone else
who will.

We're washing away,
slave-like.
They can't go to Panama to complain.
In Kenya,
they turn a blind eye.

Alarming.
If Kenya had strong laws
and a booming industry five years ago,

we might not have seen this piracy
turn into such a big business.

We're doing our best,
a lot of things have been neglected
for a long time.

Kidnappings

JUSTICE

This case took place
almost simultaneously
in three different countries.
The boy was abducted in Los Angeles
and the ransom demands
were immediately made
to the father
in Taiwan,
by a subject in China.
Then,
all of a sudden a simple investigation,
becomes internationally significant,
because it is crossing
the international border of…
three countries.
The father demonstrated cooperation
and bravery through the whole ordeal;
it was very difficult for him.
I don't know
if I could have held up as well,
not knowing whether
or not my son was alive.

This sends a message,
that neither Taiwan
nor the People's Republic of China
are places to hide
if you are contemplating this type of crime.
(The kidnapping) was the very first
real-time investigation
and it went very smoothly.

Typically they need someone
to identify the victim,
usually in Taiwan
or the United States,
someone to do the job
and someone to collect the money,
usually in China;

until this point,
a criminal who gets to the mainland
could usually feel pretty secure.

Big spender.

The Kilogram

SOCIETY

International Measurement System

Yes,
Oui.
Le Grand K,
the greatest revolution
in measurement
since the French Revolution,
heir
and the spares,
the electric kilo.

If we stay where we are
and someone did
accidentally drop the kilogram
or if there was a contamination
that we couldn't control,
then the whole system
has got no head.
We're in chaos,
that the thing
that's really been worrying us,
I think,
for maybe 15 years
or more
is just how vulnerable the system is,
by depending
just on that one little piece
of platinum-iridium.

Those units,
those constants chosen now,
include everything we know,
everything we have always known
and provide that springboard
for us to pursue those things
that we don't know,
was just leaving me
in puddle of tears.

We future-proofed the system,
we put in place a system
that doesn't depend
on something
that is 140 years old.

Kingdom of Bhutan

UNITED NATIONS

> White Gold

Bhutan,
the Kingdom of the thunder dragon.
The happiest place on earth,
minders.

White gold.
The Tibetan plateau,
the roof of the world.
Third pole,
carbon negative.
72 percent of the country
is under forest cover
and more than half of Bhutan
is protected as national parks,
wild-life sanctuaries
and nature reserves.
Carbon negative.

Koran

FAITH

Most people see the world
and say that there's this particular number
of Muslims in this country
and that country
and that they all must think alike,
but what we found
is that when we ask this one clear question
about how the Islamic holy book
should influence national laws,
we see this huge divide.

It's a measure of the dissatisfaction people have
with the moral rectitude
of their government
and the moral tenor
of their laws,
the text is the ideal
of moral authority,
social justice,
uncorrupted values
and adherence
to social norms,
would produce a society
that is more equal.

Islamicized people
want laws to be created in an ethical fashion
with an ethical set of doctrines
and moral teachings;
people are more secular in the orientation,
influenced.

Korea

UNITED NATIONS

       Nuclear Weapon

An act of war.
Pipe dream.
An act of war.

We define this 'sanctions resolution'
rigged up by the United States
and it's followers as a grave infringement
upon the sovereignty of our Republic,
as an act of war
violating peace
and stability in the Korea peninsula
and the region
and categorically reject the 'resolution';
complete economic blockade.
If the United States wishes to live safely,
it must abandon its hostile policy
towards the Democratic People's
Republic of Korea
and learn to co-exist
with the country
that has nuclear weapons
and should wake-up
from its pipe dream
of our country giving up nuclear weapons
which we have developed
and completed through all kids of hardships.

Make positive
and constructive efforts
to de-escalate tensions.
Not inflicting
adverse humanitarian impact.
That was a good move,
a major accomplishment.
Fox News Sunday.

The likeliest impact

on the deeper cuts
in petroleum products
will be on sectors
nonessential to the survival
of the regime,
that means that the incidence
of these cuts
will fall hardest
on ordinary North Koreans.
Cutting oil supplies
will only make North Koreans rage
against the United States,
because they now have to work
more by hands on farms,
while officials will keep driving cars
using smuggled petroleum.
North Korean workers
sent overseas
have brought back home
the ideas
and cultures of capitalism
that they witness,
but now Trump is leading
the way for blocking
that route
through deceptive maritime practices.

Monitoring is probably easy,
give the United States
remote sensing capabilities,
but enforcement seems hard.
A surprising amount of fuels,
by next spring
I suspect there will be calls
for lifting the sanctions
to help prevent the fall
in food supply,
snub.
Regret.

Ku Klux Klan

JUSTICE

White heritage,
white pride,
white unity,
white power.
If you are a white student
between the ages of 12
and 17
and idealistically oriented
toward the struggle
for the survival of white Christian civilization
and values,
then the Knights of the Ku Klux Klan
invite you
to become a part of the Klan Youth Corps.

In San Diego,
the Ku Klux Klan
particularly targets Mexicans,
any Mexican worker
who challenged authority
or appeared suspicious
of one thing
or another
would forfeit his life.

Newspapers refused to investigate
cases of Klan hatred,
because editors feared
that negative publicity
might create a bad image
for San Diego
and hurt its commercial growth.

It was as thuggish
and brutal as in other cities.
The KKK in San Diego,
as elsewhere,
was primarily
a secret organization

of white supremacists–
bound by hate,
prejudice,
fear
and violence…
above the law…
who cloaked themselves
not just in white hooded sheets,
but in a polluted form of patriotism
that was an attempt to mask
the base nature of their cruelty.
The anti-union sentiment
that still exists here
probably did have its roots
in the wobblies era
and the white supremacist nature
of the Klan
still exists in U.S. politics today.

San Diego had been a Southern town
for a long time,
a lot of Southern sympathizers
after the Civil War
settled in Los Angeles,
there was some carryover from 1912.
Linkage of immigration
with radicalism.
It was the first real scare.
The KKK had their own radio stations–
they were the ultimate purveyors
of fake news.
The Klan was chasing the wet-backs
across the border.

SPORTS

Kung Fu

You need to have a calm heart to practice,
this composure is very important
for practicing
traditional Chinese martial arts.
If your heart isn't at peace,
you can't keep doing this work
in today's society;
there are many distractions,
for example,
you see other people living
in the large houses,
driving nice cars
and you start to feel anxious.
You think,
'*I need to go make money.*'
You can't practice martial arts
with that kind of mentality.

Composure.
Zhongguo wushu,
Chinese martial arts.
Higher standards
when I come here,
I never hurt my knee
or other parts of my body,
Mr. Zhang has a very scientific method.
Outsider.

The more people I can pass this on to,
the more change this art will endure.
I was hurt many,
many times,
but there was a time
when I could put
my Kung Fu into practice
and see how effective it was
Zhongsan-style.
My father told me
that if I don't carry this on
I would be a criminal of history.

Kurdish Refugees

IMMIGRATION

The truth is I have lived in Japan
for such a long time,
all I want to do is work
and carry out a decent life.

Fair share.
In reality,
there are so many people
who are waiting
and are facing a life of danger,
there are companies that want
to hire them
and need laborers.

If you see my country,
there is a lot of bullying
and people being killed,
I can't even speak anymore.
Warabistan.
I want the Japanese government
to understand that real refugees
are in trouble.
You see what's happening in Europe—
terrorism,
crimes,
lots of social unease,
well-accepted.

Sometimes I see
that they get into flights
and the police have to come,
it is a little bit scary.
Japan is such a peaceful country,
we should not think about countries,
but about the world.
We are all citizens of the world,
right?

Lake Placid

VENUES

L

*"We're famous
for the winter
and weekends are busy,
because of ski season,
but in summer
it is seven days a week."*

Miracle on Ice,
at least 70% of the market,
maybe 80% are second homes
and it has been that way
ever since the Olympics,
Great Camps 1980 winter.
There are two kinds of second-home owners–
those who use their places
for the whole summer
and those who come occasionally
and mostly rent them out.
We're famous
for the winter
and weekends are busy,
because of ski season,
but in summer
it is seven days a week.
Forever Wild.

VENUES

LGBTQ

Lesbian, Gay, Bisexual, Transgender, Queer

Nightlife is a really tough sector
to work in,
the hours are friendly
for the punters,
but quite anti-social
for those of us
on the business side of things.

It was always
the same old celebrity meet-and-greet,
instead of something
that was genuinely fun,
creative
and interesting,
it really blew my mind,
wonderful.

I got really frustrated
with these clubs
that had thousands of pounds of budget
and were happy to blow it all
on a Disk Jockey,
but wouldn't give even a fraction of it to us,
we could have made their nights pop;
it felt like quite lazy booking.

None of the banks wanted to invest,
in a month
recommendations helped to turn it
into a permanent fixture
of the capital's club scene.
We grew up very naturally,
because we had no money
to grow it any other way,
our early years
were basically us
scrapping around

to find free Wi-Fi,
everyone
and their friends
wanted to be part
of what we were doing–
we would go to a booking
for five drag queens,
but turn up with 20.
That really impressed clients,
many of which were used
to talent
turning up
for an hour
while they kept the taxi running.

Liberal Democrats

GOVERNMENT

> Presidential Election

If she's going to get anything
done as president,
she is going to have to have
a mandate,
but temperament doesn't
give you a mandate
to do anything.

Secretary Hillary Clinton's decision
to aggressively court Mitt Romney's
base has her looking more
and more like Mitt Romney every day;
she is not just running as
the alternative to the other guy.
She is running on a progressive policy agenda
that she seriously believes
will make a difference
in people's lives;
if she wins,
it will not just mean
a rejection of Donald Trump.
It will be a call to action
on the issues she has championed.
Her policy proposals are admirably detailed,
but they cover so much ground
that their whole is less than the sum
of their parts.

Clinton is not likely to emerge
with a legislative mandate,
she will have to start from zero
in terms of seeing all
her policy proposals.
They will not have been sold
through this process.
We didn't see that the people
voted for that.

We see that the people voted
against Donald Trump.

We need the broadest popular front
against Donald Trump,
the challenge for the left is,
if that's all we do,
we're saying anyone one degree
to the left of David Duke
is O.K. with us.

It's up to us,
double-edged sword.
Republicans in Congress won't grant
as easily after election
that we won a huge mandate
on progressive issues,
but thanks to Donald Trump,
we might have more progressives
and majorities in Congress.
I'd rather have a Republican minority
in denial about what just happened
than a Republican majority standing
in the way.

Libya

UNITED NATIONS

        Facebook

Keyboard warriors.
Digital heroes,
everyone has Facebook
and uses it for business;
politicians,
officials,
fighters…
You ask them,
'*What's your email?*'
and they'll give you
their Facebook username.

Both sides use it for propaganda
and with it a disinformation campaign
focusing on accusing the other side
of excessive collateral damage
or intentional killing of civilians
and framing the enemy
as serving foreign interests
or having mercenaries
and foreign fighters fight in their ranks.

Facebook control.
Made in the United A Emirates,
lies
and fabrication.
Working hard to fight abuse
on our services,
particularly in conflict zones
like Libya
where Facebook can be used
to incite violence
and spread hate,
terrorist
and extremist content
and graphic material.
Global safety

and security teams,
these content review teams
are located in over 20 sites
around the world.
Including sites in North Africa–
working around the clock
to review reported content.

What he is doing
is coming up with terms
that are sowing hate
and division
and you're having people here
from its side
responding to him in kind,
it's creating problematic dynamics.
People say they're watching for fun,
but this is not something
to be laughing about.

It's not about discrediting,
but putting as many versions out there
as possible;
people will get overwhelmed,
if you create enough confusion,
no one knows what to believe.

Limited Liability Company (LLC)

ECONOMY

They're used to doing illegal things,
the idea is to try to separate the criminal
from the crime
and that's what they're used for.

You don't have to tell the State
who the owners
of the Limited Liability Company are;
the state of California does not know
who the owners of a California LLC are
if the owners don't want them to know.
The fact that someone has a financial interest
in a company shouldn't necessarily
be public information
whether you own stock in a small,
private LLC
or that you own stock in an entity
that's trade on the Nasdaq
or the New York Stock Exchange,
it's not a matter of public information.

You could set up a string of five,
six,
seven LLCs in different States,
it's going to be hard to trace
all the way through.
Where does the shell game
finally stop?

There's no way for the bank
to verify that the information provided
is correct.
The bank is going to say,
"*Who owns it?*"
We'll say,
"*We do.*"
They'll say,
"*Show me some evidence.*"
It's not clear what that will be
beyond the statement of the person
opening the bank account.

HEALTHCARE

Longevity Proteins

Human Longevity

"Longevity protein".
The effect of SIRT6 deficiency
is like turning
your biological clock backward
by half,
it means a fetus could only develop
to 5 months old
in the mother's womb.

This means SIRT6
is a highly probable candidate
for a human longevity protein
that can regulate our lifespan
and development,
these will be important
future research topics,
a new window of research
has now opened
for the discovery
and research
of a more human longevity protein
in the future.

Lurid Lawsuit

LABOR

Harassment Scandal

Rampant sexual behavior in focus.
An bearable environment,
to encourage sexual intercourse
at the workplace.
A lot of people were afraid
to be in the media,
we were scared of everything
that was happening.
People privately assumed the worse–
that the upload allegations
are all true
or they assume the opposite–
that the allegations are salacious,
crazy
and can be ignored.
Regardless,
they don't want to risk their career
by publicly talking about
a connecting node
for the entire industry.

Our employees are our greatest asset:
These allegations are entirely without merit.
We let you down and we are sorry cancer.
I tend to be fairly passionate about things
and wear my heart on my sleeve,
looking back,
there are definitely ways
I would handle this differently.
Refraining from public relations activity.
We do not have comments to offer.

There was a lack of leadership
to cultivate a healthy work environment
and investors who failed
to take a more active role in oversight,
the only way to resolve these sorts of problems

is to control them head on
and that is precisely
what no one seemed prepared to do.
To acknowledge the depths of misogyny.
Renders it so dysfunctional misogynistic
and lewd culture.
If I were to boycott every organization
that exhibited such culture
and behavior publicly
or behind closed doors,
I would be severely limited in my options,
honestly,
I wouldn't hold my breath
that there would be any left
unless I moved to Wonder Woman's
home island.

Backpacking in Europe.
Freelance users experience designer.
Elizabeth had several incidents
growing up that targeted her physical safety
and developed her sense of right
and wrong.
Short,
sassy
and blond.
Take it
or leave it,
womanly tasks,
mommies.

A lot of things
could be avoided
if there is an open line
of communication,
once you have five people,
male
or female,
at the start up
you need external Human Resources.
Not having someone
to go to talk to
about your potential concerns
just makes it so much worse.

Malaria

AMERICA'S NEW TRIUMPH

*"We helped create
two new multilateral
institutions,
we've had Gavi,
which is the thing
that makes sure
all the kids
of the world,
get vaccines
and the Global Fund
to fight AIDS
Tuberculosis
and Malaria,
making sure
that developing
countries
get access
to the life-saving tools
for all three
of those diseases."*

We're far richer today than ever—
the world,
the United States
and you know,
the Technology community
is the extreme example of that,
even in my neighborhood,
I'm not the richest guy!

Malaria from the globe.
Gene drive.
If you stand still,
you go back toward the peak,
which was 1.2 million
deaths a year
and you can't do eradication
with the existing tools.
Crossroads.
Game-changer.
Persuaded.
It's going to another decade
before this is ready to use,
but in another decade,
malaria will still be here.
Malaria remains one of the big killers
of the world.
We have to eradicate it—
it's time to tick that box.

Entirely re-engineer ecosystems,
create fast spreading extinctions
and intervene in living systems
at a scale far beyond anything
ever imagined.
The deadliest animal in the world.

This could be the year
of the last polio case,
fish bowl.

That was radical at the time
and now it is not at all.
At the foundation,
it is about every child
having an equal chance to live–
that where you're born
doesn't mean
you're 50 times more likely to die.

It's also like Microsoft,
in taking advantage
of the great innovation
in science
that brings us new tools
and better ways
of doing delivery.
We helped create
two new multilateral
institutions,
we've had Gavi,
which is the thing
that makes sure
all the kids
of the world,
get vaccines
and the Global Fund
to fight AIDS,
Tuberculosis
and Malaria,
making sure
that developing
countries
get access
to the life-saving tools
for all three
of those diseases.
They've been a tremendous success.

Giving pledge.
I'm optimistic
that almost all the people
who make huge money in technology…
will be serious about philanthropy,
there isn't a sense

that it's a dynasty
and that their kids
are going to run the company.
Everyday there's people coming up
here to talk with us
about education,
disease
or research things.
You'll get to the point
where you'll say:
'*Hey,
what is there besides work?*',
because you will go
from a labor-supply
constrained era
to a case
where you don't have that shortage.
Work won't be the central,
almost religious activity
that it is today.
That's an inevitability,
then you'll have all sorts of philosophical questions
about purpose.

Malta

UNITED NATIONS

         United Kingdom
A young inexperienced government
that was bold enough
to do things
that unthinkable previously.
Making Work Pay.
Zero unemployment.
Driven by domestic demand,
imports of goods
and services
are gaining momentum
and exports
are forecast to continue rising,
in line with growing demand
in Malta's main trading partners.

Malta's economic growth
remains one of the strongest
in Europe.
Reaching the desired fiscal position
has not been easy,
we brought our import bill down
so we have an external current account surplus–
due to our emphasis on energy,
as well as tourism
and exports.

We registered the highest rate of growth
6.6 percent–
in the eurozone in 2017
and the major indicators.
Growth Domestic Product,
labour market development,
industrial machine imports–
all point to further expansion
in the economy.
Malta's relations
with the United Kingdom
are still strong,

Brexit will have an impact
and any slow-down
in the UK economy
could have a reductive effect
on foreign demand,
as would a depreciation
in the pound,
but with regards to the future,
we have always been an honest broker
and friend to the UK
and this will remain a priority.

When the docks were closing down
some ten years ago,
SR Technics
took Malta Enterprise
up on its suggestion
to use maritime staff
in the aviation business.
The staff was taken to SRT's operation
in Switzerland for training
and company executives there were struck
by how flexible
and willing to learn they were.

Risk-managed investments.
We are open to ideas,
good at listening
and ready to take calculated risks.
We take the ball
and we run with it.
We attract investment,
financial services,
iGaming industries
and so on,
because of our efficiency;
not only our advantageous taxation.
We have excellent lawyers,
accountants,
friendly
but tight regulation
that is neither stifling
nor lax,
access to policymakers

and decision-makers,
a pleasant environment
in which to work
with great communications in terms
of IT (Information Technology) infrastructure
and flight connections.

Malaysia

GOVERNMENT

When it comes to the election,
forget about everything
and think only of winning.
I know
I'm not popular
with all the people;
remember,
I am 'cruel'
or a 'pharaoh'.
That's all right.
In politics,
you get called all types of names.
This time,
we are together
to replace the government,
the government has been there
for more than 60 years.
It is time it goes.

Mahathir's candidacy
is a kind of Hail Mary pass
from the opposition
that has spent the past three years
beset by infighting.
The reason Mahathir
was named as the candidate
for prime minister
is quite straightforward:
There is nobody else,
his role is to win the election
and hold the position
until someone else comes,
we are not supporting Mahathir
as a person,
we are supporting
the reform agenda
he has committed to.

Arrogant.
Yes,
I picked him,
I encouraged Badawi
to pick Najib
as his deputy,
which means
he would become
the next prime minister.
I was instrumental
in the fall of Badawi,
also.

This particular prime minister
believes he can buy support,
with money
he can buy everybody.
So how does he get money?
He steals the money.
For us
it is a dictatorship,
the rule of law
is no longer enforced now.

Marine Life

NATURE

The color jumps out at you
there are organisms of every size
and shape
and color imaginable,
from the finest sea stars,
up to seals,
sea lions
and sharks.
The prevalence
of marine life on these things
is just extraordinary.
Unusual.
It's more productive
than the most pristine coral reef
in the most remote part
of the Pacific Ocean.

Moving the state's rigs–
to–
reefs program forward
is important,
because it will help protect
the ocean environment
from the excessive damage
and pollution
caused by fully extracted oil rigs
from the ocean floor.
Artificial reefs provide
unbelievably robust marine life,
which is good for the ocean,
and the program creates massive
funding from the oil companies
that will be used
for environmental programs.

The question becomes,
'Are we going to let
the companies off the hook
for something that they willingly

agreed to decades ago?'
The fundamental debate is
whether nature designs
a better ocean
than human beings design.
These are places
in the ocean
for millions
and millions of years
that have evolved
a certain range of species
and a certain type of habitat
and that created
a balanced environment.

Once you alter the natural habitat,
you introduce an artificial
mix of species.
If you have an artificial environment
that brings invasive species,
a dumped oil rig
is not a coral reef
by any stretch of the imagination.

All these studies,
regardless of who is funding them,
tell us that these platforms
are ecologically significant,
even though they are not very many of them
and they don't have a big footprint,
they are unbelievably productive.
These things are expensive to study
and nobody want to fund it,
it tells us a lot
about how much they like that habitat,
if you give a fish a choice
between living in a natural reef
or platform,
they prefer the platform.
Those platforms have
been in place for 50 years
in decommissioning a platform,
you are killing zillions of animals–
or taking away a home.

The Marines

MILITARY

The Marine Corps was worried
about an Obama presidency,
the 202,000 number was contingent
upon Marines staying in Iraq,
then the 202,000 number
was not defensible.
I would call it unofficial wartime standards.
If you think about the standards
a decade ago,
the Marine Corps found reasons
to turn people down,
because it needed so few people.
Basically,
your standard is going to go up
or down based on the available pool
of recruits
and demand for them.
It's a value judgment.

SKILLS:
Aviation
Combat arms
Elite WarriorIntelligence
SmartTough
SET:
WANTS TO CHALLENGE
THEMSELVES

First-termers are re-enlisting
at the highest rate ever
and that's taken a great deal
of pressure off our recruiters,
no one expected the numbers
we've seen in re-enlistment;
very small in comparison
to other services–
our image of a smart,
tough,
elite warrior continues to resonate

with the young people
seeking to join the Corps.

There are more reasons to look at
the military because the public
are worried about their jobs.
I think that they think
that the standards have been lowered,
yet we have not changed our standards.

We pretty much raised our hands up
right away,
we said we needed more barracks.
We were able to convince them
to fund us;
the bottom line is,
unless you get them
through recruit training,
you can't strengthen the force.

The Marines
usually have an easier time
recruiting,
because their advertising
is much better
and they focused
more on recruiting
people who aren't looking
to make the military
a career.
This appeals to people
who are looking to do
something exciting for a few years,
then they'll get caught
with a big manpower bill,
the Marine Corps
it's kind of betting on the future.

Marriage

SOCIETY

Never both be angry,
at the same time.
Never yell at each other
unless the house is on fire.
If one of you has to win
an argument,
let it be your mate.
If you have to criticize,
do it lovingly.

Never bring up the past.

Neglect the whole world,
rather than each other.
Never go to sleep with an argument,
unsettled.
At least once every day,
try to say one kind
or complimentary thing
to your life's partner.
When you have done something wrong,
be ready to admit it
and ask for forgiveness.
It takes two to make a quarrel
and the one in the wrong
is the one who does the most talking.

Mix love,
happiness,
then add in some faith.
Blend in understanding,
tenderness
and lots of patience.
Add forgiveness.
Toss in laughter.
Generously serves the whole family.

Marriage Aux Personnes De Meme Sexe

SOCIETY

Hollande

C'est incontestablement
un texte gene'reaux que
vous avez aujourd'hui.
Sans retroactivite.

Oui.
Votre histoire recontre
en ce jour cellede tous un pays.
Nous avons attentu 2014
cen'etait plus.
A un an pus parce
que nous voulions
nous marier
le jour de notre
20 anniversaire,
mais ca ne vous empeche
pas de celebrer les 5 ans
de la Lou Taubira
on en a bave'
pour en arriver la,
mais ce jour-la
etait magique.

Lo 12 Otobre 2018,
now feterums
nos 5 ans de mariage.
Cettee journee'
resteragravee'
dans ma memoire
pur toujours.
Dire oui a l'homme
que j'aime depuis
bientot sept ans.
Jet'aime cheri.

Ils predisaient.
La de'cadence

de la societe francaise.
En fait,
il n'y a eu que
plus d'amour
et de bonheur.
Bisous les rageux
de la Mani f pourtous.

Mars

GOVERNMENT

        NASA's Jet Propulsion Laboratory

Touchdown confirmed!
Flawless,
this is what we really hoped
and imagined
in our mind's eye,
sometimes things work out
in your favor.
What an amazing day
of our country.

In the coming months
and years even,
history books will be rewritten
about the interior of Mars,
sols.

Now we start our work,
every single thing
had to go right.
Parking lot.
It's going to be awesome.
I can't wait to start seeing marsquakes,
decided to rest on its laurels.

Mass-Produced Plastics

NATURE

The first global analysis
of all mass-produced plastics
ever manufactured.
The ensuing rapid growth in plastic production
is extraordinary,
surpassing most other man made materials,
the same properties that make plastics
so versatile in innumerable applications –
durability
and resistance to degradation –
make these materials difficult
or impossible for nature to assimilate,
thus,
near-permanent contamination
of the natural environment
with plastic waste is a growing concern.

We didn't want to tell the world
what needs to be done,
but we wanted to point out
how large the challenge is,
to hopefully spark off a great discussion;
reduce,
reuse,
recycle.
I think the simplest
and most effective strategy
is to reduce the amount of plastic we make
and use,
currently we aren't doing a good job of doing that.

We've passed a statewide plastic bag ban,
we have many municipalities across the state
that have banned plastic foam food-ware
and have taken other steps
to reduce the amount of single-use plastic
that is being consumed
and therefore have the opportunity
to potentially become marine debris,
but there's clearly much more work that we need to do.

Mauritania

UNITED NATIONS

The duty
and fairly elected president
was deposed
by an unelected military figure.
Mauritania has all the features
of a potentially self-correcting
democracy;
the military shouldn't be stepping in.
If there's a correction to be made,
it should be made by the people.

What is going on in Mauritania
is a coup d'état organized
by the rebels who we sacked
by the president on Wednesday morning,
it's a coup against the constitutional
legitimacy in Mauritania.

This was a constitutional government,
democratically elected.
This coup comes as a form of protest
to the president's early decision
to sack the head of the presidential guard-
a move that the military establishment
perceived as a threat to its position
within the Mauritanian political system,
the military thinks the coup
would meet the demands of many sectors
in the society that seem dissatisfied
with the government.
This coup d'état shows that the military
establishment considers itself the guardian
of the democratic experience
and holds for itself the right to intervene
whenever the democratically elected
government does not meet
the demands of the masses.

Medical Negligence

JUSTICE

No win,
no fee.
You must prove
both breach of duty,
you must prove
that treating clinical
did something
or failed to do something
which no other
reasonably competent practitioner
would have done
or failed to do.

To prove causation,
you must prove
that the breach of duty
on behalf of your treating clinician
caused you to suffer
an injury
you would not otherwise have suffered.
In other words,
you would not have suffered
your injury
if the clinician
had provided
the correct standard of care.

If you wish to bring a claim,
the onus is on the claimant
to prove their claim.
You will require
supportive medical evidence.
Our solicitors
will recommend
obtaining expert reports
from independent medical experts.
Without supportive expert evidence,
it will be very difficult
to pursue your claim.

Medical Schools

EDUCATION

        American Association
Association for Medical Colleges

The growth of the University of California
San Diego medical school
has been nothing short of remarkable,
comparable schools
have been getting $250 million,
I'd be happy with $300 million.
That would be transformational.

See one,
do one,
teach one.
Today,
we allow everyone
to advance at their own speed
and they can practice
as much as they want
on a simulator,
the simulations back then
were so primitive
you couldn't really use them.

We've changed
to a much more active learning,
in small groups,
with fewer lectures
and more situations
where the students work things out
for themselves,
this is the way that things stick
in your head.
The research output
of the medical school
is every bit as important
as the number of students
who are graduated.

Physicians really view their role
as working in partnership
with the patient
and they collaborate
with health care providers,
other doctors
and nurses.
No matter how smart you are,
no matter how well trained you may be,
you need help
in terms of getting your patient everything
they need.

Mental Health Inmate

JUSTICE

Epidemic ignored.
We are paying the price
for decades of inaction,
that's why I think
ultimately
we are where we are.
People have been sending out
the warning and saying,
'The day will come
when it's going to hit
a critical mass,'
and we are at a point now
where our criminal justice system
cannot handle those that are mentally ill
and we don't have
the appropriate therapeutic beds
and facilities to deal with those
who are coming into the criminal justice system
at a rate that is just completely overwhelming.

This kid needs help
and support
and the only thing he's going to get
is three square meals
and all the weights he can lift.
Without proper 24-hour supervision,
he would in all probability injure himself
in considerable risk
or harm.
He would also in all probably act out
and injure someone else
and would re-enter the judicial system
as an adult.

If a kid never bonds with their mom,
it's hard for them to bond with anybody else;
he would talk about his mom.
He didn't understand why
she wasn't around,

he was a good kid;
he really was.
Once a youngster get institutionalized,
he gets into it
and he just keeps on,

I think once you're involved in it,
it's hard to get away from it.
I'm quite positive he never got the help
he should have got
and I don't mean to say
that the law enforcement agencies,
whether it was sheriff's department
or a police department,
I'm not saying they did it just to be ornery
and mean;
I'm saying that once he got involved in this mess,
he just kept on getting involved.
Society has lost a lot of kids,
instead of helping them,
they hurt a lot of kids–
by putting him in prison like that,
it only makes the anger worse.
He can't rationalize why he's there,
so therefore,
we're faced with this horrifically immoral decision,
we have to go ahead
and incarcerate that person in an environment…

There should be a facility available in Oklahoma,
a long-term secure facility
where they can be humanely treated
as a mental health consumer,
rather than a prisoner.
Without viable mental health treatment options
all along the continuum of care,
the criminal justice system
is not always able to lace individuals
in a setting that will adequately address
their mental needs,
while also ensuring protection of the public,
until there are more treatment options,
the criminal justice system
will continue with this struggle.

When dealing with mental health issues,
there is a delicate balance
in finding effective treatment
for an individual
and protecting public safety,
primarily due to a lack of resources
and treatment options for mental health,
the criminal justice system
is not always able to find that balance.

'I'm building a bomb to kill myself,
I'm 15,
I stole my mom's car
and I ran away from home.'

'Where were you going?'

'South.'

'Why?'

'I don't know.'

If you've got resources,
find something.
We don't know what to do with him.
We didn't realize he had any developmental
or mental issues at all,
he didn't think law enforcement would show up.
He thought the railroad would show up
and give him a ride.

What his case illustrated is that that's not enough,
because formal services have failed this young man,
he was in formal services
and he literally tried to escape them.

I have to follow the law,
I have to treat people fairly
and I have to keep cases moving
and get them to a completion point.
In the process,
I have to remember

that every one of them is an individual
and that they have different abilities
and different needs.
Judges have to care for the victim,
for the offender
and for the public;
I don't want to say too much more,
but you have to remember
they're people in a secure states-operated
or approved facility
serving the long term needs
of the mentally handicapped.
You got general population inmates
and mental health inmates
and the general population
generally takes advantage
of the weaker inmates.
Once you get the cells full,
the people out here will suffer,
they're grown up in that
and they haven't had those resources
to get the care they need.
There just needs to be better mental health care
in Oklahoma,
is what there needs to be
and I guess in the whole United States,
but I know here for sure,
because we've had not luck,
none whatsoever.

Metropolitan Water District

NATURE

There have been ramifications
from these drastic cutbacks
in regards to revenues,
the agencies
had not assumed
that we would see
such drastic cutbacks
from the state board.
The district uses
a methodology
whereby
we collect.
80 percent
of our fixed operating expenses
on the monthly
operation charges,
only the remaining 20 percent
is added
to water rates.
We should be allowed
to establish
local conservation targets
based on
our urban water management plans
and our actual water supply conditions.
The state's cookie-cutter approach
to statewide mandates
was ill conceived
and unfair to the residents
of San Diego County.
We look forward to returning
to the carefully constructed approach
to water supplied
and conservation
that the region has been implementing
for decades
without intervention
from Sacramento.

Minimal.
It would be the end
of agriculture,
up here.
Strong,
financial margins
are expected
to be notably weaker
in fiscal years
2015
and 2016
as state water conservation mandates
take hold.
Fitch Ratings expects
rate increases
and/or changes in rate structures
to be placed by fiscal 2017
to mitigate
reduced water demand
related to the drought.
"AA."
"AA+."
"AA"

There are very few places
in California
that have actual shortages,
for a great many of these agencies,
they didn't have a shortage
until the State of California
forced one on them.
We are leading
with the state
to have a different policy
over the long term…
something that allows locals
to tailor their drought preparedness
to local circumstances,
to invest in local supplies
so that people
can continue to use water
in reasonable
and beneficial ways.

In a typical year,
we discharge about a million
and a half-acre-feet
of highly treated wastewater
into the ocean,
even if we could fake
just 50 percent,
that's 750,000 acre-feet.
It's a lot of water
and when you go back
to how short people were
in 2015,
it's almost inexcusable
to be discharging that much water
into the ocean.

Migrants

IMMIGRATION

U.S. Citizenship
and Immigration Services
is making the process
of applying for immigration benefits
more efficient,
secure
and convenient,
we continue to add new forms
that applicants can complete online.

Our website is one of the most visited
of all federal agencies
in the United States;
we have approximately 12 million
unique visits each month
and we have renewed our website,
put in online our most solicited services
right in the main page.
Visitors now have access to breaking news,
for example if there is a closure
in any USCIS office.
Visitors can also have access
to the most looked up tools
like how the citizenship process works.

Our final goal is to show information
in an easy way
and that anyone can see
the process of their case,
migrants now have a lot of access
in our website,
they don't need to go to our offices anymore
and it doesn't mean that our doors are closed
for them,
it means that they now have more online access.

MILITARY

Military Academy

United States

False comfort.
The list goes on,
because if you target Americans,
we will find you
and justice will be done
and we will defend our nation.

Strong headed
and bighearted,
many of the threats to our security
cannot be solved
by military force alone,
we have to draw on every tool,
all elements of our national power.

How will it alter the conflict?
What comes next?
When we ask those questions,
we prevent the kind of mission creep
that history teaches us to avoid,
when I'm no longer president,
I will sleep well at night,
because I know
that men
and women like you
serve to keep us free.

Millennials

SOCIETY

Baby Boomers

Positive about their financial future,
saving for retirement,
what we have here is a classic
mismatch between perception
and reality.
Millennials
and Money.
Wisdom of Experience.
Lessons learned from Millennials,
Generation X
and Baby Boomer Investors.

Many Millennials are introduced
to investing at work,
the Millennial investor is significantly
better off investing today
as a new entrant to the workforce
than workers 30 years ago,
there is something in their DNA
that make them want to own
what they know
and love;
it told us that young people know
what it means to own stock.
They weren't buying a pack
of bubble gum,
they were buying part of a company
and they knew what it meant.

Millennials are everyone.
They are Uber drivers.
Engineers.
Workers at BestBuy.
People in the military.
They want to invest,
but many just don't understand.
Many have no idea you don't

have to be rich to invest. Young people don't need to be scared of investing. They just have to start.

SOCIETY

Retirement

Gold-plated.
Defined benefit.
Opt out.
My parents
don't have an amazing pension
and they encouraged me
to be in a better position
than they are.
I now contribute £80 pounds
each month
through a self-invested
personal pension.
I save my contribution
into a readymade portfolio
and then with take relief
I get from the Government
I have a bit of a gamble myself.

My husband has now said
that he will continue
the contribution each month,
as my retirement is important
as well
and we don't want to miss out
on those payments,
we know that we want to go traveling
when we're older
and go on cruises
in our retirement
and for that
we need a good pension.

I'm self-employed,
no one else is going to save
for my retirement,
because I don't have that security
of employment;

I thought it was really important
to start saving for the future.
At the time...
I was not a homeowner
and I felt like it was one of the few assets
I could put together myself,
you don't have to contribute
that much,
but it also seemed
like a wasted opportunity
not to invest
when the Government will help you
out a bit,
too.

At the moment
I've gone through
a few job changes
and I've had more outgoings
than I'd planned,
like getting a new car
that I needed for my new job.
On top of that,
keeping on top of the mortgage
is eating up a lot of cash.
I would like to retire early.
I don't want to be working
until whatever the Government's retirement age is
at that point.
I want to retire in my 50's,
but the big thing at the moment
is I have a lot of short-term debts
I need to get over.

Rising housing cost,
soaring student debt
and now wage inflation
have left millennials with stretched budgets.

They have been brought up in an era
of over-protective mollycoddling.
They don't have to witness the slaughter
of beef cattle
at the local abattoir,

just get them to hold,
touch
and smell a nice juicy steak,
they're bound to cook it better.

Millennials

SOCIETY

Vegans/Vegetarians

Rip
and tip.
Customers,
particularly younger ones,
are quite scared
of touching raw meat.
If they are not used to it,
they may think
'*Ugh!*
I'd prefer someone else
to do it for me',
it's important to touch meat
and even be exposed
to some bacteria,
the more that the food is processed
and packaged,
the more supermarkets can charge.

We will then butcher it down.
I'm a butcher's daughter
and I actually think that,
if you're going to eat meat
you should probably kill it
once in a while.
Meat,
but without the bones.
If that's your attitude
then why eat meat
in the first place?

It seems fair
to both sides of the debate.
There is no meat
without the death
of a warm-blooded sentient animal...
and at the same time
to ask vegetarians to consider
to just what point of the slaughter process

that cruelty
and suffering are taking place…
How exactly would they prefer
these animals to die,
given that immortality
is not an option?
The way that over-cautious health authorities
go on about meat
you'd think
you were handling lethal weapons
or unexploded bombs.

They love the gruesome nature of it,
they love to give it a poke
and then ask questions about it.
If you don't touch meat,
if there is packaging
then you become further
and further removed
from the reality
of the animal
and the further removed you become,
the more detached you are
and the less likely you are to care,
if you care
then you are interested
in the welfare of the animal.
These days
they don't teach cooking
in schools
and a friend of mine told me
that one of his kids
did have a lesson recently,
but it was how to make
a ham sandwich.

I'm really cross about it,
it's just rubbish.
If you don't want to touch the meat
then why bother cooking it?
These kids' brains have been boiled.
If you kill an animal,
you should eat all of it,
it's only polite.

Millennials SOCIETY

SOCIETY

Video Games

Downtown Abbey.
We're always about innovation
and what the next casino experience will be.
Young people who grew up playing video games
like to socialize,
they very much like interactivity
and innovation,
they want something that uses some skill.
This stokes your natural competitive side
and encourages people
to bring people with you to play.

Our hardware production can't keep up
with the demand;
we're filling orders placed a year ago,
I think this is the future of gaming.
Slots are super successful,
but they appeal to an older demographic,
we look to the video arcade…
and we partnered
with the Australian company
that developed 'Jetpack Joyride'
which had had 350 million downloads.
We're taking hit mobile games
and making a gaming version of them.

The younger generation
does like the nongaming amenities
like shows,
clubs,
restaurants,
entertainment,
concerts
and hotels.
Those things are part of the solution
for casinos.

The next generation of gamers–
millennials
and beyond–
has been a big part
of the discussion
in the gaming industry:
'What are we going to do about it?
How are we going to attract them?
How are we going to get them
into the casino
and gamble?'
Younger generations
have never been a large part of casinos
to begin with,
casinos need to concentrate
on their core customers,
who are older.
It's not millennials
right now,
but going forward
they're to be the customer base,
they don't have as much money
to spend now,
but they will.

Miners

ECONOMY

Miracle in the Mine.
12 Miners Rescued.
ALIVE!
The Key is:
Were the sources of information,
credible?
and the answer seemed to be,
yes...
at the time.
They were attributed,
identified
and quoted;
then at some point
you have to print a newspaper
and deliver it.
I really don't know what else
we could have done.

12 Miners Reportedly Found Alive.
Jubilation in West Virginia.
Jubilation,
then Horror.
All printed copies of today's Times
were circulating,
relying in attributed sources.
It was a very confusing situation.
There's no page in the textbook
for what happened last night.
They were official
or semi-official people
repeating the same information,
until it,
became perceived facts.

In the process of being cautious,
we allowed the jubilation to go on
longer than it should have.
We were looking for all of the skilled
personnel that could get underground

to help transport these 12 survivors
to the surface–
sincerely regretted.

Only one made it out alive,
I didn't know how their information
could come out
that these people are alive...
It's misinformation
and it's awful.
All this time,
we've been told of a miracle
and that's why we're here.
We got hurt,
they lied to us.
They lied to us all along.
Why'd you tell us those things
when they weren't true
and got all of our hopes up?
The whole country was ready
for them to come out.

12 are alive.
Fresh air.
It was all reality,
but they just lied;
we were looking for them
to come through that door,
man,
it didn't happen that way.
It hit people's hearts so hard.
*"What in the hell has God done
for us?,"*
but just a few minutes before...
we were praising Him,
because we believed
that they were alive.

Nightline.
We refused to run it,
until we had specific confirmation
that was double,
triple,
  quadruple sourced.

I sometimes have the sense
that readers think
we've got these insider channels
to everything,
that there's some way
we have of crawling along
the search team
and that we know
the honest-to-God true facts,
but for some reason withhold it;
failure of skepticism.
The reporter has an obligation
to say to the governor,
"How do you know?
Who told you?"

One of the Lost Coal Miners.
We don't know where
the good news came from,
when I heard all of this
going on,
I said to my trooper...
"Do you know
what's going on?
Has anybody called us?"
he said *"no."*
I can relate.
You grab hold
of every little thing you can,
news like this can spread
like wild fire
and it did.
Everyone has worked so hard
and there's no blame to place,
on anybody.

Only one miracle.
The one of the lost miners.

Minimum Wages

LABOR

It was brutal.
It was really racking up
credit card bills,
making many multiples
of what use were making
at Betterworks.

The better off
are getting better off
and the worse off
aren't getting any better off.
Economic gains are not spreading
as uniformly across the population
as they used to.
The fact that those people
weren't gaining
as much while we were expanding,
that's troubling.
It's an indication
of how we are doing
as an economy.
Even if the field is expanding,
it's relatively easy
to find people
to fill those jobs
without raising compensation,
this is a big experiment,
in areas like Fresno,
a majority of workers
are likely to be directly
or indirectly affected.
Research suggests
that a minimum wage
set as high as $12 an hour
will do more good
than harm
for low wage workers,
but a $15-an-hour
national minimum wage

would put us in uncharted waters
and risk undesirable
and unintended consequences.
Although the plight
of low wage workers
is a national tragedy,
the push for a national
$15 minimum wage
strikes me as a risk not worth taking,
especially,
because other tools,
such as the earned income tax credit,
can be used in combination
with a higher minimum wage
to improve the livelihoods
of low-wage workers.

A raise of 3 percent is an insult,
frankly,
we teachers say we didn't get into teaching
for the money
and that's true,
but it would really be nice
to have money to live a good life,
if you took the wage down
and cut them in half,
it would make it easier for certain businesses,
but you can't function that way,
because we're a community.
It's a matter of economic justice
and it makes sense.

There is a glut of work to be done
I think it's strange
when I see my friends who are teachers,
something I think is immediately useful
and they can't find jobs,
whereas I have to be really selective
about what jobs I take.

Just as a benefit of this policy
are likely to be greater,
because it covers a greater share
of the work force

than for the past minimum wage increases,
the risk of these costs
is also higher
it's very unclear
how that's going to stack up.
There's so much cynicism
and anger
to have the governor
and legislative responding
in a positive
and constructive way
to our members
is really important.
Wow,
we really do matter.

Mir Space Station

AMERICA'S NEW TRIUMPH

Spacewalk.
Today the Mir crew was busy
trying on their space suites
and preparing for the spacewalk
in them.

Oxygen candles.
Everything is all right
and there are no problems
with oxygen.
The Electron system
which produces the oxygen
on board is working fine;
the understudy team
is trying to simulate every situation
the cosmonauts might face
when they get into Spektr,
a module attached
to the station's core.

They acted like a single team,
regardless of whether they were Russian
or American,
this is a good example
for the future.

Mistress Dispelling
SOCIETY

I thought I was in a marriage before,
but I now see
something better,
this is real living.

When I discovered the affair,
I confronted my husband,
we fought bitterly
and I kept on asking him,
'*Why-why,*
when I have–
followed you,
so many years?'
At first he expressed guilt,
but after all the fighting,
he just didn't want to talk
to me anymore.
That's when I sought help.
Dispelled.
We've been through a lot
together,
I don't want to give all this up.
Separation has never been a concept
I have thought about
and also I am approaching 50
years old,
there's just not a market
out there
for a woman like me.

We have 33 ways to dispel a mistress,
in marriage there are all kinds of problems
and one is having an affair.
It's very serious,
bad for the family
and bad for the stability of society.

Little thirds.
There's one ultimate way

of dispelling mistresses,
we believe them,
we get intimate pictures
or videos
and then we give them
to the clients.
A kept woman.
An adultery map.
We take the measures
that are needed,
we represent the sights
of the original couple.
The clients asks us
to do what we are doing
and mistresses are the ones
who break those standards.

Mistress – seducer.
I act as the bait myself
and the whole team is there on hand
to offer expert support,
I have to understand
the different angles needed
to please the woman,
what she wants.
For example,
if she fancies a luxurious lifestyle,
wants luxury products,
nice restaurants,
we satisfy her.
In my experience,
most of the mistresses
are after financial rewards.

They say that the divorce laws
were written to make men laugh
and women cry,
also,
outside of the cities
it's seen as shameful
for a woman to divorce.

Of course I still love him.
There are many things

I still love about him
and now I know
what the problem is
with our marriage.
I know how to manage marriage.

A mistress is a tumor,
so the first thing to do
is to get rid of the tumor.
After this
the relationship
between the couple
is healthier.
It's like learning to drive.
It's tough
to get a driver's license,
but any 18 year old
can get married.
We teach them the right path
to go down
the road with safety.

Modern Architect

AMERICA'S NEW TRIMPH

Rethinking Pei:
A Centenary Synposium.
New York Times,
'the year of I.M. Pei...
the high priest of modernism.'
To many people
I.M. Pei
has become the pre-eminent designer
of modernist monuments
of our time,
the best bank building in the world.

The site had one important advantage,
because it was located
just out of the airport flight path,
the new building was not restricted
by the height limit
imposed on all buildings
to the north,
a tall building would permit us
to overlook
some of the most prestigious buildings
of Hong Kong,
with a panoramic view
of the harbor
and Kowlown beyond.
Windy City.
Mega-structure.
Vertical Knife.
X.

Probably the most innovative skyscraper
structure built anywhere to date.
It is in the view
of many who have seen it,
the finest modern skyscraper
since Mies Van der Rohe's
Seagram Building
was completed

over 30 years ago,
Architectural Record.
One of the most important
cultural icons
for the city of Hong Kong.

Mongolia

UNITED NATIONS

Election Fraud

Right step.
There was a massive election fraud.
Museum of Election Fraud.
Strong stuff from the strong party.
Fraud,
I don't think this election
has put a question mark
on the democracy in Mongolia.

Everything was in the hands
of the government—
just look at the millions
of tugriks spent on billboards
and on pop star concerts
in Ulan Bator,
we had fourteen years
of democracy,
freedom of speech.
These fourteen years
have changed the mentality
of the people.

Mortality

GOVERNMENT

You're talking about an area
that is five thousand square miles.
Los Angeles county is multicultural
where practically every race
in the world is represented.
We go from Malibu to Wrightwood
To near the San Bernardino County lines.
We see it all.
It goes back
to the Menendez brothers.
I grew up in the 50's,
we had idols back then.
You would have never seen
something like trashed babies.
All these cases give you
good perspective on how to live.

He always took care of himself,
he ate very healthily.
You would think he would die
from old age
not something this tragic.

People think I'm a bad mother.
There is always this feeling
that this makes no sense,
you have family members
blaming themselves
for not behaving properly.

Mortgage

HOUSING

Home Loans

If this proposal becomes law,
it will amount to a new tax
on homeowners,
costing them hundreds of dollars
more per month
and thousands of dollars
more per year,
the last thing potential homeowners
and those looking to refinance
into new loans need
in their market
is higher mortgage payments.

Leaders put up loan modifications,
but they're just tacking on
some payments at the end
or allowing people not to pay
for a certain amount of time,
they're delaying the problem.
They're not remedying it,
long term.

We should be giving families
every reasonable tool
to ensure
that they can keep
a roof over their heads.
Small changes
to an outdated bankruptcy code
could help over 600,000
at-risk families
keep their homes–
that should be our goal.
We believe
that all the provisions
are very important
and hope that the Republicans

will allow us to pass the bill
by the end of the week.

It would introduce
a major new element
of risk
into mortgage contracts
and that risk
would be elevated
for sub-prime borrowers,
there's going to be a hell of a fight
over this thing.

This bill will have more impact…
than any other option
currently on the table,
it should be considered
in committee first.

Mothers

PARENTS

Just have more potential things
they could do
instead of being a parent,
like going to college
or grad school
and having a fulfilling career,
lower-socioeconomic-status people
might not have as many opportunity costs–
and motherhood has these benefits
of emotional fulfillment,
status in their community
and a path to becoming an adult.

The education patterns
do help drive inequality,
because well-educated women
are really pulling ahead of the pack
by waiting to have kids,
but if going to college
and achieving
an upper-middle-class lifestyle
seems unattainable,
then having a family
might seem like the most accessible source
of meaning to you.

In places where people have children
earlier
and younger,
it doesn't mean they're less happy,
but they are less gender equal
in terms of economics,
it feels like no one here
has babies under 35 anymore.

We were just having a really good time,
we love to travel,
we were really happy
we found each other

and I think I sort of believed
you can have a baby
when you want.
I have more confidence
that it's not going to be that challenging
to pull it back together.
We're dying to take him places
and just show him
that the world is large.

People here don't have a population
going from high school to college,
there's no thoughts
about getting your degree,
becoming independent
or traveling the world.

Mount Everest

NATURE

Mountain Climbers

There were more people on Everest
than there should be,
the easy headline is,
'*Overcrowding is killing people on Everest,
but the root cause...*'
is low cost guide companies
bringing in a new demographic
of climbers who don't belong there.
Limiting the number of permits
isn't the solution.
People should have to have climbed
an 8,000 meter peak
and they need to tighten up
who can guide these,
because right now they let anybody guide.

Death zone.
Once you get above about 25,000 feet,
your body just can't metabolize
the oxygen...
your muscles start to break down,
you start to have fluid that builds up
around your lungs
and your brain,
your brain starts to swell,
you start to lose cognition,
your decision making
starts to become slow
and you start to make bad decisions.

Members of the 7 Summit Club
have scaled the highest peak
on each continent,
death zone.
With a single rate to the summit,
delays caused by overcrowding
could prove fatal,

so I am hopeful my decision to go
for the 25th will mean fewer people.
Unless,
of course everyone else plays
the same waiting game.
Dehydration,
exhaustion
and tiredness
after being caught in the jam
of climbers,
collapsed as soon as he reached the summit.
I have had bottlenecks on mountains,
before,
but not this many people
at such a high altitude.
Lost its spirit of adventure.

Incompetent climbers.
The landscape on Everest has changed
and things seem to have come
to a head this year.
Utterly remarkable.
These people are complete beginners.
When the going gets tough…
they become very slow
and they're unable to get through
the obstacles
and the more technical sections.
That's what creates the bottlenecks.

If you were to restrict
the number of permits
down to say 200,
you could still have
100 incompetent climbers
within that mix.
You'd need to provide
a climbing course of life (CV)*
with a certain level of experience,
before you're able to set foot on the mountain.

* CV: Curriculum Vitae

SOCIETY

MTV's Spring Break

Southern California summer,
you can do it.
I'm here to portray an image
that San Diego is fun
and worth your while.
I grew up watching MTV
every summer
and always wanted
to be a part of the Beach house.

This is great.
TRL,
Hot Zone.
Say what?
Karaoke.

We found a place in San Diego
that gives up proximity
to the beach
and gives up proximity
to the people
who can drop by.
The biggest success
we've had in the last couple of years
is when real people
get involved in our shower.
Today,
it's more like a nine to five businesses,
we don't shoot at night
and we don't shoot on weekends;
unless it's approved by the city.
We work incredibly hard
to be good neighbors.
If we aren't,
our programming isn't going to work,
because we'll have problems
with the police
and the mayor.
Even when you're not on TV,
you are!

You're at the coolest party of the summer.
Have some fun.

This lady outside just hooked us up!
It's awesome.

MTV is the only thing I watch.
This is so cool.
I'm going to be here all summer,
I can't believe
I'm this close
to Blink 182
and Carson Daly!
TRL Superstars
Total Request Live,
Aliens Exist,
Adams Song,
All the Small Things
This has been so much fun,
except I thought
it was going to be sunnier.

Everyone's really nice,
we're meeting some cool people,
but I'd say
this is more interesting than exciting.
They've put up a beautiful set
and are bringing a lot of nice,
young people to Mission Bay
and publicity is good.
This will affect the city
in an incredibly positive way.
Viewers will see the beautiful weather,
a lot of beautiful people
and the fun we're having in San Diego.

There's a good chance
you'll see us at the beach
at the roller coaster,
and at Sea World.
Anyone who has a movie
or an album coming out
will possibly stop by.

MTV Network

ECONOMY

           Advertisers

Source: SPIKE TV
                MTV &
                CMT

Get Moe
Bourne Ultimatum
Men of Action
Trick My Truck
Pod busting…

The results are amazing,
in many of these messages
we're seeing 100 percent retention.
We are increasingly being asked
by advertisers to create messages
for audiences in our voice.
We're looking to redefine
the commercial experience,
we're re-trying to change
the product-placement paradigm.

Truth campaigns
Real World
Mystery Science Theater 3000

That's the idea here;
we want to blur the lines
between the commercial breaks
and the entertainment content.

The Hills
TRL
C.S.I. Guys
C.S.I.

Viewers keep watching
right through the commercials,
good commercial content
is good content.

Murder Case

JUSTICE

Stun gun.
We have known about the use
of a stun gun in this murder
for many months.
At the request
of law enforcement authorities,
we have not previously disclosed it.

No member of the family
has ever owned
or possessed one of these devices.
It must now be clear
to any open-minded person
that this vicious crime was committed
by an outsider.
Although,
if the grand jury
says there isn't enough evidence
to indict,
the district attorney
can cover his rear
by saying,
"*I told you so.*"
This case is bizarre,
you couldn't make it up
on Lysergic acid Diethylamide.

We are conducting an investigation
and we are not going to comment
on the details.
Under an umbrella of suspicion
we're honing up on our research,
because we don't do
a lot of grand juries
and we don't like the secrecy
surrounding them.
Still,
if forced to make such a decision,
we have to be very careful

about who we immunize,
so we don't immunize the person
who committed the crime.

I felt the detectives questions
were not very penetrating.
He asked,
whether we had any duct tape
or white nylon cord in our garage.
I said,
"We don't have a garage."
He went onto the next question.
When he asked whether I
or anyone I knew
owned a stun gun,
I was flabbergasted,
how could it have been used?
If it's critical to the case,
why wasn't it mentioned before?

The Museum of the Bible

FAITH

Conclusions on the status
of the remaining fragments
are still forthcoming,
to encourage guests to create
their own souvenir rubbings...
and serves as tangible
and dramatic introduction
to what awaits guest inside.

The museum of the Bible
invites all people
to engage with the history,
narrative
and impact of the Bible,
it is nonsectarian,
meaning it does not promote
any particular religion.
It is the hope that everyone,
whether they have a faith
or not,
learns something new
about the most popular book
of all time
by visiting the museum.

Explore the knowledge
of the Bible
and Holy Land.
Washington Revelations:
Flying Theater.
Flew.

Bible in the World,
Crucifix Pumps.
Elvis Aaron Presley.
Stranger in a Strange Land.
East of Eden.
I Know Why the Caged Bird Sings,
as a writer,

she kept the Bible close at hand
to read aloud
for inspiration,
Evan Almighty.
Comedy of Biblical proportions.
The Ten Commandments.
History of the World Part 1.
Fury,
Shalom.
The World of Jesus of Nazareth.

Museum of Modern Art

VENUES

It's a rethinking
of how we were originally conceived,
we had created a narrative
for ourselves that didn't allow
for ourselves that didn't allow
for more expansive reading
of our own collection,
to include
generously artists
from very different backgrounds.

The bulk of the discussion
has really been the shift from a system
that in some ways was outdated–
photography,
media –
into one in which we're thinking
about the entire presentation as a whole,
today we're saying:
of course there are many histories,
that collection represents
those many stories,
don't repeat the dogmatism
of the past.
Reassurance and surprise,
you can have a suite
of integrated spaces
and discipline spaces
together for a much richer experience.

A Revolutionary Impulse:
The Rise of the Russian Avant-Garde,
it allows us to open the narrative
from our own holdings,
to the different stories.
Making Space:
Women Artists
and Postwar Abstraction,
Making Space.

It's time to give
the White Guys a rest,
they're looking tired.
Strategic acquisition,
Frank Lloyd Wright at 150:
Unpacking the Archives,
it's a continuation
of the whole idea
of taking down the silos–
less regulation,
more fluidity,
it's a better way to show art.
It makes more sense.

I call it a cross between archaeology
and surgery,
there's no place to point:
That's the new thing.
It's everywhere,
to expand
and enhance the quality
of our galleries
so we can show more
of our collection in new
and different ways,
to provide more public space
and better circulation
and whenever possible to connect
the museum to its physical location,
to open the museum
even more to the street.

Musical Genius

AMERICA'S NEW TRIUMPH

While my Guitar Gently Weeps.
Greatest performer I've seen.
A true genius.
Purple Rain,
When Doves Cry,
1999,
Little Red Corvette.
Raspberry Beret.

I was born epileptic
and I used to have seizures
when I was young,
my mother
and father didn't know what to do
or how to handle it,
but they did the best they could
with what little they had...
From that point on,
I've been having to deal with a lot of things–
getting teased a lot in school–
and early in my career,
I tried to compensate for that
by being as flashy as I could.
What's happening now
is the position that I've always wanted to be in,
I was just trying to get here.

For You.
Prince,
Why You Wanna Treat Me So Bad?
I Wanna Be Your Lover.
Purple Rain,
1999,
Around the World in a Day.
Purple Rain,
Dearly beloved,
we are gathered here
to get through this thing called Life,
Let's Go Crazy.

Darling Nikki.
Sign o' the Times.
Nothing Compares 2 U.
When You Were Mine.
Manic Monday.
Slave.
The Artist Formerly Known as Prince.

MuslimFAITH

FAITH

      The Hajj

Here I am,
Lord.
I am here to serve you.
The Hajj–
I have traveled all this distance,
left my home
and my business,
here I am,
Lord.
I'm available for you.
I am your servant.

Hajj lessons.
You have to be as natural
as God created you,
but you do rave to take a shower.
Please!
So,
don't worry.

You're spending all this time
getting ready,
running around
and you almost don't have time
to think about the spiritual experience;
it won't hit until we're actually there.
No,
it'll hit me on the plane.
When I won't have anymore
lesson plans to do,
the bathroom situation,
longer than Disneyland's
it'll be like camping—
just with 3 million other people.
Stoning the devil.

Finally the year,

if we're not going together,
I'm going without you.
You hear the names
of the mosques
and holsters,
but to actually be here—
It's just annoying,
I thought I would be walking
in the footsteps of the prophet
and at times I certainly did feel that,
but being in the middle of all this
modern luxury did take a little
away from that.

Everyone wants to get better—
to be more of a moral person,
an ethical person,
I want to become someone
who has piety
and wisdom.
Peace bear upon,
oh prophet of God.

Myanmar

UNITED NATIONS

Int'l committee of the Red Cross
State Law Order Restoration Council.
Visit Myanmar Year.
Crush all internal
and external destructive elements
as the common enemy.

Visit Myanmar year.
We said that if any foreigner
visits our cell for one night,
then he will know
the real Burma.

It smelled very awful,
so bad you can't even imagine it.
Actually,
it was very rare
to see a rat.
Everyone was after them.

Visit Myanmar year.
They saw it made
them look bad.
They think we are rivals,
but we are not rivaling them.
It is propaganda.

Emerge into the sunshine
immaculate and serene.
There is no misery
that manifests itself in rags
and sores.
Golden Earth.
The lady,
the stunt actress of democracy,
puppet doll,
England returnee
mild that women.
Mrs. Aris,

some of the voter
wrongly cast their vote,
personality cult
super political actress.

The fact is
people turn off the television
when the news is shown
only after the news hour,
they switch the television on again
to view Chinese morel.

There is a catastrophe in Burma,
it is what happens with an epidemic
when you do nothing
dramatically.

The government actively encourages
the investment of narcotics profile
into the Burmese economy.
No part of the strategy is to wean
the ethnic organizations
from heroin production
or to affect the shortage
of foreign investment.

Posters who no longer can work
often are either abandoned
without medical care
or assistance
or are executed.
A target for greedy soldiers
and bureaucrats.

Myanmar

UNITED NATIONS

Rohingya Genocide

We didn't allow
the United Nations
Fact-Finding Mission
to enter into Myanmar,
that is why
we don't agree
and accept any resolutions
made by the Human Rights Council;
false allegations
made by the United Nations agencies
and other international communities.

Perpetrated on a massive scale,
including acts of rape,
sexual violence
and mass killings.
Zero tolerance
for human rights violations,
collect
and preserve proof.

Stomach churning.
Global pressure
on Myanmar
to respond
to the United Nations' probe
is growing
and Asia must be a central part
of that.

Aung San Suu Kyi
won the Nobel Peace Prize
for her fight
for democracy
and freedom
up until 1991,

the year she was awarded
the prize.

Clearance operations.
The civilian authorities
have spread false narratives,
denied the military's wrongdoing,
including of the fact-finding mission
and overseen distraction of evidence;
through their acts
and omissions,
the civilian authorities
have contributed
to the commission
of atrocity crimes.

National Aeronautics and Space Administration (NASA)

ECONOMY

*"Pursuing opportunities
to generate
greater excitement,
awareness
and understanding
about space."*

NASA has not seen a proposal
for such a show.
The agency has to see a proposal,
before it makes any commitment.
Pursuing opportunities
to generate
greater excitement,
awareness
and understanding
about space.

We were told
NASA was involved.
If they're producing this thing
through NASA,
that's the powerful attraction.
They told us
that this had been given
(a stamp of approval)
an endorsement from NASA.

I'm skeptical
that either of these space shows
will get off the ground.
I'm laughing at the idea of NASA
reaching me as a viewer.
Talk is cheap.

Survivor,
now,
that's a show;
I can actually do this.

The networks
not only remain enthusiastic
about the reality genre,
but the next iterations
are all about one-upping the others.

With shows like
'*Who Wants to be a Millionaire*'
and '*Survivor*'
already being several years old.
The Europeans,
are already onto the next wave.
Jailbreak.
Boot Camp.
The Big Diet.
Life on Mars.

National Aeronautics and Space Administration

GOVERNMENT

NASA

These missions
typically are billion-dollar class missions,
the most costly,
the most complex,
but the most capable
of the fleet of scientific spacecraft
developed by National Aeronautics
and Space Administration (NASA),
they produce tremendous science returns
and are a foundation
of the global reputation of NASA
and the U.S. Space Program.

Stop thinking about…
flagship missions.
There always is this question
of balance
and a question
of what exactly does balance mean;
we reaffirmed that,
yes,
these large missions are important,
there are some science questions
you cannot answer
any other way.

As the report says,
not all strategic missions are large,
there are strategic scientific objectives
that can be met with spacecraft
that would fall in the small
or medium classes.

National Anthem

SPORTS

Borat!
Deutschland,
Deutschlanduber allies,
Germany,
Germany above all,
I thought I was the epitome of Ignorance
and I've never felt more disrespected
in my whole life,
let alone in Fed Cup
and I've played Fed Cup
for 13 years now
and it is the worst thing
that has ever happened to me.

In no way did we mean any disrespect.
This mistake will not occur again.

I thought,
what is that?
and when I listened further,
I realized it was 'Die Stem.'
I couldn't believe my ears.
It was an offense
to the Spanish nation,
Livin' La Vida Loca.

The Star Spangled Banner.
Shake Your Bonbon.

National Association for Advancement of Colored People

GOVERNMENT

      (N.A.A.C.P.) Presidential Election

Unless we change policies,
we will not change results.
He's alienated a number of minority voters,
and that's reflected in his low numbers,
you have to do the bare minimum
and he's not even doing that.

As is the case with many other groups,
Donald Trump is in a race
to the bottom,
he will likely have to get more
than 65% of the white vote to win.

I am now looking at opportunities
for Mr. Donald Trump to get in front
of key patterns
in the African-American community,
particularly civil rights groups
and faith groups;
particularly black colleges
and universities.
The Apprentice.
We have to make an effort,
it's unacceptable to say,
'*Oh,*
it's just too late,
we are not going to try
to do anything.'
The Apprentice.
Birther.
Disavows.
My African-American.

We didn't get any reason,
we just got an email declaration.
My view is that candidates

who run for public office
should work to appeal
to the very segment
of the electorate.

We've never seen numbers this bad
for someone at the top of the ticket,
this is a much deeper
than simply not agreeing
with Donald Trump on the issues.
This is a much deeper
rejection of him.
No.

Every cycle
except for this one,
the Republican presidential campaigns
have reached out to me
to help them.
He's a billionaire
and so his life doesn't have
to include black people,
it would be great if he went
to a N.A.A.C.P meeting
or just interacted with blacks more–
and not necessarily for political gain–
but just to understand our struggle
and what we go through.
Would it have necessarily moved
the needle?
Probably not,
but would it have indicated
that he has an interest across
racial lines in a business attempting
to serve the community
and fulfill his agenda?
Without question.

National Security Agency (NSA)

GOVERNMENT

Misinterpreted.
Foreign.
Not true.
Vast quantities.
Troubled by allegations
of the government intercepting traffic
between our data centers
and we are not aware of these activities.
We have strict controls in place
to protect the security of our data centers
and we have not given access
to our data centers,
to the National Security Agency
or to any other government agency.

Google cloud Exploitation.
Public Internet.
Google Cloud,
get around clouds.
A retrospective look at target activity,
added
and removed here!

I do not believe
the United States
should be collecting phone call
or emails
of friendly presidents
and prime ministers.
Mayor review
of all intelligence collection program
it wasn't satisfactorily informed
certain surveillance activities
have been in effect for more than a decade.
With respect to National Security Agency
collection of intelligence on leaders
of United States allies–
including France,
Spain,

Mexico
and Germany–
let me state unequivocally;
I am totally opposed,
unless the United States is engaged
in hostilities against a country
or there is an emergency need
for this type of surveillance,
I do not believe that the United States
should be collecting phone calls
or emails;
the President should be required
to approve any collection of this sort.

We have already made some decisions
through this process
and expect to make more,
not accurate.
We have intel relationships
that are already very close,
there are other types of agreements
you could have:
cooperation,
limits on intelligence,
greater transparency.
The countries on the top
of the list for those
are close European allies.

100% wrong.
Misinterpreted,
this was about a counterterrorism program
that had nothing to do with French citizens,
if the French citizens knew
exactly what that was about,
they would be applauding.
Disingenuous.
It's a good thing.
It keeps the French safe.
It keeps the United States safe.
It keeps our European allies safe.
This whole each other on what
is really legitimate protection of Nation–
state interests;

I think is disingenuous.
Sometimes our friends
have our relationships with adversaries,
we need to be respectful
and we need to be accurate;
it needs to be overseen...
but we should collect information
that is helpful to the United States' interests.

Natural Gas

NATURE

Black outs.
The people
who control blackouts
are threatening blackouts
if they can't keep
Aliso Canyon
natural gas storage facility open.
This is a threat,
this is not a report,
it is not responsible
to determine
what natural gas goes
to what location
it is based on
inflated estimate of the demand
for electric power;
under estimates
of the capacity
of other Southern California Gas
gas storage facilities
and other unsubstantiated
or flawed data.

Since gas travels
through pipelines
at a relatively slow rate,
approximately,
30 miles per hour,
rapid changes in demand
at these plants
quickly draws down supply
in the pipeline operating
pressured in the line drop
and must be replaced quickly
both to maintain operating pressure
and to continue to meet demand;
also it's the only facility
close enough to respond,
on a timely bans.

To further stabilize
the single most volatile component
of the Department of Water
and Power's operating expense,
thereby helping
the Department of Water
and Power achieve its goal
of maintaining stable,
retail electric rates
for our customers.
The only thing keeping that gas
in Wyoming out of the system,
the band leader
of that transportation system
is southland California gas
the fact that the Department of Water
and Power
and the Southern California
Public Power Authority members
together own natural gas reserve
in Wyoming
is not relevant
to the technical report
or the action plan,
ownership of reserves
does not provide
higher priority to service.

MILITARY

Navy SEALs

Danny leaves behind a legacy
that inspires us today
and serves as a brilliant example
known as heroism;
encouraging the future generation.
Years from now,
people will look upon this statue
and be reminded of the valor
of a son of Colorado,
whose country he was proud to serve.

As a boy,
Danny used to play right here
in this neighborhood.
When people come down
to this park,
I want them to be reminded of Danny
and all of our service men
and women who contribute so much,
yet ask so little.
I hope his statue reminds people
of the sacrifices
our military make every day.

Danny gave his life selflessly
serving our nation.
On behalf of the U.S. Navy SEALs,
we are proud to call him brother
and will forever honor
his warrior spirit
and sacrifice.
This statue is more
than a tribute to one man,
it is a lasting reminder
of the honor,
courage
and commitment
that Danny
and all of his teammates embody.

Extraordinary courage in actions
against the enemy.
Operating in the middle
of an enemy controlled area,
Danny fought valiantly against
a numerically superior
and positional advantaged enemy.
Forced to defend his teammates
and himself in a harrowing gunfight;
until he was mortally wounded.

MILITARY

Navy Ship Repair

Anticipate the possibility
of a downturn this fall,
we are adjusting
our hiring technique
and business plans accordingly.

Since the Iraq war started,
ships come in very briefly
and then they have to go out,
quickly,
sometimes within just 48 hours.
So,
our ship repair business
has dwindled down close to nothing.

We haven't faced off anybody,
but we haven't been doing any hiring either.
It seems that a lot of money
has been getting redirected to the war,
leaving less for repairs,
but the slowdown in the ship repair business
does affect our overall volume.

At the pace these ships are going now,
they're really taking a beating–
they're steaming continuously,
without spending a lot of time
in post for the tender love
and care that they should get.
It just seems that the money's not there
to do a whole lot on repairs.

Orders for new ships
at National Steel and Shipbuilding Company
have been very strong,
as a result,
they have a remarkable employment program;
especially for welders.
They're taking people off the steal

to get their shifts completed
and out the door.

Although we are seeing a higher
operational tempo for those ships
and submarines in there,
all the required maintenance
for those assets are being periodicity,
mission accomplished.

Higher operation tempo.
Ship maintenance.
Ship maintenance gives us,
for the first time,
the flexibility to support continuous
maintenance aboard the ship.

The Navy had under funded
ship repair,
they underestimate the amount
of money needed for repairs.
The money spent in repairs
is worth every penny.
Once you lose those trades
involved in repairs,
you never get them back.
Once the ships are gone
for two
or three months,
you have to pay off people,
but when they come back,
you have to hire
and train those people,
which adds to the costs.

SPORTS

NBC Olympics

Going past one billion minutes–
I'm impressed,
excited
and overjoyed,
we expect an O.K. crowd,
but it went viral,
and went to a shootout;
the numbers rose dramatically
and we had to add more video
sources to back it up.

Take gymnastics,
yesterday,
do I stay up until midnight
to see how they did
and avoid all social media
or watch it live?
The answer was to watch it live
and celebrate with the rest of the country.

We pointed a camera
at the Rockefeller Center Christmas tree–
it was like Yule log–
and people watched it,
if you think about it,
that was pretty advanced for 2002.

Netflix

SOCIETY

They're trying to be Walmart.
We're trying to be Starbucks.
Amazon's business strategy
is super board:
Meet all needs.
The stuff that will be amazing,
right?
We can't try to be them.
We're never
going to be as good as them
at what they're trying to be,
what we can be is
the emotional connection brand,
like HBO.

Our customers watch
lots of other videos.
They watch videos
on YouTube and
we're not trying to
replace that,
we're not trying
to meet all needs.
Crouching Tiger
Hidden Dragon:
Sword of Destiny,
Cultural moments.

Netherlands

UNITED NATIONS

I have stayed
in five different safe houses,
it's a life you don't wish
on your worst enemy.
Meanwhile,
they are still walking
the streets of the Netherlands,
because the police can't arrest them—
there is not enough evidence.
I say that those who choose to kill
our democracy
with radical,
fascistic Islamic ideas
don't deserve the rights
of our democracy.
Once again we will have to wait
until something else terrible happens,
before we do anything.

They know about the planning
and radical meetings at his house,
the intelligence service knew
he was radicalize very fast.
He should have been on the list
of the top 10.

Un-Dutch.
It's amazing
that those kinds of things escalated
as they have.
There is a great fear
of Islam in Holland,
but on the other side
the Muslim community is also afraid.
You have two groups
who are afraid
and who don't speak
to each other

and that's not good,
for the society.

There's no age limit,
if they feel the need
to go for Jihad,
they go.
We know there are armies
in Pakistan
and people are going to them.

I saw that guy lying there,
the police all around,
the terrorist shot him,
stabbed him
and cut his throat;
like an animal.
Many people agreed with Van Gogh.
There is too much crime happening.

The Moroccans
and Turks
are ruining everything,
the government gives them $950 a month,
in unemployment.
You see them in the cafes all day.
Playing cards,
plotting their plots against us.
The police are scared of them.
Najib
and Julia.
It's the end of democracy,
if the answers to an argument are bullets
and knives.

Both did everything
to tease
and irritate the establishment;
it's a frank,
Rhetorical Dutch Style.
It's a tradition in polemics:
You go over the top
to try to amuse people.
They said:

*"I perform pyrotechnics
you shouldn't take anything,"*
I say,
as well,
"seriously."

New Millennium

SOCIETY

It moves us very often
to a sense of helplessness...
Here we are—
Jews,
Buddhists,
Christians
and Muslims.
We try to speak,
we try to fight prejudice,
promote understanding
and do something together,
but there are people
who use death as an instrument,
as a means of persuasion.

Diminish the plight
and pain of people.
I see a large,
yet typical,
paradox for our era
in the fact
that through contemporary
humanity has been aware
of these dangers,
it does almost nothing to confront
or avert them.
It is fascinating how preoccupied people
are today with all kinds
of catastrophic prognoses
and how very little people
take these into account
in their everyday activities.
It is necessary to understand differently
and more perfectly
the true purpose of our existence
on this Earth
and of our deeds.
Maybe the greatest task
we have here

and now is to open our lives
to a new opportunity;
to explain
that what has happened,
did happen
and what may happen,
is completely different.
Govern administrators,
rather than nations.
True valor is not found
in declaring war,
true valor is rising up
to the circumstances around us.
Our lack of ethics
has led us to apathy
and our inaction
is simply immoral.

Universal responsibility.
I believe that the very purpose
of life is to be happy;
it is a mistake to place
all of our hopes for happiness
on external developments alone.
The key
is to develop inner peace.
The motion of purpose
of intention
is a human projection.

New York Stock Exchange (NYSE)

ECONOMY

It's hell–
what do you think?
I'm not going to give up hope,
there's still time.
It's our eighth session
of being down.
It's a sad time,
as tough a time
as I've ever seen...

Everyone is rushing for the gold.
Everyone borrows money,
farmers in Iowa need to borrow.
It's not just people in Wall Street.
This is a crisis for everyone,
Irrational exuberance.
Morbid.
I think we're already in a depression,
we skipped over the recession.
Soon enough,
we're all going to be wearing fedoras
and standing on the corner,
asking for bread.
It could be particularly frantic.
People want to say
the world is coming to an end,
but I'm not going to.
If you go outside for 10 minutes
to get some air,
people will come up to you
and say,
"oh my God,
you work there?
What's going on?"

We've been trying to send
positive vibes into the building;
maybe when the market comes back,
you just hope it works itself out,

somewhere,
somehow.

The Annotated Fed.
You should have seen this coming–
We did.
For me,
it's about letting people
have a voice in a situation
in which they are otherwise voiceless.

I'm over it,
it's surreal.
An industry just collapsed,
everything I've worked for is gone.

I think it's time to buy
a few acres in Vermont
and grease up that shotgun,
it's bad.
I think we should buy
as much gold as we can.
There's a lot of guilt,
there's oozing regret
and within couples
or people who rely
on financial experts
there's also a lot of rage.

It's the greed factor kicking in.
It's
*"I'm the guy who calls the bottom
and won't that make a great story
this weekend."*
A lot of people are saying
they don't want to see
how the movie ends.
When in doubt,
get your tail out.

SPORTS

NFL Draft

It's amazing,
This is great for the city.
E-A-G-L-E-S.
This is excitement.
He thinks Joe Montana
and Jerry Rice are walking
through that door,
they're not.

I had to come over for this,
I've been watching them
build this site for over three weeks.
I'm surprised
there's no heckling
with the Cowboys fans,
the intention is to move
it around.

With the X-number pick,
the insert name of
your favorite team here
then select.
Boooooo.
Terrible pick.
Another stupid choice.

You can see that
this is going to be an event
that will make Philadelphia proud,
where's the band?
There should be some type
of entertainment,
like a concert.
Why not?
It just doesn't make sense
not to do that.

Nigeria

UNITED NATIONS

    Lagos

He doesn't believe
I have any rights of my own,
if I say no,
he beats me.
I said:
"*Wow.*
That is not
what I want in life."
They told me
I am not a small girl,
if I didn't want to be married,
I should get divorced.

Beating is normal.
I shouldn't make him so angry,
whatever my husband says,
I should submit.
A cry for help.
In this society,
a woman must do everything
she can do to make her marriage work,
if it fails,
the woman gets the blame.

Should I stay,
because of the baby
and then end up getting killed?
Marriage to you
and a slavery relationship!
Happy family.

An African man believes his wife
is like a piece of property,
like a car,
like a shoe,
like something for him to trample on…
our men need to be educated.

Our mothers,
our fathers,
our sons,
the whole society
needs to be overhauled.

It is like it is a normal thing
for women to be treated
by their husbands as punching bags.
The Nigerian man thinks
that a woman is his inferior…
right from childhood,
right from infancy,
the boy is preferred to the girl.
Even when they marry out of love,
they still think the woman
is below them
and they do whatever they want.

I am an organizer,
I am a leader.

If you tell your wife
she puts too much salt
in the dinner
and every day,
every day,
everyday there is too much salt,
one day you will get emotional
and hurt her.
We men in Africa,
hate disrespect
and you can't imagine yourself
beating your wife?
You can't imagine yourself
being pushed to that level?
Some people just push you
over the edge
and you do things
that you are not supposed to do.
For God's sake,
you are the head of the home,
as the man.
You must have a home,
that is submissive to you.

Nigeria

UNITED NATIONS

Presidential Election

The worst thing
is they've been saying
we're well prepared,
only to cancel
at the eleventh hour!
it's just not done.
It's not done.
Continuity.

The Buhari administration
hopes to disenfranchise
the Nigerian electorate order
to ensure that turnout is low
on the reschedule date;
you can postpone an election,
but you cannot postpone destiny.

They didn't postpone yesterday.
They postponed on the day,
something is fishy.
Remain peaceful,
patriotic
and united
to ensure that no force
or conspiracy
derails our democratic development.
So much money wasted,
how many people are dying
of hunger in this country?
they do what they like.

The one-week adjustment was a painful one
for Independent National Electoral Commission's
late decision
and denied needling in its affairs,
but necessary in the overall interest
of our democracy.

Why wait until 2:30 am
when most decent Nigerians
have gone to bed?
it's a huge shock…
why didn't you inform us 48 hours before?
If materials don't get to a state capital
by the day before elections,
you might be in trouble,
things weren't being communicated.
I feel so bad.
We all prepared to perform
our civic responsibility,
it came too late,
it came too late.

Nightlife of Gazi

UNITED NATIONS

    Istanbul

An alternative source
of information.
I believe I was imprisoned,
because I am willing
to show the inequity
I witness in Turkey
every day,
but I was about to stay motivated,
because I believe
I have done the right-thing.

I often felt in danger,
but I learned how to navigate.
Wipe out.
The drug trafficking,
the prostitution,
the dog fights
and the protest–
at first glance,
these activities seemed different,
but they all had the same roots,
the same motive.
Turkey has given certain ideologies a platform–
and anyone with opposing thoughts
is vilified.
They have been pushed into the night.
That's what I photograph.

In modern Turkey,
anyone with any sort
of marginalized sexual orientation
is obliged to conceal their sexuality.
I was allowed to witness acts
at odds with the conservative image
of Istanbul.
They trusted me enough
to open themselves up

for my camera.
Being able to photograph that
was an amazing experience.

People might be repressed during the day,
but when the lights go off,
everything suddenly explodes.
He found a way
of expressing his fight
against an invisible power–
by showing the darkness
in which his subjects live.

My duty is to document the things around me.
I try to be as ethical as I can.
I will never share the identities
of my contacts.
This,
I believe,
was a reason behind my arrest.
Taking photographs of people
in Turkey has always been hard,
everyone is suspicious.
As a photographer,
you can be an agent,
someone from the state
of constant paranoia,
but we are finding ways to exist,
to be out there–
and chase the truth.

North American Free Trade Agreement (NAFTA)

OPEN DOOR POLICY

Fair deal for all.
There's been talk
about creating
more a regional manufacturing hub,
I think
there's actually some openness
to that.
There's a point
at which it is cheaper
to import directly
and forget about NAFTA.

Dumping lumber.
If NAFTA were functioning properly.
Ultra-filtered milk,
there was a loophole
in their restrictions,
we found it
and proceeded to exploit it
and that made them upset.
Buy American,
Hire American.

Nursing Home

HOUSING

Her second life focuses on friends,
trips
and the goings on
around the nursing home complex.
Old friendships are renewed
and new ones are made,
though she outlives them all.

Her legs had grown weak.
She used a silver chair
that she pulled in front of her
to steady herself.
I kept hearing '*Merci madame*'.
My generation had dreams.

She gave the impression
that her life—
her true life—
had ended with her daughter,
of whom she often spoke
in the present house.
Sometimes she would tell a joke
or slow a flash of anger
at the mention of her daughter's death.
More often,
she stared straight ahead.

She had been lonely everyday
for the past 25 years,
ever since her daughter
had died of cancer,
she still had 3 sons,
8 grandchildren.

Everybody around her has died,
one after another
and she's the only one left,
but when she thinks about death,
she is afraid.

She has started recording
to break the solitude,
so she wouldn't forget–
the unhappy events,
otherwise,
everything is lost forever.

Years passed.
The woman died,
as did other friends,
inside
and outside the Arepa Nursing Home.
Her step-sister developed dementia.
Even her now had trouble walking.
She had been lonely for 25 years,
they're the one to blame for dying.
She's angry.

Birthday or not,
she knew that no one would call,
drop a note
or stop by to check on her.
Born in early 1900's,
she never expected to live this long.
One by one,
family
and friends had vanished
or grown feeble.
Ghosts of the living
and dead,
now dwell all around her.

Oceanographer

AMERICA'S NEW TRIUMPH

*"We were working
with a very sophisticated
animal,
who was showing
comprehension
of simple sentences..."*

In contrast to the learning process
that seems required for chimpanzees,
the dolphins at our laboratory proved
capable of understanding
gestured language instructions
given through television images
of people the very first time
they were exposed to television.

Went surfin',
slave no more
and let my people go.
We were working
with a very sophisticated
animal,
who was showing
comprehension
of simple sentences;
like,
'*Fetch the ball*'
and '*Touch the ring*".
'*The Wrong–Way Whale.*'

Oil

ECONOMY

    United States

Continue to plague…
a so-so chance
that half the country
will see $4 by Memorial Day.
This is just insanity.
It has nothing to do with oil,
nothing to do with supply & demand.
It.
Nothing lasts forever.
I don't know when it'll end,
but I know how badly,
it's like watching a man
fall off a building.
You know what happens
at the end.

Makes us poorer
than we would otherwise be,
there's a hit to real income.
It's a drain on your purchasing power.
Continue to plague.
Cost recovery
through surcharges
is becoming increasingly different.

It's impossible
for a normal business
to keep up with it.
You just can't do it,
because it costs so much,
drive it into the ground.

We'll just manage
to get everything
into the Yaris
to be stuck in traffic
with the high cost
of fuel,
it's not worth it.

Okinawa

MILITARY

        Marine's Camp Schwab

We mourn with Okinawa,
We were super nervous,
almost sick to our stomach.
We are at a new law,
in a nutshell,
it's unsustainable here...
operationally,
strategically,
fiscally
and politically.

But I had just been preaching
on standing firm in one's faith,
someone needs to stand up for hope.

He works on the base.
Before,
he was a Marine,
before,
people didn't think
we should close
all the bases,
but after this incident,
people are afraid
and really angry.
Not even half.
After 70 years,
we are all family here.

As a junior high school kid,
I remember doing a weekend
home stay one of the U.S. bases.
I stayed with a black serviceman,
his wife
and two kids,
it was a change to experience
American culture,

which I only knew from Television
and movies.

If you get the community relation right,
the politics fall into place,
this creates a situation
of moral hazard,
there is a need
to create a dialogue
to bring unity,
this is where
God is challenging us.

Olympic Boxing

SPORTS

For us,
the Olympics are every athlete's dream,
you can't stop them.
We should open the door
and make that dream come true.

I consider them professional amateurs,
they are professional players
of the rounds.
I tried to adapt
to the three-round matches,
but it was difficult to adapt.
If any of them jump in that ring,
there's going to be a fight,
they box with a lot of older boxers
back home,
so they're used to the rough,
rugged tactics.
More mature,
stronger
and more experienced
over less-skilled
and less-experienced.

Such a mismatch may well lead
to catastrophic bodily injury,
including a variety of neurological,
ophthalmological,
orthopedic
and maxillofacial injuries;
amateur and
professional boxers.
Distinction has been artificially
created by the development
of the pro boxing organizations.
This isn't like the Berlin Wall
coming down,
it's a very important step,
but it's an incremental one.

SPORTS

Olympic Chefs

I thought,
this is an opportunity to do something
that can make a difference,
this is not just a charity;
it's not just about feeding people,
this is about social inclusion,
teaching people about food waste
and give hope to people
who have lost all hope.

We are a generation of young chefs
who are not competing with each other,
but who want to share
everything.
They knew how to take the food
that would otherwise be wasted
and turn it
into amazingly delicious meals.

People right now
just don't trust each other
and most of these companies didn't
want to get involved in a project
they thought could get messy.

Oh my God,
he takes banana peels
and makes incredible ice cream
and you know,
we ate food from Italy!

SPORTS

Olympics Games

Rio de Janeiro

The city has never felt so safe,
they just materialized out of nowhere,
which is something I've never seen before.
Pacification.
The safest city in the world.
it's nice to see soldiers.
patrolling the streets,
at least where I live,
it could be a lot worse.

The assault on the American athlete
is what happens to us in Rio every day.
State of calamity.
'WELCOME TO HELL.'
It was shocking to see,
as far as I can tell,
nothing has changed.

The government through a snap
of their fingers
would bring peace
to the city that has lived
through so much violence
in the past few years.
It doesn't do any good to have
this show of thousands of extra police
unless you tell every Olympic athlete
to walk the street with the policeman
by his side.
Police forces are invading
the favelas every day
and killing people,
which is outrageous.
How can anyone hope to
bring peace by spreading violence?

SPORTS

Olympic Golf

One of the greatest golf trips
I've ever been on.
I've never been so happy
with a third-place finish in my life.
This is a greatest sporting event
I've ever been a part of.
I got to go to the Masters
for the rest of my life,
but it's just golf.

Once we got down here,
we realized what a great
experience it was.
I was very excited about golf
in the Olympics,
at least one of us
will get to the Olympics.
So from the beginning,
he really embraced it.

With the flags and everything,
It's as emotional as
I've ever felt about a win.
Honestly,
bless athletics,
it looked great,
but it was a half-empty stadium;
there was nothing half–empty
about this place today.
It was an amazing atmosphere.
Podium jackets.
Being a part of this,
I don't need anything else.

Olympic Spirit

SPORTS

　　　　　　　Pyeongchang 2018
　　　　　　　　Winter Games
The Olympic spirit
is the most important symbol of peace
in this world
which sees so many conflicts,
so many victims.
The Olympic spirit
allows people to be together
from all over the world,
to respect each other,
to serve the themes of tolerance
and mutual understanding.
These make the basic element of peace possible.

Snowboard cross has a special place for me.
It was my sport,
my main passion for a time.
My obsession with pictures
from the start is born
from my excitement
at the snowboard cross start.
The adrenaline,
the excitement
and the potential
are at the maximum there.
As soon as the race starts,
that excitement turns into pure energy,
you are giving the best
and the finish is a big relief…
and then you climb back up
to the start
and it starts all over again.

The biathlete coming in
from a hard ski
needs to focus
on slowing his heartbeat
so he can hit his target

with split-second accuracy.
If he misses,
there is a penalty.
All the elements came together
as the same split-second
that the athlete fired the rifle,
as witnessed by the bullet
easing,
leaping into the air.
The whole experience
has been insane.
You hear so much
about the Olympic Games,
but actually being a part of it
is a completely different story.
To share my story with the world
has been amazing.
It's been four years of preparation
for this event.
It's so important for us,
there's so much hard-work in it–
so many hours of training,
so much blood
and sweat–
and now we're Olympic champions again.

Africa is the home
of so many very successful Olympic athletes.
Africa is a continent of youth.
That is why
we want to take
the Winter Youth Olympic Games'
athletes 2022 to Africa.
The International Olympic Committee
will provocatively approach
a number
of African National
Olympic Committee
to evaluate the feasibility
of such a project.
Fireworks of Victory.

To win
in three different Olympic Games

involves very hard-work
over many years,
so many thoughts
are going through my head.
So many people helped me.
It is always good
to have a great team behind you
and they all did a very good job.
Sports can make the world one,
together,
when people win
they are happy
and when they lose
we all feel sad together.
We need some time to understand
that we won Olympic gold medals,
our goals remain the same–
to enjoy it
and show the audiences what we can do
through expressing our emotions.
It was something very special
and we will think about these moments
with the end of our lives.

Building a peaceful
and better world
through sport
and the Olympic ideal.
Dove of Peace.
Bell of Peace.
Imagine.
Games of New Horizons.

Olympic Winter SPORTS

International Olympic Committee

For humankind to live together
in peace,
respect
and harmony.
The Olympic athletes showed us
what the world could look like,
if we were all guided
by the Olympic Spirit
of respect
and understanding.

While recent years
have seen improvements
in gender equality in sport,
we need more,
we need to do it quickly.
These recommendations
aim to make substantial change
and swiftly.
The International Olympic Committee
is in a prime position
to lead the way
in bringing purity
in gender equality
and this decision
is a great step forward
toward achieving our objectives.

Outstanding services
rendered toward world peace
and development of sports
in the development of sports
in the Republic of Korea.
Essential role in marking these Games
such a success.

Unwavering faith in the Olympic Spirit

and in his belief in the unifying power
of the Olympic Games.
Bridge-builder.
Had greatly contributed
to the reconciliation process
between North
and South.
Agree.

The main objectives
I would like to focus on
are the implementation
of this great strategy
that we have all worked so hard
to bring together.
We also need to ensure
we continue to improve
and be proactive
with our communications.
This will help us to build
a strong global athlete community
that is truly reflective
of the athletic representatives.

SOCIETY

Online Dating

Baby Boomers

It was just like old times,
a deep
and strong love for each other,
I am so happy.
I do believe God had a hand in this…
You sure I'm old enough
to get married?

I think so.
It's not every day
that you get
a wedding invitation
via text–
from your 77-year old Aunt.
We are all family now.

The definition of 70
or even 80 now
has really changed,
I think that window
of healthy living,
as well as long life,
make people feel more ambitious
and more entitled to…
begin a relationship.

That story gives other inspiration
and belief in their own
possible good future.
Part of being vital
and being young
is being with a partner.

Online Girlfriend

SOCIETY

       Exhibitionist

Tip.
More often.
More explicit.
Fitness model.
70 percent of my fans are men.
I'm a thick girl.

Basically,
only fans are online,
go-go dancing,
having sex for money is appealing,
Tumblr was filled
with the most extreme sexual experiences
you could see
and I think a lot of people
were turned off by that.
It's what they're looking for.
They want more intimate experiences.
They want a boyfriend experience.
They want to fantasize
about someone
that they want to have sex with
and not fell disgusted by it.

How to Make Love Like a Porn Star:
A Cautionary Tale,
Porn went the way of all media.
If you have a known name,
it's much easier
to make you services,
the whole industry did a 180,
when I started,
there were actually websites
that would out famous porn stars
if they escorted,
because it was shocking,
for lack of a better word.

Now,
all talent is looked at
as they are escorts
and those who aren't
have to come out
and say so.

Typical working-class.
I was raised well,
I went to audition after audition,
eventually,
I realized I wasn't good enough
and it was quite hard to accept at first.
Popular with day laborers
and construction workers.
You can get porn for free,
guys don't want to pay for that.
They want the opportunity
to get to know somebody
they've seen in a magazine
or on social media.
I'm like their online girlfriend.

Opioid Overdoses

COMMUNITY

I think that gets people's attention
when we have celebrity deaths.
This affects everyone,
people start questioning
their own behavior more.
They start to think
maybe they should seek help
themselves.

Self-administered fentanyl.
Deadly synthetic drugs.
Over 30 percent of American adults
have chronic pain,
and it's higher the older you get,
most of these people
don't see themselves
as being addicted.
They just see themselves
as following their doctor's orders.

We don't know that opioids
can help people
with an acute
flare-up of pain,
but the vast majority
of pain studies
do not go beyond
three
or four months.
If you're still taking an opioid
six months later,
we don't know
if it's working
or not.
We get all ages.
We get patients
who will come in
from their late teens
to their 70s.

In the last two years,
there is a pattern of doctors
prescribing fewer opioids,
we're right in the cusp
of a change.
It's very difficult to get people
to surrender their opioids,
it's easier to keep people off
opioids than to get them
to give them up later.

Organization of Petroleum Exporting Countries (OPEC)

ECONOMY

It's too little,
too late to really rescue
the gasoline market this season,
but we could see some easing
by the end of the summer.
I would argue
that we are really robbing
Peter to pay Paul;
by that I mean some of the excess
production capacity
that we were counting on
for year two-thousand
and one
is being put into the year two thousand
marketplace.

It's OPEC-mania today,
the market doesn't seem to know
what to make of it yet.

We're pleased
that they listened
to the arguments
that we made,
hopefully,
this will have a good
psychological effect
on the market soon.
Hopefully,
it will mean decreases
in gasoline prices,
but that's not certain.
Such an action would give
the public some respite
from the untenably high priced
without harming our environment;
this is an administration devoid
of an energy policy–

we're depending upon crude.
I would hope the administration
could convince our friends
in the Organization
of Petroleum Exporting Countries
to open the spigots.

The worst may be over.

I am deeply concerned
about the conduct
of the oil companies,
which may have led
to these unreasonable price hikes.

The Oscars

SOCIETY

Bohemian Rhapsody.
A Star is Born,
Roma.
It's going to have an entertainment pace
throughout it.
It's going to be fun to watch
and we get to honor
all the folks
in these 24 categories,
GMA.
We Will Rock You.

Black Panther.
Is this real life?
Is this just fantasy?
We welcome Queen
Will
Rock
Adam Lambert to this year
at the Oscars,
Shallow.
A Star is Born,
Special Guest.
The Place Where Lost Things Go.
Mary Poppins Returns.
When a Cowboy Trades His Spurs for Wings,
The Ballad of Buster Scruggs,
I'll Fight.
RBG.
All the Stars,
Black Panther.

If Beale Street Could Talk.
Roma's:
The Wife.
Green Book.
A Star is Born.
Vice,
Bohemian Rhapsody.

The Favorite,
Roma,
Green Book.
Black Panther.
Roma.

What I've learned
through this whole experience
is that women,
we're nurturers,
that's what's expected of us.
We have our children
and we have our husbands,
if we're lucky enough
and we have our partners,
whoever;
but we have to find personal fulfillment.
We have to follow our dreams.
We have to say,
'I can do that
and I should be allowed to do that.'

This is what we say:
we've asked the people
to stick to the 90-second rule.
From the time that the name is called
to the time they exit the stage
they have 90 seconds,
we are asking them to do that,
because it is a kindness to the people
that are following them,
so everybody else is going
to fall into the same pattern.

Oscar Winners

SOCIETY

> The Oscars

It's amazing.
It's like winning the lottery.
It was Gary's wife
who texted me
to say I'd been nominated.
'*Lucy Sibbick,*
Bafta nominee sounds pretty good.'

I've always avoided public speaking
and I thought,
'*oh my god,*
I'm going to have to go
to these awards.'
After that it went crazy,
it all happened so quickly.
We went to Los Angeles
for the Guild Awards
and the Oscars,
which was an incredible experience.
It's like a military operation.
I think there are more people
working behind the scenes
than at the actual ceremony.

It was just nice to be there
with so many people
who work really hard
and put everything
into what they do.

I thought if I enjoy painting
people's faces,
working on Darkest Hour
was incredible
in so many ways.
The make-up was challenging
and interesting

and I was able to work
with some amazing people.
It was a really stressful shoot
as we were such a small team,
but it paid off in the end.
It's such a prevalent thing
in our industry,
I experience it all the time.
It's a male dominated industry.
Part of what makes the special
for me is in our business,
women don't get noticed
in the way they should.
Even when you contribute
something to a conversation
it's not acknowledged
until a man next to you says it.
It does feel like women
are more of a part of things
now.
They've always been there
and it's good to see
that increased recognition.

Owl Habitat

ZOOAMERICA

The government cannot continue to destroy
these forests while simultaneously
contemplating a plan to protect them.
Viable population–
option nine
and we don't have any idea
how many acres
and owl
habitats are disappearing.

Judge William Dwyer's ruling
was the beginning in terms of setting
the framework for the Clinton era.
It was the case that made forests
an issue in the 1992 campaign,
which led to Clinton's forest summit
and led us down a path
that we see here now
in the Pacific Northwest,
I would look closely at the people
who are really behind the case,
their agenda is clear
and has been for a long time—
zero cut on national forests.

None of the alternative presented
address what our government deems
to be the most serious threat
facing these forests—
catastrophic wildfires.

Painter

AMERICA'S NEW TRIUMPH

*"I came
from a very frantic
background,
where a million things
were always going on
at once,
I think
it was more
of a spiritual battle."*

Painting has always been parallel
to my human experience...
the more clarity I get in my life,
the more clear my paintings become,
I am essentially looking into a mirror,
but when I look at the painting,
I imagine that I'm observing
the world thinking,
what's going on?

That was something
I was kind of shy about,
because I wanted it
to be in really subtle form,
of showing worship,
I feel like I have to be
so careful
when I talk about my faith
in the context of my paintings,
because it's such a journey,
even for me.
It's personal
and I certainly
don't have all the answers,
but it is central
to who I am.

I remember the way
he had the father embracing
the son
was so natural
and loving,
I think that story
is really applicable
to everybody's life.
I came
from a very frantic
background,
where a million things

were always going on
at once,
I think
it was more
of a spiritual battle.

I would just listen
to him talk
about poetry,
philosophy,
sunsets
and beauty–
but not in a cheesy way.
I started to want to create
things that are beautiful.
I reconnected
in trying to figure out
how we are supposed to be
as humans.
From my perspective,
if we were created
we must be created
for some sort of purpose.

Learning to draw
and paint become a parallel
to learning how to live
healthy–
just slowing down
and breathing,
being careful
and honest,
my hands are my favorite
part of me,
so I wanted
the hands
to play a really expressive,
very dominate role,
it brings us back
to the Greeks
and Romans
and it's our investigation.
It's just like how we want
to understand

the flowers that we are painting,
we want to know it really well–
whether it's studying anatomy
or understanding general forms,
we are all human,
we are all going to die one day
and I want to paint humans
that are having a real human experience…
making an incredibly beautiful painting,
because there is beauty
in the world
is a good enough reason
to do it
and there's so much to be said
about why our culture needs that.

Palestine Liberation Organization (PLO)

OPEN-DOOR POLICY

Carry out its duties immediately.
Lift the siege,
let people breath,
electricity,
water,
salaries,
medical–
instead of explosion.
Administrative committee.

From my point of view,
immediately.
Justified what the President has done,
he was in pain,
because he was putting
his people under pressure,
but he felt he had to.

The only language they understand:
forcing compromise in Israel
and Palestine,
now,
it's a grand concession to dismantle it,
requires time.
From an outside perspective,
they have almost no control
in Gaza today,
so it's better than nothing,
but they look at it as,
why should I take on the burden
and blame?

Generous efforts.
Leadership.
An expression
of Egyptian concern.

Palestinian Liberation Organization (PLO)

UNITED NATIONS

Instigated moves.
In a game of chest of negotiations.
Where are the masses?
Where is the anger?
Where is the pride?

If he had acted immediately
to stop the violence,
he would have been seen
as a collaborator,
with the occupier.

The next few days will tell
whether Arafat is in control
or not.

It is the Israelis' right to know
whether Arafat is with us
or against us,
whether he is the architect
of the riot–
or their victim.

The political people
need some dead
and wounded,
this is their plan–
it's the politicians on both sides
that play games with our blood.

I think Arafat was more surprised
than the Israelis
at the extent
and with the way the street exploded.
Arafat relies on his own instinct
and judgment,
rather than on careful,
analytical examination
and hard evidence;

he is not out of touch.
He quickly adapts
when confronted by a situation.
He knew it could be extremely serious,
but the extent
of the intensity
of the feeling
was the surprising part.

Heartbreaking.
If he is moved,
why doesn't he come
and intervene in the situation now
and stop the Israeli killing?
Martyr of Al Qaeda,
we are going to continue our struggle!

What kind of cease-fire?
A cease-fire takes place
between two armies.
It is one army,
the Israelis,
who battle with rockets
and our people in the streets.
When they take back their soldiers,
it will finish the problem.

When I spoke about cease-fire
understanding,
I meant that they will not shoot
and we will not respond.

Panda

ZOOAMERICA

Two very long drinks of water,
to act like the perfect mother.

It's developmentally right on,
very careful.
She picked it up
in her mouth very gently
and rocked back
into her resting position.
We're well into the fifth day of life...
and she's getting bigger every day.

We're not out of the woods yet
with Bai Yun,
we're making fresh formula everyday...
and our incubator is on
and ready to go.
As a general rule,
first time mothers
across the board are less successful
than mothers who have raised
children before.
We've had a lot of time,
to prepare,
we try to simulate
the natural situation;
panda pillows
pandas need to foe of swaddled.

Panda milk substitute
is a mixture of dog milk replacement,
human milk replacement
and dehydrated whey–
a milk solid.
We hand-raised a Malaysian sun bear
two years ago
and that animal
was an excellent model for us,
to go on,

she was weaned
and is now a normal
functioning adult.
Nobody's milk is better
than mother's milk;
we've been conditioning Bai Yun
for milk collection every Thursday
morning for the last two years…
it's a non-event for her.
High-fiber,
low-energy
we cultivate sixteen species
of bamboo
on San Diego Zoological society
to meet their requirements.

Paparazzi

COMMUNITY

    Celebrities

Editors have blood
on their hands,
you should be ashamed.
In the immediate aftermath,
they were the villains.
They were blamed right away,
we're living in the 21st century,
when everyone has a smart phone,
they all have cameras
and that makes everyone a potential paparazzi,
if anything,
it's gotten worse,
not better.

The British national papers
did cut back on paparazzi pictures
and when it comes to royals,
they won't touch them,
they don't want to upset them
for fear of being left out
of something in the future.

I always believed that Diana died,
because her driver was drunk
and speeding
and because she was not wearing
a seatbelt.

Parents

SOCIETY

Baby Boomers

One child.
To put it bluntly,
the birth of a baby
is not only a matter of the family itself,
but also a state affair,
among regular people,
among scholars,
there's enough consensus already
about the policy,
it's just a matter of time
before they can lift this policy.
'One Child' policy.

Without the introduction of measures
to encourage fertility,
the population of China will drop
sharply in the nature,
women cannot decide
what happens
to their own ovaries,
one child,
planned birth.

Economic
and social development,
the generalization
before us only had one-child,
so in their mind
having only one child
is the normal thing,
I think we really need
to have a sense of urgency–
from the top down
and the bottom up–
to encourage families to resume
a healthy birthrate.

Two child.
To eliminate the concerns
of the masses
and sustain the birthrate,
we need to focus
on the practical difficulties
in fertility
and child-rearing.

This kind of family
should be given more support
and should have more invested
in child welfare:
early education,
maternal
and child health,
although elders can help us
look after the kid,
they cannot once their health worsens,
raising a child is stressful,
it costs money
and manpower.

Pawnbrokers

ECONOMY

If it weren't for me,
by the 15th of the month
the whole town would go dark–
they couldn't pay their utility bills.
The sector we deal with is living
paycheck to paycheck,
they don't want to lose what they have.
We have to be aware of the economy,
if they're coming in to get gas money,
what can they actually afford to repay?

Lost all their money
and need to pawn something
so they have gas to get back home.
I assume every one of those
represents a guy out of work.
Everyone has sad stories
and you can't believe all of them,
but I feel bad for the people
who need gas
or for the mom with her baby
brining in the junk
that I can't take.

If I can just get even
and be really,
really careful,
I can get back on my feet.

Personal Interpreter

UNITED NATIONS

        U.N. Arabic Interpreter

Just can't take it anymore.
His interpreter just collapsed,
this is the first time
I have seen this
in 25 years.

This is the best team
in the world–
most heads of state
prefer to use United Nations interpreters,
because then–
no matter what happens–
they can blame the interpreter.

It's not just that what he's saying is illogical,
but the way he's saying it
is bizarre.
However,
I think
I could have made him sound
a lot better.
Khadafy has a habit
of repeating the same phrase over
and over again,
which is good,
because if you don't understand
what he says the first time
you can get it right the second
or third time.

Peru
UNITED NATIONS

Lima

Psycho-social operation.
The greatest contribution
to regional security
is coming from Peru,
precisely the nation
that was left out of the trip.
We're not very concerned about the matter
as long as they were getting the money
in cash.

The message of all this
is that Montesano's
cannot be removed from the government,
because he is the strategist
of Peru's successful secret service
and it minimized the start of the dialogue
between the government
and opposition.

In 1998,
we sold Peru
ten-thousand automatic rifles
for half a million dollars;
verified the identity documents
of the Peruvian generals
who took delivery of the shipment
at Queen Alia International Airport.
We came to know afterward
that the Peruvian authorities
had discovered that part of the weapons
had gone to the leftist rebels
in Colombia.
Secret operation of the Peruvian government.

SOCIETY

Pet Microchips

Dog Owners

The results
of our Freedom of Information requests
are somewhat surprising
and what we found most of the note
was how much the fines charged by councils
varied across the country.

Microchipping is a simple
and cheap procedure
that doesn't hurt a dog
in any way
and it's vital
for responsible pet owners
to obey the laws.

We'd urge dog owners
to take steps
to get their canine microchipped.
Firstly,
for the health
and safety
of their four-legged friend
and secondly,
to comply with the law
and avoid potentially hefty fines.

Philanthropy

AMERICA'S NEW TRIUMPH

My childhood ambition
was to get into philanthropy.
My intentions were not,
ideally,
good ones.
My goal was to have people
admire me.

This is an effort to talk about our future.
People on the outside are telling us
what we should be doing,
but we as the people on the inside
ought to have a say in what we can
and can't do.

The capital for philanthropy
is moving westward.
Six of the fifteen largest foundations
in the United States,
today,
are in the West;
in 1980,
it was zero.

We are a sector
increasingly under attack in the real world.
People don't know
or care if they're served by a for-profit
or by a non-profit organization.
It's incumbent for us to demonstrate
that we can provide quality service
at an affordable cost
and not hide behind non-profit status.

Try to figure out whether to reverse
policies such as:
welfare reform,
venture capital,
leasing firms,

an amazing array
and an enormous amount of specialization
for businesses.
We don't have that in the citizen sector.

The idea of the old establishment
educating the new money
is diminishing.
The belief
that new money ought to kowtow to
and respect old money
has been completely extinguished.
The whole future of new money
is in electronics and entertainment.

People will always try to break
new ground.
We just can't predict
what
or when.
They'll be doing wonderful things–
There will be philanthropy,
just not real soon.
The gap in wealth
and income inequality
are the two biggest obstacles to overcome,
before philanthropy is possible.
For the people,
who believe they're doing God's work,
they're dangerous.

Philanthropy

AMERICA'S NEW TRIUMPH

Women of Dedication,
All-Stars,
Champions of Giving.
I feel honored to be in this group,
I look at what a privilege
and blessing it is to be involved
in philanthropy.
I really feel fortunate
and I consider this to be the renaissance
of my life
and it brings me great joy.

Women's Witticisms.
I go into those nonprofits
thinking how I am going to help,
but in turn,
I've received so much back;
such as great friendships,
memories
and life experiences
I wouldn't have had otherwise.

It can be done with a smile,
a kind word
or showing gratitude.
Focus on the little things,
but do it wholeheartedly
and with love in your heart.

Philippines

UNITED NATIONS

Banking

We would like the public
to remain calm amid rumors
that there are other banks
experiencing problems
similar to those that led
to the downfall of Urban Bank.
The financial system is very stable
and some banks are being hit
by rumors;
sound
and stable.

They are ready to infuse
the funds needed to keep them running;
unfortunately,
as the bigger banks consolidate,
from time to time you
will see some of the banks
that have their own peculiar problems.
Accounts amounting to five thousand Pesos
and below will be paid
in full while accounts
amounting to five thousand pesos
and above will be paid the equivalent
25 percent of the deposit account,
but not to exceed 25 thousand pesos.
The retaining amount,
of the injured deposit,
will be paid
as soon as the consolidation
and examination of deposits
are completed,
by the Philippine Deposit Insurance Corporation.
We estimate the examination
to take another week
or two from the initial pay off;

first come,
first served.

These are the same groups
that are spreading the rumors,
via text message.
We would like to assure
the general public,
especially our valued clients,
that there is no truth
to the rumors being circulated
through text messaging
and by some quarters
that the International Exchange Bank
is going to be downgraded
from a commercial bank
to a thrift bank.
The truth is our equity
is three billion
and five Philippine dollars
way above the required two billion eight
for commercial banks.
As of today,
International Exchange Bank
has total nets of thirty-four billion
and is considered a commercial bank
in the country with fifty-nine branches nationwide.

The bank continues to grow
and in fact is looking
at the possibility of acquiring other banks.
We are a commercial bank
and will continue to be so.

In a situation like this,
there's something you can do,
but to prove that
you are able to meet your obligations,
the owner
of Philippine Communication Bank
exposed of the families
Luy of International Copra Export Corporation,
Nubla and Chung
of La Suerte Cigar and Cigarette's factory

and Chief Executive Officer Isidro Acantara
assured the public
that the reported withdrawals are isolated
and in no way affect the bank's continued stability.
Philippine Communication Bank
remains financially healthy
and will meet all its obligations,
as it has done for the past sixty years,
being the fourth oldest bank
in the country.

This gives the other banks
more reason to merge.
There is big room
for more merges.

Philippines

UNITED NATIONS

Impeachment

It's official now
that the impeachment rap
is before the Senate,
we have indicated the president.
People lower.
Impeachment.
Midnight cabinet.

My conscience is clear;
I did not become president
to take in money.
A single centavo.
I appeal to you not to through with it,
we have a crisis.
Let's join hands
and pull out of this,
for the sake of the nation.

If President Estrada is arrested
I want it to serve as a lesson
to all police officials,
it would be an honor
to go to the president
and ask for a presidential pardon.

Poets Anonymous

SOCIETY

Please keep my name out of the press.
You know,
like the first family
or someone really famous.
I wondered what that would be like.
The billboards are an antidote
to the commercial spectacle
that bombards all of us
as we travel around the city.
I was very surprised,

I've never met a group of people
who didn't want publicity.
They're just down-to-Earth people
who love poetry
and want to share it.

This material,
I understand right down to the core.
I think all political art,
ultimately has the power
to elevate us
and change our minds.
If you will,
the Buddhists believe
there is a bardo–
a pause where change is possible.
Someone who knows
we all recommended
we speak to one another.

I like the culture
and the way the project
faces with society.
If I look at my own history,
I see this is the kind of thing
I do well.
I like people
who are doing it their own way.

We've published
more than fifty books,
catalogues
and other weirdness;
an important part of the operation.
Very busy.
This is not a nonprofit organization.

Very interesting,
very curatorial,
it's something to change the day
a little bit as they zoom around
the city in their cars,

I want to give full credit
to these people.
It was not my idea.
I am delighted
that I can communicate,
in some small way
what they were after.
It took a love of ground work.
They did all the research
to make sure the billboards
covered every part of the city
and bought the space.
It was a huge,
huge task.
This is one of the most altruistic projects
I have done
and also one of the most fun.

They tend to be a good medium
for reminders,
but not for getting people
to think deeply,
because we pass them so briefly.
Nevertheless,
they might raise
some general awareness,
it's not something
one would do lightly.

A real antidote to all
those commercial billboards
are blank space
or silence
or trees.
Probably most important
about them is they're not trying
to sell you something.
Presuming this is not some hidden
marketing play,
could they all be poets
with the same publisher?

Poetry excerpts
is a wonderful idea,
they inspire us to think.
We discussed billboards,
but the cost was enormous.
I think they're terrific,
they have that sort of colloquial
combination of metaphor
and wit.
Each one is a little snippet
of what keeps us alive.

JUSTICE

Police Officers

Loadbearing Vests

We were surprised
by just how big of a difference
the vests made
in how officers rated their pain,
when they went from the vest
to the belt,
there were really big jumps
in the levels of pain
they reported.

Knowing I'm helping the police officers
who keep us safe
is pretty special;
it feels like I am giving them something
in return
for what they do for all of us.
That's an amazing feeling.
I'm incredibly fortunate
and grateful to have had the opportunity
to pursue this research.
It is so special to lead a study
that went so far beyond the university,
it's the best feeling in the world
of knowing that I helped Eau Clair
and other communities.
It opened my eyes
to all the possibilities out there
and has sparked an interest
in continuing to pursue research
in the future,
so I can keep giving back.

My experience as a McNair Scholar
has been nothing short of amazing,
this program opened my eyes
to the opportunities out there
to further my education.

The program set me up for success
and provided me with all the necessary tools
and skills needed
to take on a research study
and to take on graduate school.

In 10 days,
I learned more about our civil rights history
than I did in any historical class
I've taken in my life,
there was something
about standing in the exact location
where a specific historical moment took place
that felt so much more intense
and real.

It was during this trip
that I realized learning really does go so far
beyond the classroom.
I never thought I could do all that I have done,
experience all that I have experienced
and gain all that I have gained
during my undergraduate career.
I would tell any current
or future blue gold
to take advantage of the opportunities
this university offers.
Go out there,
work hard,
have some fun
and make your dreams a reality,
because anything is possible
with an education
from the University of Wisconsin – Eau Claire!

Political Action Committees

GOVERNMENT

Stealth Political Action Committees
black hole groups.

If Sadam Hussein,
the Sicilian Mafia
or the Cali Cartel
want to dump
one hundred million dollars
into the American presidential election,
they can do it…
They can do it,
they can do it legally
and they can do it enormously.

It can be done with zero money–
there's no filing fee.
there's no particular overhead cost
if it's being run by volunteers;
if everyone volunteers their time.
Every dollar raised could be spent
for the five-twenty-seven committee.

The rush is on,
it's overdue for legislative reform,
the potential for abuse,
which was always there,
it's now being rapidly exploited.

They are only going to go
into races where an investment
of one million dollars
or more
in a House of Representative race
has a good chance of tilting the balance;
they want to have influence
over which party will be the majority party
in the congress.
It's going to mean a lot of politics,
probably more than most viewers

and readers want to see;
they will also see,
more negative campaigners,
vs. more negative campaigners,
because there outside money-funded campaigns
are more negative than candidate ones
and they will have a hard time knowing
who is paying for those commercials.

They can come in at the very end
and literally decide a race
just by the sheer volume of advocacy....
At the precise moment
when voters are starting
to pay attention.

We fully comply with the law
as it exists today.
We are fighting congress
to reform campaign finance laws
to get big money out of the politics
and to add restrictions
on issue advocacy.

Political Power

JUSTICE

It makes you sick
that something like this can happen
and you have no power,
of course you help a friend
I used my relationship
with the governor
to help my son,
I'd do it again.

We continue to grieve
over the losses related to our son's
involvement in this tragic accident
and pray daily for God's healing grace.
Our son has paid his debt to society
and will continue to meet all legal
and financial obligations
to the victim's family as agreed.
He is committed
to continuing the woe
of healing,
self-reflection
and spiritual growth;
we respectfully request
privacy at this.

Repugnant.
Back-room dealings
were apparent,
I don't believe he's reformed,
I take pleasure from the thought
that he will screw up
his life again.
I don't think there will be away
out of this mess again.

The crossing.
Before running for office
the governor
had been a movie star

specializing in playing
larger than life heroes –
men willing to sacrifice
everything to do the right thing,
he was now back in Hollywood,
trying to be a movie star,
once again.

Just another horrible blow
you can't fathom
what they're going through,
it's like they keep getting kicked in the gut.
People always say,
'It's who you know,'
and I always say,
'No,
it's not.'
I guess in this case,
it is.

Politics

ECONOMY

New economy.
New economy.
New economy.
High technology is the key
to a political transformation
taking place in California.
It's surprising
how few California politicians
even seem aware
of what's happening.

New economy.
Information age.
I think the person who works
in the computer industry
thinks differently
than the person who works
in the defense industry.
The political impact
of California's new economy
has implications
on how they perceive
politics,
parties,
and ultimately on how they vote.
They're not real civic-minded,
that's true,
but they do vote.

I'm really looking
at the decision being made
on short-term
and long-term capital gains,
in my age bracket–
not being married
and not having a lot
of tax write-offs–
I'm in a very,
very high tax bracket.

This community
is still philosophically Republican,
you have a group of people
who are pro-economic growth
and anti-government regulation.

New economy.
One place the Republicans
are falling down horribly,
is when they try to approach
extreme divisiveness on issues
like race
and welfare–
understand that to be productive,
they need to be positive
and engage in teamwork.
The idea of dumping on one group
to advance yourself
just isn't rational to them.

So,
I identify more
with the social issues of Democrats.
Of course,
now,
I have more financial issues
that are traditionally the issues
of Republicans.
They don't have really strong
political ties–
they just want to make
sure the government
leaves them alone.

Presidential Campaign

GOVERNMENT

My team has been amazing,
it's actually a team of unity.
It's evolving,
but people don't understand that.

Senator Cruz.
Lying Ted.
Whether he will be able
to maintain this tone
or indeed if that will be productive
for him.
Lying Ted.
Get him out of here.
No shift in tone,
message
or policy at this point
is going to erase anyone's memory
of how Trump has been conducting himself
and his campaign for many,
many months now.

It's about Paul…
He got smart
and hired one of the best
in the business
and he's learned quickly
that Paul knows a lot more
than conventions.

Crooked.
Rigged.
Only to see him reflexively return
to bashing his opponents
and everyone else in the party.

Doing nothing Congress,
it's the economy,
stupid.

Presidential Campaign

GOVERNMENT

Web log,
Media Gate keepers be damned.
Snapchat election,
there was no news cycle–
everything was one big fire hose,
news was constantly breaking
and at the end of the day
hardly anything mattered.
Things would happen;
24 hours later,
everyone was talking
about something else.

This is radical stuff,
hit refresh.
Oppositional research,
ties to 1.
He says Islamic States of Iraq
and Syria
'ISIS is attacking me;'
this was debunked in eight minutes
by Twitter,
cable talked about it
for three hours
and it went away.
Hillary Clinton said that she was under sniper fire
in Bosnia
and that has stuck with her
for 20 years.

Remember to round up 11 million
undocumented immigrants
and deport them;
lied about President Obama's birth certificate.
The constantly churning news cycle,
many seem like news from another area.
It's important that they not be forgotten.

An emblem for a lack of attention span
in our politics.
It's about being in the moment.

Presidential Candidate

GOVERNMENT

        Moscow, Russia

There are many people like us.
We are declaring a voters' strike.
Going to the voting booth right now
is to vote for lies
and corruption.
Not against me,
but against 16,000 people
who have nominated me,
against 200,000 volunteers
who have been canvassing for me.

Maybe we would be interested
if you were running.
We would like to point out
that the conviction remains
and therefore,
we are forced to propose
a draft
Central Election Commission resolution,
the point of which is to deny registration.

First,
we are turning our headquarters
into a strike headquarters.
Second,
we are organizing monitoring
of the voter turnout.
Third,
we are campaigning
against these elections.
We're being asked
about street protests against
the Central Election Commission decision,
of course we are going to organize protest actions
across Russia.
We will prepare it carefully
and of course it should happen across Russia.

They will damage our prospects
for the future,
if we don't stop them…
and only you
and I can stop them.

Presidential Nomination

GOVERNMENT

Persuasion team,
the official Ted Crus slate,
you have to think of this whole process
as having two different tracks to it.
There's the primary process–
that's about winning
and allocating delegates,
the story that will really be more important
to what happened in Cleveland,
is the delegates–
selection track.
They're two connected,
but separate skill sets.

The nomination process
has reached a point
that requires someone familiar
with the complexities involved
in the final stages.

Unbound.
Unfair.
Many more volunteers.
Either before Cleveland
or at the convention in Cleveland.
Together,
we won all 21.
On every round of the ballot.
This process just doesn't work well
for our kind of campaign,
it's an insider's game.
Senator Crug
is certainly good at playing
the insider game.

It's not an inconsiderable organizational drill
to make sure you have loyal delegates;
confusing.
It is complicated,
it is archaic.

Primates

WORLD WILDLIFE

We never kept more than five-hundred
at a time
or for more than three months.
Medical research.
I have to start from scratch,
I have to make this place
financially viable again.
We are resourceful people
in the West Indies,
I believe we can continue to use them
in a humane way.
I hope to,
because I would feel miserable
and I don't know what I would do then.

We're up to our ears at the moment,
we'll have to look after them,
until they die
and they live to about 30.
They can ruin someone's livelihood,
the way they take a piece of fruit
and bite it,
throw it aside,
take another,
bite it,
throw it aside;
they're lovable,
but they're really destructive.

Most famous would like to see
every monkey dead.

It's difficult to find areas
far from farms on a small island,
it's difficult to find areas far from farms
in a small island,
more as rescuing farmers
from the monkey than vice versa.

I do believe for these animals
there are things worse than death;
they actually go mad from confinement.
It should be a crime to do this.

Productivity

ECONOMY

       Individual

Source: Lisa Belkin, Writer for the N.Y. Times

Cheaper by the Dozen.
Unproductive.
Personal development expert.
The average full-time worker
doesn't even start doing real work
until 11:00 A.M.
and begins to wind down
around 3:30 P.M.
Not productive.
Personal productivity coach.

The longer you work,
the less efficient you are.
Play a lot of tennis,
a down of football
or an inning of baseball;
have a pause in between.
It's best used in spurts
where we work hard
on a few focus activities
and then take a brief respite.

We are in a knowledge-worker world.
If you were building me a building,
I could measure the number of bricks.
If you were loading a truck,
I could measure the number of boxes,
but I can't simply count your words.
That doesn't measure quality.

Prozac

SOCIETY

Like a zombie.
It's sad to watch this.
You find...
suicide,
murder,
rape,
arson.
How did they convince us
that this is therapeutic?
As firm as I am on the dangers
of these drugs.
I'm afraid of withdrawal,
because if people quit
and don't know how to come off
the right way,
we're really going to be in trouble.

When a story like this broke is brewing,
people think,
"If this medication
can possibly be related to a bad outcome,
I'd better get off it now,"
we're talking about millions
and millions of people
who've been treated successfully
with these drugs
and stopped treatment
without any kind of dramatic changes
of behavior.

Electric Zap.
You're going to get some unpredictable
reactions if you have millions of people
taking them
and gone off.
The potential for violent behaviors,
suicide
and particularly
impulsive suicide exists;

with the sicker the person
coming in the front door,
the more likely they are to have a bad crash
when they go off.

We do see these extreme reactions.
It's not a horse race.
No one says you have to have to be off
medications in three weeks
or even three months.

The Neurobiology of Aggression and Rage.
Untoward post-treatment effects
seem to prove to pretty significant reactions.
Excruciating slowly.

Psychotherapists

COMMUNITY

You're doing fine,
call
and check in
with me
in about,
say,
two months.
'Go out
and contract
a fatal disease
and nothing
little
bothers you
anymore.'

Oh,
gosh
it's such a joke
in New York,
isn't it–
that someone spends 20 years
on a sofa
in therapy,
certainly,
people do see therapists for years,
but it's not that they're going two
or three times a week
for 20 years.
They're checking in
as they would with their regular doctor.
It's often a long-term relationship.

Keep your socks up.
Focus,
just focus,
cured.
Doing fine.
A shrink saying she has cured you
is the most frightening diagnosis imaginable,

having been in therapy for 30 years,
I find that is unthinkable
and utterly impossible.
Could it be
that you really didn't need a shrink
to start with?!
I suggest you consult a psychic
immediately.
Milly has a highly effective one.
Even I went to see him
when my shrink was on holiday.
He predicted
I should see a shrink.

We are continually faced with stresses
and strains throughout life,
but if your level of distress is low enough
and you are functioning
in the various areas
of your life that are important to you,
then you may have enough
for that course of therapy
this particular trauma
affected all sorts of people
who would not normally seek help,
the threshold for seeking help
is reached sooner.

Wait a second,
your shrink says you're fine,
that you're cured
and you're writing about it
in the newspaper for everyone to read?
I think she must have been kidding,
right?

Racism

COMMUNITY

Shamelessly perpetuates.
Subhuman,
warlike savages,
rubbish,
sympathetic tribute.

Po-faced.
It's not racist,
what's racist about it?
I tell it as it is
and I tell it with humor.

It shamelessly perpetuates
a centuries-long artistic tradition
that seek to portray Native people
as subhuman,
warlike savages.
It is time for this racist tradition
in all of its forms–
whether art tapestries
or football helmet logos–
to end,
once
and for all.

This tapestry forms
part of the British Empire
and Commonwealth Museum
collection held in storage.
It is not on public display
and there are no current plans
to put it on display.

JUSTICE

Raping and Murder

The possibility that he
(David Wayne Stoker)
was innocent...
Low-life scum drug dealer.
Dismissed.
This defendant helped
the distinct attorney office
(Terry McEachern D.A.)
solve a murder case.
Yes,
the record indicates
that that had happened,
is that of substantial importance?

I don't even know
whether I was wearing
white
or blue socks on that day,
and I really don't think
it matters.

Twelve jurors believed
that the witness was credible
and reliable.

I told him
(Terry McEachern)
I didn't mean to sign it.

When we went to trial,
we were a hell of a lot better
prepared
than the district attorney's
office.
Ladies
and gentlemen,
yesterday
when I was talking
to you

all the lights went out;
I don't know,
maybe that was a message.
Today it rained,
maybe that was a message;
maybe the rain drops
are the key issues,
but that's what you have to decide,
today.
The system.
Justice.
I don't know,
but that's what ya'll are going to do.

I think the judge knows
I would take this case
and maybe dispose of it quickly.
He probably thought perhaps
I would roll over
and play dead.

I don't know
that he would have to believe everything,
knowing he
(Carey Todd)
was paid
or he got a deal.
I would have had a harder time believing
this testimony.
If I had known
some of those things,
I'm sure
it would have weighed
on me (us).
Direct tie.
I was really surprised
we did
what we did
with the amount of evidence
we had,
that says the lawyers
have not been the crown jewels
of the legal profession;
That kind of statistic should

embarrass every right thinking Texan.
You desperately look
for sufficient people
for these cases,
I think he did
a quite credible job.

Recreation

SPORTS

I was in a gym all my life.
Some people are born
and raised to play the piano.
I was born
and raised to be an athlete.
I'm a little bit of a daredevil.
I had never even water-skied,
but when I started knee boarding
at seventeen,
it was a complete challenge.
That's what I like the most.
I absolutely love the sport,
It's a whole new lifestyle.

To tell you the truth,
the water
and the outdoors
were the main reasons.
It was that simple.
I was doing very well
as a gymnast,
but it required
a full-time commitment,
because of the high level
of competition,
because of the Russians
and I couldn't give it that.
My quest for perfection
in barefoot jumping
comes from
'*The Russian Way*,'
the only way to be a perfectionist
is to be a perfectionist.

I dated a few cheerleaders.
That's part of the reason I played.
The danger factor in skating
is what keeps you going.
It was like that in football.
The higher level you take it to,
the scarier it gets.

Recreational Classes

SOCIETY

Baby Boomers

Let me show you my diamond necklace,
it's a way of giving back,
especially in a retirement community.

We teach people
how to prepare to be a clown,
like makeup
and costume,
then how to be a character,
I always say to be your best self,
if you don't have a character think
of something when you were amazed,
like being amazed by a sunset.
Let your clown be amazed.

As a senior,
I think it gives you a lot of self-confidence,
it also gives you a chance to play
and it gives you a chance,
that if grandkids don't live nearby,
to interact with children.

On the outside,
I may seem quiet,
but on the inside of me,
there's a clown
who wants to come out.

Happy Birthday.
Gigs.
It's all clean,
family-based fun,
we are a nice alley;
we have rules
like you can't spray water on a clown
without permission
or make them the butt of a joke

without permission.
We keep clean fun
within the clown community too.
We are a family,
we are there for each other.
A lot of times we've dressed as clowns
to go to the funeral,
because the family wants it,
in this day
and age,
especially what we see
on Television with the spooky clowns,
we're fighting that right now.
Immediately people see you
and get scared,
because that's what they portray
in movies.
What we see is the opposite–
the sparkle in a kid's eyes.
It could be children,
the disabled,
seniors–
it's just a chance
to get whoever you meet smiling.

I think clowns show a side of vulnerability
when they're a little bit timid.
To try things out
and not be afraid of others' criticism,
these people who moved
into Laguna Woods
have been takers
most of their life
and now they're becoming givers,
clowning is a great way to give.

Referendum

UNITED NATIONS

Second Brexit

Disorderly.
Risk of failure.
Forensic annihilation.
Very worried.
Little point.
Put no deal back on the table.
There are still difficulties,
still a risk of failure.
On 25 percent of the text,
we don't have an agreement.
If there is no agreement,
there is no orderly withdrawal;
there is a disorderly withdrawal
and there is no transition.

Single market a la carte.
No way.
Cherry pick.
This is the moment
where the British government
has to stand firm
and ensure
it is delivering
on the referendum vote.
We have got to put no deal back
on the table.

Includes as an objective.
In negotiations…
the establishment
of an effective customs union.
Walking a tightrope.
We're not opposed
to any form
of democratic engagement.
We've not ruled anything out.
My preference

is not another referendum,
but a general election.

We are confident
that in the coming months,
if all sides work together
productively,
we can achieve a solution
to the Ireland-Northern Ireland border
that works for everyone involved.
A fantasy island unicorn model.

Refugees

IMMIGRATION

Syrian

All Canadian people are very nice.
A lady comes to our house,
every week,
twice a week,
to study English with me
and another lady comes
to the house of all Syrians
and bring gift for the children.

Humanitarian leadership.
Canada's contribution
is a drop in the bucket,
but my view
would be
it's an important drop,
because we're offering permanent homes,
in the context of North America,
it is sizeable,
it is admirable.
Civil society consensus.

U.S. politics is more polarized
than Canadian politics
I would argue
and it has created a kind of wedge issue
so refugees have become conflated
with terrorists in the United States,
they are just…
ramping up for the presidential campaign
with the prime
and there is quite a different geopolitical positioning
in a relation to the war on terror.

I understand that the overwhelming majority
of refugees are feeling violence
and bloodshed
and pose no threat to anyone,

however,
if even a small number of individuals
who wish to do harm in our country
are able to enter
to Canada
as the result of rushes
of refugees resettlement process,
the results could be devastating.
Jumping the queue.
Boat people.

Remote Control Device

SOCIETY

It's almost like men think
someone's going to announce
the meaning of life
over the television one day
and they're afraid
they're going to miss it.

We are multitaskers.
For us,
commercials are a cue
to do something else,
like finish doing the dishes
or empty the cat box
or make a pot of coffee.
Men aren't like that.
They want to keep watching
television.
I really wonder
if men are just wired
to watch television
the way they do.
Maybe men are still hunting–
and they just don't want to miss
the next antelope
that runs across the screen.
You'd think
we'd all know by now
that there really isn't that much worth
watching on television.
With men,
more is better,
the more functions it controls,
the more they like it.

You've heard the expression:
'males don't want to know what else is on.'
Even in households where wives
earn as much as their husbands,
women

and men believe
that the woman's paid work
is secondary.
Women
and men think
men are entitled to more
leisure time at home.
They've been out at the rat race,
so they've earned their time to relax.
For women,
home is a more complicated place–
it's a place of both work and leisure,
but women feel guilty about leisure at home.
They don't feel as entitled to it.
In our study,
some women said
they're unhappy
about their husband's behavior.
When asked,
if they've brought up
their husband's upsetting behavior,
most of them said,
naaah,
they're not going to mention it,
it's not important enough for them
to disrupt the family's happiness–
which is also one of women's
primary responsibilities.

I'm one of the most power-driven
remote-mongers you'll meet.
It's really awful.
I'm terrible,
but I do it.
Much of this behavior is unconscious.
I would never say that men
are deliberately trying
to annoy their wives–
it's not like that.
It just happens
and it comes from men
being in a position of entitlement.
I don't even watch commercials anymore,
despite having taught advertising.

You can just zap 'em
and that has a lot of people
in the industry very,
very worried.
They have kind of lived off
this confidence game
for a long time–
they've charged rates
as if people
were actually paying attention
to commercials.
I can watch two
or three shows at once–
it's usually easy to pick up
the thread of many dramas,
films
and many sitcoms,
certainly,
while being rewarded
by hearing a good gag
or two by continually watching.
The revolution in this industry
has been that television is now
under the user's control.
We don't have to sit
in front of a televion set
and watch three choices programmed
at the convenience of the networks.

Frustrates them,
it drives me nuts,
I don't understand why
it has to be click-click-click.
I don't think he's doing it
to have the remote
and use it.
There's no way
you can tell what's on each channel
when you're going that fast.
I think the majority of them
probably spend the day
working for someone else,
not necessarily doing
what they want to do,

so,
by God,
if they can grab a little more
control of their lives
when they get home,
they're going to do it
and that's okay.
It's just selfishness.
The way sports are structured
may be related to the way men
use the remote-control-device–
there's a lot of down time in sports,
there are free throws,
timeouts
and in football
there's hardly any activity
most of the time.
So it's easy for men
to keep up with
multiple sports events–
even if they miss a play,
they'll get to see the replay.
I'm not optimistic about change,
for now.

Our gender interaction
shapes patterns
where men are advantaged
and privileged
over women.
I don't see that
becoming any different.

Renter's Law

HOUSING

Tenant Protection Ordinance

No-cause.
Substantial change.
As far as I know,
no place else has taken
this sort of approach,
replicate
and improve.
I think our relocation ordinance
is unique
and the only one of its kind
in the country.
It is clear
that the City Council tool is working
for cutting down evictions.

A rental housing catastrophe.
Really great first step
for a city to take,
I see it more as displacement
mitigation.
Preempting.
The doctors of old
who thought that applying leeches
would help a patient.

Draconian.
Mom
and Pop.
I'm a guy who owns a duplex
and I'm getting stymied
by city government,
I want my property back.

Bill of Rights.
Extremely low income.
Really big
and important protection

for tenants
in a moment of crisis.
It doesn't solve all of our problems,
who has three months
of money in the bank
that they just can just pick up
and move.
We rent
because we are not in a position
to buy.

It was the first whiff
I had ever caught
that there was anything on our side
as tenants.
It was the difference
between us feeling
like we would end up living
on the street
or sleeping on a friend's couch–
or being able to stand up
for ourselves.
It was just radio silence,
like a pit bull,
having that extra cushion
allowed me
to look for a new place
from a position of strength;
if I didn't have
the relocation assistance,
I feel like I would have experienced
a lot of paranoia
and uncertainty.

Republican National Convention

GOVERNMENT

It would be a wide-open rodeo,
it would be a multilevel chess game.
Much excitement is in the air.
If Donald Trump continues to win states,
but does not achieve the magic number
od 1,237 delegates,
yet still win a majority of the popular vote,
I suspect there will be a lot of upset people
across the country,
however,
the election law states
that a candidate must receive 1,237 delegates
from primaries
and caucuses
or it will be decided at convention.
There is no getting around that.

There are so many 'What if' scenarios
that it can make your head spin.
Some of those uncertainties
will become more clear
after the March 15th primaries.

Not a fan
of not giving the nomination
to the candidate
that has the most votes.
Unorthodox.
He has grown the party,
no one can fault him for that.
The enthusiasm behind him
is much greater
than either of the Democratic
candidates at this point.
It's looking more
and more like it's possible.

Those conversations will take place
ahead of time

and people will know
who their second choice is
when they arrive at the convention.
I don't know if that's Trump,
some polls show other candidates
running stronger against the other side
and he has not
yet been as critically examined
by the media
as some of the other candidates.

Trump can pull in independents
and some Democrats-Cruz can't,
he needs to have
an effective delegate defense strategy,
to make sure they'll stick with him,
there's a realignment of the electorate
and they're coalescing around Trump,
because they're tired of being promised things
that never happen.
The Republican Party put itself in this position
by not paying attention to the frustration.
If he has the most delegates
and isn't nominated,
there could be a significant backlash
and we hand the election to Clinton.

Retired

SOCIETY

Retired.
That was the one word that stung,
it's a negative word.
It creates the impression
that you've left the busy,
active world.
A work in progress.
"What do you do?"
"I'm retired."
It depends on who's asking,
'*self-employed*'
it sounds more dynamic,
there's a stigma to say
'*retired*'.

Emeritus.
The phone stopped ringing.
That is the stereotype
and it's very real.
What has happened to American culture
in the last century
is that we've created retirement
as a new stage of life,
but we haven't caught up
until that social reality.

I say,
*"I do some consulting
and I am doing a lot of volunteering,"*
it's an identity thing.
Even though I'm retired
from all the primary things
that I was doing,
one of the reasons I keep my hand in
is my identity
is tied up with what I did.

People have their own little firms,
maybe a second phone number

or a fax number,
but there's not much going on there,
a bunch of retired people.
Formers.

I do a variety of things,
retirement is not viewed
as an occupation.
"What did you used to do?"
"I'm still working."
Less acceptable to say,
"Hey,
I'm having a good time
doing my own thing."
I got used to it,
about five minutes,
to revel in it every day.
"What do you do?"
I tell them,
"I do everything–
I do it all."
people lose interest
if you're not is a position
to help them.

I have no shame in putting myself
in a position where I could retire.
My mother-in-law asked me,
"Did you get fired?"
when I left the firm,
in a society
with a premium on youth
and energy,
when people leave careers before 65,
people wonder
whether they were leaving voluntarily.

Retirees

SOCIETY

Baby BoomersNations advocacy going for older Americans

Source: RetireeWorkforce.com
         Seniors4Hire.org
         RetirementJobs.com

It's been difficult,
I don't know how
I will pay for fuel oil
for heating.
I can't walk into a grocery store
and buy what I want.
I don't look forward to Christmas,
because I can't buy gifts this year.

We've definitely seen an increase
in the sense of urgency
in terms of jobs;
now there's a growing need
in the opposite direction.
A lot of these folks who are hiring
are in their 20's
or 30's
and they think people in their 60's
are ancient.
If it comes down between you,
with a lot of experience
and a younger person;
I feel they're going to go
with the younger person.

The job market has changed,
employees are accepting
job applications online;
interviewing has changed,
so it's important to keep up.

I think companies
certainly are looking to retain

their own people over 65
and it's not going to be unusual
at all for people to work
till age 70.
Whether they're as willing to hire
someone over 65 from the outside
remains to be determined.

Retirees

SOCIETY

    Early

We were thinking
we've got the time now,
but how do we finance it?
It's been a help
for Cathy's peace of mind.
Unless you've actually lived
through it personally,
you don't fully appreciate
some of the nuances
of the deaccumulation phase,
there's a lot of angst around,
how am I going to get
my paycheck in retirement?
There are still some risks to it,
these funds are a tremendous fit
for an underserved marketplace.
The mathematics
of this are beyond what most people
could really be sophisticated
or it's not that they're stupid.
It's just that it's complicated.

Guardrails,
A midcourse correction.
It resonates,
Retirees have had a lot
of life experience.
Not all of it good.

Retirement

SOCIETY

Companies could lose everyone
who remembers how they handled
the last economic downturn.
We always had the policies,
but until now,
only the savviest employees
asked to use them
and only the savviest managers
said yes.
That's where older workers
get a chance to say,
"Hey,
we tried that 10 years ago
and here's why it didn't work."

They're letting older employees
wind down gradually,
so they can transfer their knowledge,
before it leaves for good.
We're educating our managers
to offer new jobs to people
who want to retire;
it's quite scary,
what could potentially happen
on some of our nursing units
if they retire at traditional ages.
So,
we've taken a fresh look
at our pension calculator
to see if we can make
it financially worthwhile
for older workers
to ratchet down now,
rather than just leave;
we hear it time and again,
that people would retire
if they didn't have this opportunity.
Going to be a lot fewer young workers
to go after,

this way.
We get to hire the people
who are playing into retirement elsewhere.

Winter is CVS's busiest time in Florida
and it's when I want to enjoy
the beaches
and golf.
I don't call it partial retirement;
I call it working.
It no longer feels
like I'm doing the same old thing,
I see no reason to retire now.
I feel like I received a gift.

I can't see a downside for anyone –
I'm helping new people
get their act together faster
and I'm helping people
spot where the pitfalls
in new mainframes might be.
I really like doing this,
so why should I retire?

They all know
that workers are getting older,
but only companies on the cutting edge
are focusing on ways to retain them.

Most employers are not even making it
for people who want to stay,
let alone giving them incentives to stay.

They're made to feel like lame ducks
if they announce their retirement
too far in advance.
When someone's retirement
will leave a real talent void,
you find a way to keep them;
degree of criticality of knowledge.

Retirement Savings Plans

ECONOMY

       Profit Sharing
       401(k) Plans

Sources: Center for Retirement Research
              At Boston College
              Federal Reserve
              Employee Benefit Research Institute

The current 401(k) system
has not turned out to be as secure
as we want it to be–
it has not provided the level
of savings that we want it to.
It's kind of failing in a number of fronts.
Should there be a serious reassessment?
Absolutely,
if you're not really managing
your assets well in these critical years,
it's going to have a huge impact
on your retirement years.
One of the lessons that we're learning
is consumers are having a really hard time
grasping the concept of risk.

In July,
my plan was looked on
at best as a noble idea,
but completely unrealistic…
I was viewed as thinking outside of the box
and now I'm in the box.
The market might recover from a crash,
but people don't recover
from aging.
For many people
the market will recover
two years after they're dead.

What happened in the '90s–

and there's still a little carry over–
is that some people are expecting
returns in their plans
that are unrealistic,
a very efficient savings machine.
The average 401(k) participant is 45,
there is plenty of time
for the historical correction
that comes
from these kind of situations to occur
and for people to be in good shape.

Exchanging the equity investments
in your retirement account
for Treasury bills
is not a sound long-term investment
strategy
and will subject retirees
to substantial inflation risks.

The Great Risk Shift.
We suddenly found ourselves,
without anyone making a purposeful decision,
in a world where the primary plan
was this 401(k).
In the wake of this financial crisis,
I think a consensus is emerging
that we just can't have a retirement
system that exposes people
to this type of risk.

Right-to-Die Law

JUSTICE

It gives me a great peace of mind
to know
that I will not have to die
slowly
and painfully
as a cancer patient.

Quality palliate case,
spiritual case
and emotional support
and a respect for our human dignity
are the compassionate response –
not a lethal dose of drugs
from a physician.

Robocall Scam

ECONOMY

Hello.
Oh,
hi there!
I'm sorry,
I was having a little trouble
with my headset!
Can you hear me?

Conversational agents.
Chat bots.
On every front in development
of conversational agents,
there's a huge emphasis
on making them more sociable.
The vision right now
for conversional agents
is moving seamlessly
among various tasks,
that clearly is not out of the realm
of possibility.
Um,
uh-huh,
these things
are all being pursued,
social bot.
Converses coherently
and engagingly
with humans
on popular topics
and news events
for 20 minutes.

This stuff
is all coming together now
in a way
that's getting very close
to artificial intelligence,
can you hear me?
Careful human engineering

with an understanding
of the human dynamics
of conversations
and what will sound natural.
2001,
we're really at a tipping point
for so many elements
of the technology.
We're in a golden age
of machine learning
and Artificial Intelligence,
we're still a long way
from being able
to do things
the way humans do things,
but we're solving
unbelievable complex problems
every day.

Can you hear me?
If someone call
and asks,
'Can you hear me?'
do not answer *'yes'*,
just hang up.
Scammers change their tactics
as the public catches on,
so be alert
for other questions
designed to solicit
a simple yes answer.

Romania

UNITED NATIONS

The people's reaction was:
*"Why should we support
the ones who don't need us?"*
That was the moment
of his downfall.
The people thought
with their hearts
rather than with their minds.
The reform...
began gradually
and conveyed a lot of fear.

Six years after the overthrow
of Communism,
Romanians waited
for a miracle
and when Constantinescu came
along,
we thought it was a blessing,
but there was no such miracle.
A second tier,
as a former Communist.
One wrong move
and Romania will be on standby again.

I think that Iliescu's return
to power would mean isolating Romania
from the European Union
and the North Atlantic
Treaty Organization,
it's something the ruling power is using
to benefit them
in the elections.

Whoever wins the election,
Romania's policy will continue
to be pro-Western.

Iliescu's victory

will be an unbearable
problem.
He represents the period
when the will for strong reform
didn't exist in Romania.
It was the period of constitution
and hesitation.
Their image is very bad
in all polls…
they think it's,
because of the criticism
from the press.

Warehoused in residential facilities,
wasting away,
Romania is where we prove
that the concept could work.

We have given them a chance of life.
Now we have to give them a future,
they advise us,
we have people who love us.
They helped me go through
the grieving process.
I always say
that all these children are my own.

The rich say there is economic growth,
but the only thing growing
are their pockets.
The people wanted a real government
to bring them work,
not just pretty words.
The women have seen
how there has been inflation
in the kitchen
and in caring for their children.
We deal with that
and we saw we were on the precipice.
If you do not have enough
to feed your children,
there is nothing you can change,
but you can change the government.

Romantic Love

SOCIETY

Their sexual arousal
seems to be relatively indiscriminate–
they get aroused by both male
and female images.

I'm not even sure females
have a sexual orientation,
but they have sexual preferences.
Women are very picky,
yet most choose
to have sex
with men.
It's popular among male academics
to say that females preferred smart guys;
such genes will be quickly selected,
in males,
because new beneficial mutations
will be quickly apparent
and will have more
variable brain phenotypes.

Male homosexuality
is evolutionarily maladaptive.
A maternal immune response
to succeeding male pregnancies.
Most males are quite stubborn
in their ideas
about which sex they want to pursue;
While women seem more flexible.
I think most of the scientists working
on these questions are convinced
that the antecedents of sexual orientation
in males are happening early in life,
probably before birth.
Whereas for females,
some are probably born to become gay,
but clearly some get there quite late in life.

Romantic love can last 12 to 18 months
is a universal human phenomenon.

Romantic Relationship

SOCIETY

You complete me.
I'm close to you,
because I'm afraid to be alone,
I could stay home forever–
and so could he–
and be 100% happy.

He doesn't feel bad
and I don't feel bad,
he's got to have things
outside of me.

Attached at the hip.
Michael
and I are together constantly.
We get ready for bed at the same time
and we go to bed together.
Occasionally,
I still need my alone time.
It's a little hard for him,
since he doesn't seem to have the same need.
He has been wonderful
about listening to what I have to say.
We just keep talking about it,
communicating with one each other
is just so important.

Suffocated.
Get out.
Loss of self.
We are supposed to look
for the person who completes us,
who makes us whole.
We miss each other,
when we're apart,
but it's important
to maintain your relationship;
eventually you're going to run out
of things to talk about.

You can still have that wonderful sense
of trust
and dependence
and still be whole.

Come together.
They appreciate
and embrace the similarities,
but also the individual uniqueness
that they bring.

If a couple is too close
and wants to change that,
they can resolve it
by becoming stronger.
They are unique individuals.
Each with their own friends,
interests,
passions
and each growing
and learning about themselves.

Straight-talk for Men About Marriage:
What men need to know about marriage.
Couples could spend 24 hours
and 7 days a week together
and not be considered too close
as long as each partner
is able to keep his
or her own identity.
Emotional boundaries.

Rummage Sale

COMMUNITY

We are getting a whole lot
of storage containers this year
and we've got a million drawer organizers,
it makes sense.
If you had all of your stuff
in containers
and you're getting rid of your stuff,
you no longer need the containers.

When we get calls,
for when people are ready
to drop things off,
the urgency has changed;
they don't want to wait.
They're like
"We're got it
and we've got to get it out
of here now!"
It didn't used to be that way.

San Diego likes sparkles.
They are really coming back,
Gone Girl.
I think we are really literate
here in San Diego,
All the Light we Cannot see,
the Goldfinch.
I feel like we know
what is The New York Times
best seller list.

We never define
what anything is for;
we never say,
"*That's a curtain rod.*"
If you want to wear a curtain rod
around your neck,
you can.

We get people's wedding albums
and frames with family photos in them—
it's hard for people to let go
of somethings;
if they give them to us,
in their minds,
they aren't throwing them out.

Salt

COMMUNITY

*"We'll stretch
what salt we have,
for as long as we can
and hope
for warm weather;
that's all we can
afford to do."*

We did the only thing we could:
tell the public to drive slow.
There was no way
we could have a brand-new storage dome
and have it empty...
we'll make it last as long as we can.
We'll stretch
what salt we have,
for as long as we can
and hope
for warm weather;
that's all we can
afford to do.

Our mines in the United States
and Canada are going 24-7
and we're subcontracting
with salt companies
from South America
and Europe;
even with all that,
our supplies are short.

They're telling me...
eight to ten weeks before you see it–
in eight to ten weeks we'll be in January,
by then,
snow will be on the ground
and it'll be too late.

Companies are selling their stockpiles
as quickly as they can produce it;
no one can keep up.

Samoans

JUSTICE

      America

Nationals.
We're proud of the United States
and we want to be recognized
as part of it.
I see young men
and women who go to war
to fight for the United States,
they are willing to die for a country
that is not fully theirs
and for a nation
that doesn't fully accept them
as citizens.

Inhabited by alien races.
Development of the American empire.
Politically incorrect.
Views of race of imperialism.
All persons born
or naturalized
in the United States
and subject to the jurisdiction thereof
are citizens of the United States.

To persons everywhere,
whether in the states,
or in the Territories,
or in the District of Colombia
unequivocal promise
of birthright citizenship,
singled out persons
born in American Samoa.
Branded them with an inferior,
subordinate status
that deprives them of the full rights
many of them have fought to defend.
Shall be nationals,
but not citizens,
of the United States at birth.
Natural-born citizen.

San Onofre Nuclear Generating Station (SONGS)

GOVERNMENT

        Nuclear Waste

Fatally flawed.
San Onofre Nuclear Waste Problems,
thin walled,
steel.
Gouging.

With a double walled fuel tank,
if a leak occurs it can be detected
and the storage container
can be repaired
or replaced
before any gasoline is released.
At San Onofre,
we certainly should expect
that some kind of leak prevention system
would be in place
to contain extremely toxic
high-level radioactive waste.
Explosive energy
greater than that
of several large sticks of dynamite.
Enormous amounts of heat.

I find that virtually none of the protocols
that should be expected
for the safety handling
of this dangerous material
are present.
I find that personnel
and companies are being hired
virtually off the street,
no specific qualification standards
are present
or for that matter even required.
Training is not specific to the risks
of the material involved
and there is not fully-qualified

and certified team
assembled for this highly-critical operation.

Potential Economic Consequences
from an Event
at San Onofre
Nuclear Generation Station
Interim Spent Fuel Storage Installation,
much better storage configuration
technically defensible storage facility.

If an accident,
natural disaster,
negligence
or an act of terrorism
were to cause a large-scale release
of radiation,
the health
and safety of 8.4 million people
within a 50-mile radius
would be put at risk,
complete analysis
of canister loading procedure
and comprehensive risk assessment.
Reliable canisters that can be monitored,
inspected
and repaired.

Santa Anita Racetrack

VENUES

Source: National Trust for Historic Preservation
         One of the country's most endangered historic places
         Los Angeles Conservancy

It's one of the most recognizable
historic sites in California.
If they go forward
with these plans,
it would be a tragedy.
The final outcome
would be infinitely better
if this historic resource
were thoughtfully redeveloped,
not obliterated.
Remodeling of the interior
of the grand stand area,
Santa Anita is a true gem
in the West.
Pressure has got to be brought
to bear to save
this wonderful place.
Can you imagine the anguish
if they tried to do this
to Churchill Downs
in Kentucky?

There doesn't seem to be a concern
by the owner
of Santa Anita
about historic resources.
The most popular place
with young people in the nation
is Art Deco Miami Beach
and here we have something
that looks like Miami Beach.

Year-round,
destination entertainment center
which will be appealing to families.

Very preliminary.
Magna Entertainment Corporation,
the racetrack's parent company
has submitted nothing to the city;
the model was shown
twelve months ago
to small groups of people.

Saudi Arabia

UNITED NATIONS

     Riyad

We wake up each morning
complaining about management,
not legitimacy.
We never debate direction,
we debate its focus,
speed,
style emphasis
and colors.
We cannot sit by ourselves
and say we don't need others,
we are part of the international community;
we have to live
and work with it.

We are in the process of inventing ourselves,
all of the indications are that we are opening,
but what are the consequences?
We will have to deal with it as it comes.

Desire action.
The reputation of the United States,
in the Arab region,
has dropped to zero;
too biased a stand
makes an awkward situation
for America's friendly.
It's a delicate situation
and not to be discussed now.
If the perception of the United States
doesn't change,
it will weaken the arguments
of those who say we should totally open up
and plug in with the world.

People say it's too risky.
An image of impatience
is bad for rulers;

I think they want their government
to cut the right figure
and Abdullah has satisfied that desire.
The crown prince
is a master politician
in a way that Saudi Arabia
hasn't had for a while
in terms of reading his own public.
I don't think he's in anyway anti-American,
but he is more openly critical,
than Fahd would have been.

Scandals

COMMUNITY

The newspapers,
bewildered at the sudden absence
of a war communiqué
flung themselves on this.
The mob in cry after their murderer
did not notice
or was delighted to notice
the concomitant shortness of news
about the Peace Conference.

The stories go on forever
and they have a numbing effect…
They invade your life
and you really can't hide away from them.
This is the same blockbuster mentality
that you see in publishing,
in Hollywood
and in other entertainment areas.
What is '*Hamlet*' if not a scandal
on the highest level?
The king is murdered by his brother,
who lusts for the king's wife.
It's a high,
canonical story.
You can't say these things
are merely bread
and circuses for the masses.

People are fascinated,
but they have a limited attention span,
most scandals end pretty quiet…
someone like Rita Jenrette
says she and her congressman husband
once made love on the capitol steps,
but you forget it all a week later.

When you see that a large number
of subscribers are checking out stories
about Monica Lewinsky on the web,

you're going to ride that story
as long as you possibly can.

It began with the Gulf War,
because fifteen minutes after
it was over,
nobody remembered it,
the war begat O.J.
and O.J. begat Monica.

These stories create an adrenaline rush
that wears off–
and we're all addicted.
We need another fix.
If I run into you somewhere,
I can't count on
you having read DeTouqueville
or Melville,
but we can certainly talk
about Monica Lewinsky.
It's the froth we share in common,
like a glass of wine.
In times like this,
the media is the great
American butler.
The more you watch
the less you know,
opinion is cheap
and information costs money,
as the British put it;
which is why you see pundits
gabbing away on Monica
and as little coverage on television
on Kosovo
and other hot spots.
Today,
information culture is at war
with entertainment culture
and real coverage is losing.
Scandal Songs.
Living through.
Scorpio Tongues.
Ultimately,
you create a culture

that is not shocked
you surf channels on television
and hear about Monica,
so you go to the next channel
and it's Monica again,
then there's a talk show about someone
with a senior citizen diaper fetish,
so you keep switching channels
and finally you give up.

The Death of Outrage:
Bill Clinton
and the Assault on American Ideals.
We needed Clinton to be the first father
and not a carouser.
We needed to count on him
and his lies took a great toll.
It's easier to be titillated
by Monica's underwear than the story
of the Russian soldier
who nearly hijacked a nuclear submarine
and caused a catastrophe.
Human nature responds more naturally
to sleaze and gore.
It always has.

Scandal-immune.
We all want a grand narrative,
a lesson underneath these stories,
but America is a fractured society
with so many divisions
and it's hard to tell one tale
that everyone can agree with.
When you lose that consensus,
the storyline can provoke anger,
because no one agrees.

Moral panic.
Righteous.
The message was clear,
since most Americans
felt justice
was done in both cases.
Daily Show,

we now continue our endless,
ceaseless,
won't-stop-if-you-beg-us coverage
of '*Make It stop*
Nineteen Ninety-Eight:
To Dream the Impeachable Dream'
The Metropolis and Mental Life.
An incapacity emerges to react
to new sensations
with the appropriate energy.
We have too much media
bombardment now
and you simply can't expect
people to watch the same story
over and over.
The public begins to scream things
out on its own.

School Board

EDUCATION

I was working for the district
when Columbine happened
and we were basically on our own.
Cannabis conspiracy.
I voted for you
and you alone on my ticket,
but somewhere along the line
I feel you got lost.
Save Carpinteria United School District.

Grueling,
horrible,
awful,
awful,
awful,
contentious minutiae,
lack of understanding.
Failure to function
as a cohesive body.

The governing board
views board service
as a voluntary contribution
to the community
and elects not to receive the compensation
to which it is entitled by law.

As I explained in the last board meeting,
the process is:
we make the recommendation,
the board votes on it,
we bring a resolution–
once the resolution is voted on
by the board,
then we will meet with the leadership.

The district,
for the second year in a row,
dismissed a plethora

of contractual obligations
surrounding lay-offs
and has chosen to claim
that the Education Code
designates the process
they'd like to pursue...
clarifies exactly how the union
and the district are to work together
on these lay-offs.

At times,
over the last two years,
I have spoken
from a place of anger
and resentment...
I am human
and humans are by nature flawed,
I have apologized when possible,
in person.

Scientific Spirit

COMMUNITY

Next year will be the centenary
of the May Fourth Movement,
in my opinion,
China in 1919 lacked scientific spirit
and China in 2019
will still lack scientific spirit.

Take China's Science
and Technology sector
as an example:
its level of original innovation
remains low
and its fundamental research is weak,
you can attribute these to a thousand reasons,
but the most fundamental reason
is the lack of scientific spirit.
Accompanying this,
there comes a host of ugly phenomena
like corruption
and fraud in academia,
as well as arrogance
and superficialness.

Scotland

UNITED NATIONS

The new parliament hasn't done much,
but argue about the new building;
unfortunately,
they tried to run,
before
they could walk
with this building.
The money is out of control
and so people aren't going
to trust them
with tax-raising power.
They've kind of fallen on their faces.
A little Parliament's
'*just jobs for the boys*',
I don't like it at all.
Feathering their nests.

Family values.
It is much more contentious.
The storms blow
with great ferocity,
we're on our own.
We've got to develop policy
and make a government
that wasn't there.
We actually think
it is the right thing to do,
if the ban
is rather mean-spirited
and discriminatory.
No one believes it is an essential safeguard.
This has put the nation-lit genie
back into the bottle.
There is no evidence
of risking support for independence,
cash for access.

I'm really proud
of the fact that we've got a parliament,

a lot of illnesses are Scottish
and shouldn't be decided in London.
Hopefully,
one day we'll get a parliament
with full power.
We're doing fine,
finding our feet,
putting the executive
under pressure,
that's the role of the Parliament,
after all–
to subject the government
to democratic scrutiny.
Scotland will be independent
within the next ten years.

Sculpture

VENUES

Attractions

Peace
and Love.
The commission thanks Mr. Starr
for his generous offer,
but unfortunately
the donation
did not meet the Fine Art Criteria.

They said,
sorry Sir Ringo,
thanks for your proposal,
but you're not an artist
and the work is not art,
they produced a definition of art
which is extraordinary.
They would have rejected Van Gogh
or Picasso on those grounds.

We want to be a city of love
and peace,
when you take a picture
with City Hall in the background,
it symbolizes that.
The whole submittal process
was all about the value of the piece,
it was all about this Beverly Hills version
of art.
Peace
and Love.

He said,
we'll give it another try,
so we tried
and then finally the success came
with the changing of the guard.
Peace
and Love.

Peace
and Love.
You want it to be approachable,
I think this is approachable.
I know there were other cities
that were interested,
but he said he wanted it in his hometown
and that's wonderful.
For their passion on this project…
I'll see you all at the unveiling,
Peace
and Love–
Ringo.

Sea Dragons and Seahorses

WORLD WILDLIFE

Association of Zoos and Aquariums

The goal of this exhibit
and the aquarium
is to instill that sense of wonder
and passion for these animals
in hopes that people will take steps
to not only harm the planet
that is close to home,
but the planet as a whole
and hopefully to take steps to protect it.
These are amazing creatures
that we hope are around a long time
and I think everything benefits
when we are protecting habitats
and species.
All of them.

Seahorses,
sea dragons,
pipefish
and some other funky creatures
that we have in the exhibit
are in the Syngnathidae family,
which is a type of fish,
they may look bizarre,
but they are true fish.
There are three different types
of sea dragons.
Up until a few years ago
we thought there were only two.
What we have on exhibit
are the leafy sea dragons,
that are a little more elaborate
and beautiful
and we also have the weedy sea dragons,
just as cool,
with the spots
and purple stripes.

Scripp's Institution of Oceanography
recently discovered
a few years ago
the ruby sea dragon,
which was unknown to science.
They found it through genetic research,
then they went on an expedition
to find this fish out in the wild.
No one has the ruby sea dragon in captivity.

The wonderful thing
about having both sea dragons
and seahorses here,
is more than 25 years ago,
Birch Aquarium
started the Seahorse Breeding Program
and we have been breeding
13 different species of seahorses
in captivity,
there is a lot of pressure on seahorses.
People take them out of the wild
for trinkets,
aquariums,
traditional medicine;
they are kind of one of those things
you can easily love to death.

We are hoping to do the same
with the sea dragons,
the exhibit was designed
with decades of experience
along with our Husbandry team
and the team
at Scripp's Institution of Oceanography
who studies these guides.
One of the reasons it is so wide
and deep is so that the sea dragons
have enough room
to do their really elaborate dances;
so that they can reproduce in captivity.
The weedy sea dragons have reproduced
in captivity
a handful of times
over the last 30 years,

but the leafy sea dragons
have never been bred
in captivity
anywhere in the world.

Security and Exchange Commission

ECONOMY

Very soon.
Gain one thousand percent.
He has done other investing
and has done extremely well,
he's a nice kid,
just a little different;
I just wish
he'd told me about it,
that's all I can say.

The most undervalued stock ever.
I implore investors
to be highly skeptical of any advice
they receive from the internet.
People should do thorough research
before making investment decisions
and verify all information,
before acting on it.

Self-playing Piano

COMMUNITY

Music Industry

It's a player piano,
but we call it a re-performance piano,
it is a seamless melding
of 21st century technology
and Old World craftsmanship.
We're able to actually re-create
the keystroke–
the hammer hitting the string–
in the exact way that it did
when the artist played it,
it makes it much more musically enjoyable.

But it wasn't a Steinway
and I remember my sister crying
at that time–
and I realized how powerful the draw was
for musicians to play on Steinway,
my viewpoint is you can't have too many Steinways.

Platform.
If you're at home
one night
and in your local concert hall
you've got Billy Joel
playing a concert,
it is possible today
that if you have a Spirio
in your house,
you can enjoy that concert
in real time
on your piano–
not over a speaker system,
but actually he's activating
your particular piano,
in your living room,
while you're in the comfort
of your home,

that's what we call
a remote performance
and that's something
that will be very realistic for us.

There really is a lot of opportunity
that the Spirio platform
can provide,
I hope what it does
is it actually enlarges
the group of individuals
that really appreciate
fine music,
which will again make our industry
start to grow.

Serbia

UNITED NATIONS

      Montenegro

Can anyone tell the difference
between Bosnian
and Serbian?
New.
Language defines the identity
of a people,
having the Bosnian language
brings recognition to a people
who have lived in Serbia
and Montenegro for centuries.

I speak Serbian,
Bosnian speaks Bosnian.
We don't live in Sarajevo,
we live here.
It's Serbo-Montenegran!

I was also assimilated,
the language I speak
is absolutely Serbian,
but my parents spoke Bosnian.
We want to bring back
what has been gradually lost
over the last 250 years.
Helicopter,
zrakomlat–
air beater.
Dalikovidnica,
seen from afar.

I am not against the introduction
of the language,
but the way in which it is being done.
I speak Bosnian.
My language is the most beautiful
in the world;
dangerous.

Sex Education

SOCIETY

The kids were talking about this stuff
at school
and Clemence didn't' understand.
We've talked about things,
but penetration–
that I had trouble with.
The reality is I didn't want to talk about it…
I know
they've done a good job
and she won't be shocked.

The pursuit of happiness.
We don't want to replace
the French family,
but we want the exhibit
to be another view
of what goes on between men
and women without it being…
raw.
Instead,
we promote respect,
romantic feelings,
pleasure.
In France,
kids are bombarded with sexual images–
in films,
ads,
songs,
on the Internet,
to show things
in a way that allows for imagination,
let's have children come up
with their own representation
of sex.

9-to-14-year-olds.
Calvin and Hobbes.
What does making love mean?
If a pregnant woman eats spinach,

does the baby in her tummy,
taste it too?
Love-o-meter.

Pubermatic.
Teenagers.
"*I have one breast bigger,
than the other,
is that normal?*"...
"*What is masturbation?*"...
"*I'm afraid to have my period,
is it painful?*"...
Love mural.
Zizi sexual.
Sexual Willy.

Corrupting.
We don't have the power
to shut it down;
we at least want parents
to have the power
to keep their children from it.
Crude.
Love wall.
These are not enough
about building a relationship;
it's just learning
how to kiss,
listening to kissing.
That's not about feelings.
Nadia's room.

Sex Education

SOCIETY

      Teenagers

Don't,
there's a lot of problems with porn,
but it's kind of nice
to be able to use it
to gain some knowledge
about sex.
The Real Housewives.

Here's your nose,
here's your toes,
I have a boyfriend to do that.
Guys will say,
a hand job is a man's job,
a blow job is yo' job.
Well, I guess when you put it that way,
fifth base naïve
or flawed,
relax.
If he's sexually satisfied,
then I'm sexually satisfied.

Intimate justice.
Good enough.
Driven by hormones,
very well.
My friend's mother
also asked me how it was,
if I had an orgasm
and if he had one.

Not Under My Roof:
Parents,
Teens
and the culture of sex,
with a drunken head.
Porn kills love.
Yes,

Mom,
but I've never seen it.
I know,
Honey,
but you will
and there are a few things
you need to know.

Sexism

LABOR

Venture Capitalists

I call them the
'we cool?'
conversations.
I can be friendly
without being flirty.
I should be able to,
any male Virtual Reality
that isn't re-examining
their behavior towards women
in light of recent press,
regardless of whether
or not they have been accused,
just simply isn't doing their job
as an investor
or a person of privilege
and influence.

I deeply regret
ever causing anyone
to feel uncomfortable,
there's no denying
this is an issue
in the venture community
and I hate that my behavior
has contributed to it.

It's like a death
by a thousand paper cuts,
what do you think?
While we were raising money
and building the company,
it was more like
'this is the way
the world is now.'

Spirit crushing,
I didn't know

that there was any discrimination,
the more it's front of mind,
the less it's excused.
Scar tissue.

We are taking
a lot of time
to look deeper
at how our conscious behaviors
contribute to our own role
in all of this
and how to improve,
we know that our role
as venture capitalists
in the tech community
makes it our responsibility
to be leaders.

Sexual Harassment

JUSTICE

Settled the matter personally.
For decades,
women found
that this harassing behavior
often was the price
of coming to work.
It was entrenched,
with high performers
getting a free pass.
Women have a means today
to tell these stories
and to reinforce each other's stories
and to support each other's stories
and to support each other in a way
that didn't exist
when this happened to me.
Everything is on the table
in a way
that it was never before,
it's certainly a moment to seize,
but it won't happen by its own.

Boom Boom Room,
sexual harassment
by its branch managers,
male brokers
and other male employees.
Retaliating against
female employees
who file complaints.
Just shows where women are
in the power of hierarchy
and that's why you see
repeat offenders.

This is the definition
of an imbalance of power.
We've seen time
and time again

that in a sexual harassment case,
it is the executive
who benefits
while the employee
is often dismissed,
leaving in their wake
co-workers who then may face
the same unacceptable behavior;
it's a sweeping under the rug
and they can't find each other.
It's not about one bad guy,
it's about the corporation
and the board that protects them,
when you have respected figures topple,
it creates important cracks
in the armor,
men would often just go on
after harassment accusations,
but women often find their dream
and careers derailed,
may be that can stop.

Sexual favors
in return for giving her work.
Many inaccuracies.
'*b*----'
'*ho*'.
We continue to believe
that Isiah did nothing wrong,
in addition,
the jury did not find any basis
to award punitive damages
against Isiah.

Real change needs to happen,
but women cannot do it alone,
we need men
to make the right decisions,
not when caught
in a torrential media downpour
or years later
when the experiences
of their daughters
cause them to reconsider their ways.

Men may have been terminated,
but because no one knew why,
it allowed them
to be snatched up elsewhere
where they could continue harassing.

Sexual Misconduct

LABOR

Inappropriate sexual behavior.
You want to report your bad news,
if somebody else reports it,
then it looks like you've been hiding,
which is the worst thing
you can do.
Today,
inappropriate sexual behavior
in the workplace.

A Prairie Home Companion.
The Best of
A Prairie Home Companion,
the Writer's Almanac House of Cards.
All the Money in the World.
The process of analyzing allegations
and making determinations
about misconduct hasn't changed,
what has changed
is the pressure
that employer's feel under
right now to move quicker,
to be more decisive
with the decisions
and in some cases,
to publicize their actions.

We really are a period
where there's heightened
consumer awareness,
in general,
of companies' social policies,
their environmental policies,
customer-facing companies,
particularly media
and information services,
depend on the good will
of their consumers
immediate

BETTER FUTURE | 683

and appropriate action.
Appropriate.

Old days.
Spend more time
with their family.
Balancing act.
Today.
Unusual,
completely changed the conversation.
For someone to be accused
on Monday
and fired on Wednesday,
that's unheard of
in a pre-Harvey Weinstein world,
you just never saw
that speed of action before.

Shark Attacks

NATURE

        Pacific Coast of America

More people are in the water today
than there were 10 years ago,
more people are kayaking,
swimming,
surfing
and diving,
as those ocean user groups go up,
the likelihood these types of events
are going to happen…
you're going to get more reports
and you're going to have more incidents
of physical contact
with sharks.

We don't know
what their numbers are,
there's no way
to get an accurate account,
but we know their numbers
are rebounding,
surfer.
Displacement behavior,
these types of events
really give us some insights
into their behavior,
in this case,
the shark struck his kayak.
In my opinion,
it had invaded its space
and this shark felt threatened,
it was protecting an area
it was using for food.
Apparently,
these are the same areas
sharks are using,
it turned out this shark
had come up

and was laying alongside
his surfboard.
He was trying to get to leave,
the fin goes underwater,
then comes from under to bang the board,
propelling the surfer about six feet
into the air.
When he comes down,
the surfer lands on the shark.
The shark submerges,
he crawls on the board,
these people come running
to see if he's OK.

The sharks are teaching themselves,
through conditioning,
this isn't anything
that I should be concerned with.
It is possible,
because of all the contacts
with yearlings
and juveniles,
all these interactions,
are they conditioning themselves
to ignore humans in the future,
because they realize
we're not anything important?
That's a possibility.

Sharks

NATURE

Migration

Sweet sport,
overtime,
you can predict
where you can expect to see sharks
in Southern California
and in other parts of the world,
it's exciting
when all the technology–
when you put it together with math–
start to come together
and you can make predictions,
what makes that important.
We can let the public know.

Hot spot.
Hot spot.
Once bigger,
they are now big enough
that they are not influenced by temperatures,
like a small kid,
they get colder in a pool
than an adult that has more mass.
The bigger they get,
the less temperature–
sensitive they become.

It's looking like it may be a busy summer,
but we have to wait
and see,
right now,
water temperatures are starting
where they should be starting to hit
our beaches.

Jaws.
Baby Shark.
We think they are coming

somewhere to Southern California
to give birth,
but we rarely see big adult females
near the beach.
I think they are giving birth in deeper water,
in the channels
and the babies are becoming incubated
in a warm mom.
They give birth
in colder waters
and that forces the babies
to swim to the beach.

Shopping Carts

LABOR

Got 'em!
Target.
Albertson's.
Food 4 Less.
Everyone wants a shopping cart,
but no one wants to pay for them.

You've got to be in shape
and you've got to have
a lot of energy.
When I got into there two years ago,
I thought it was hilarious,
but now I know
it's a serious business.
A great deal of money
is lost every year
and these are victims—
the consumers.

Borrowed.
Orange County
is a real political hot spot.
Junk.
We'll come back tomorrow
and probably do the same thing;
it gets frustrating!
You can get worn down
real fast,
but somebody's got to put
a stop to this.
We are not standing.
We are only trying to clean up the area
by picking up these old carts
and we just leave them outside.
If Rick
and Gilberto want to come
and pick them up,
they can pick them up.
We are not stealing.

The first of the year,
I had almost 200
brand new shopping carts;
now I have 120,
somebody took 80
of my carts
and yet they still call me a thief.

Shopping Malls

COMMUNITY

Negotiations are difficult
for retailers
when one landlord owns all the space,
if you control real estate,
then you can dictate the terms.
Be value.

By 2008,
Simon's CEO decided to
'go nuclear'
and remind Ann Taylor
of the fact
that they were
'in the process of proceeding
with documentation
for almost 50 renewals
and over 25 new factories
and full-priced stores,
we compete fiercely
for our retail tenants
and always try to offer them
the best deal possible,
we are confident there is no antitrust
or other legal impediment
to the proposed purchase of Macerich,
we believe this transaction
would benefit retailers
and consumers,
because we expect to improve the experience
at the Macerich proposes
that we're proposing to acquire.'

Smart Identification Cards

SOCIETY

Cross-Border Integration

The aim is to make Hong Kong,
Macau
and Taiwan residents
able to enjoy public services
and facilities
in ways basically the same
as mainland residents
in their place of abode,
breakthrough.

As far as the Hong Kong government knows,
there are 520,000 Hong Kongers
living in Guandong province
and more than 75,000 Hong Kong students
in universities across the mainland,
Residence Permit.
Among the three rights,
six services
and nine conveniences,
some have been rolled out separately,
but the advantage of this permit
is that it will provide a full-coverage solution,
many of the concerns
and requests I have learned from Hong Kongers
living on mainland are resolved
and fulfilled.

810000.
820000.
It doesn't matter to us
what the permit is called,
the most important thing
is that we need the code
that can be recognized by machines
and systems on the mainland
to get public
and private services,

what will happen to accounts
and services
I registered for
with my home return permit
after I get a residence permit?
Will I have to register again?

Snow

NATURE

This is something you tell to people
who are from out of the area,
they have a hard time believing it,
it's the California Christmas dream.

The teacher would not let us out of class,
I had dreams that the waves
were frozen over
and I wanted to see that.
Huh?
They had been out surfing
and all of a sudden,
snowflakes were falling on them.

Snow day.
It was very difficult
keeping the kids in class,
because the snow was all over,
everywhere,
it was quite an exciting event.

Rocky.
He was writing on the chalkboard,
but we were looking out at the snow.
What?
You've never seen snow before?
He made me come over
and wipe off his pants
and shoes.

Everybody,
was freezing.
It was pretty funny,
having snowball fights with nuns.
There wasn't a bit of snow left
by that time,
after that first one,
it was too much.

Social Network

COMMUNITY

Clickbait.
Disputed.
People tell us they don't like stories
that are misleading,
sensational
or spammy.
That includes clickbait headlines,
that are designed to get attention
and have visitors
into clicking on a link,
in an effort to support
an informed community,
we're always working
to determine what stories
might have clickbait headlines
so we can show them less often.

Disputed.
Disputed.
There's no silver bullet solution,
which is why we've deployed
a diverse,
concerted
and strategic plan,
we know there is misinformation
and even outright hoax
content on Facebook
and we take this seriously,
we've made progress fighting
hoaxes the way we fight spam,
but we have more works to do.

When she looked
under Her Couch Cushions
and Saw This...
Wow!
Ginger tea is the secret
to everlasting youth.
You've GOT to see this!

Social Unrest

JUSTICE

This isn't just,
Oh,
my gosh,
all of sudden this happened,
it's a series of things
that have happened
over a period of time
and right now
you shake a soda bottle
and you open the top
and it explodes
and this is what it is.

Multiple arrests.
At the end of the day,
he is going to support his officers,
even when wrong is wrong,
if they caught you in a backyard
or alleyway,
they'd want to beat you up.
Really viewed blocks
as less than them
or animals
or not deserving of respect.

I was like,
'You just pushed me down
and was roughing on me,
and you expect me
to tell you stuff'.
The people have been calm,
the people have not stood up.
So when will we stand up?

Unless something is done
about the uninhabitable conditions
that the black man has to live in,
Milwaukee could become a holocaust.

Solar Energy

NATURE

It's like a giant layer of cake of debt.
Sun Edison expanded much too quickly,
with probably too little thought,
substantial risk.
They sent development teams
all around the world,
spent a lot of money,
launched a lot of projects
and basically none of their gambles
paid off;
yield companies.
Solar
and wind companies
have always gone bankrupt;
frankly,
just because an industry is growing,
very quickly,
doesn't mean that all players will do well
and in fact,
one reason the renewable energy industry
is growing
so quickly
is that costs
have been coming down,
very rapidly.

Material–
weaknesses in its internal controls
over financial reporting.
Based on the fact
that they still haven't filed
their 10k,
I'm wondering
whether central management
even knows what is going on
in all their sub-offices
and development teams.
If you said every industry
where something goes bankrupt

was a poor industry,
then there wouldn't be many good ones,
would there?
Coal
and oil drilling,
there are plenty of companies
having troubles now,
but nobody is saying,
oh its totally
build on the sand.

I wish,
I could say that I'm shocked,
there's nothing more fickle
than political winds
and when they're not at your back
and you have to compete
on your own,
trouble can ensue
when a company
or business hasn't been formed
by the market forces
of supply and demand.
None of these solar power sources
can compete
with conventional power sources,
it's a completely different thing.
Keep in mind
that you don't need a multinational company
to do rooftop solar.
Basically,
you can put up rooftop solar panels
if you're a company,
with two people
and a van.

I think the industry
has been
and continues to be
much larger
than any single company,
we expect the U.S.
solar market
to more than double

this year in terms of installed capacity
that's being deployed.

Very,
very rarely are subsides
a cost–effective way
of addressing a problem,
that's because it's difficult to know
which technology to subsidize
and even if you have subsidizes
that are technology-neutral,
you don't necessarily know
how much the subsidy should be.

South Africa

UNITED NATIONS

African National Congress

Generations,
new dawn.
I don't think changing President Zuma
will change anything,
at the end of the day,
as long as you have power,
even the new president
will do the things the other guy did.

African National Congress
is the best,
it's the one that took South Africa
out of apartheid.
Yes,
it's the best.
I wouldn't vote for any other party.

The same as Zuma,
they've been together
for quite a long time.
So what can we expect from that?
I keep thinking it might change,
it might change,
let me give him some time–
but there's no change,
I'm a strong fighter,
but I guess we'll see
with this new one.
They were talking among themselves,
there was no information
we were receiving,
I was uncertain about the future
of our country.
I thought maybe there would be violence
and there would be loss of life.
I was scared actually.

A new dawn is upon us.
This is the year
in which we will turn the tide
of corruption
in our public institutions,
we are determined to build a society
defined by decency
and integrity,
that does not tolerate the plunder
of public resources,
not the theft by corporate criminals
of the hard-earned savings
of ordinary people.

That man was a businessman,
he understands what he's talking about.
Maybe we can get jobs
or something with Ramaphosa,
we'll just wait
and see,
but they're spending a lot of money
just on catering,
the money that's supposed to be helping people,
six months' salary.
They're just doing each other favors.

South Africa

UNITED NATIONS

African National Congress

Umshimi Wami,
Bring me my machine gun.

Certain negativity
and completely unacceptable tendencies
have emerged within our movement,
which threaten the very survival
of the African National Congress.
As the trusted servant of the people,
it has been for 96 years,
that these are people who abuse
their position in government consciously,
purposefully
and systematically to engage,
in a corrupt practice
and for self-enrichment.
They engage in criminal
and amoral activities driven,
by the hunger for personal gain,
acquired at the expense of the poor,
off the country.
Over the years we have seen
the persistent propagation
of outright falsehoods,
intended to discredit our leadership,
a practice that is entirely foreign
to our investment...
a practice of untruths...
that resorts to dishonest means...
and to deceit
in order to achieve a particular goal.

Definitely he felt humiliated,
we wanted to show him
that we grew tired of him
and he should definitely give someone else
a chance;

he was supposed to have handed over
the power.
We want to see the changes
that Jacob Zuma will bring.

When Jacob Zuma wins the election,
the whole of South Africa
will die,
because these people are not there
for the people on the ground,
who are suffering in this battle.
I just felt so angry
that they showed him
they didn't want him
to be the president.
He (Thabo Mbeki) felt very painful,
because he's worried about the people
and what will happen to them
if this person seized the control.

South Africa

UNITED NATIONS

   Johannesburg

Catastrophe injustice.
Clean up.
A disastrous venture based on a set
of colonial–era laws
and policies that were a tool
of segregation
and social exclusion.
For its part,
the government must recognize
the virtual state of emergency
that now exists,
allow unhindered access
for humanitarian operations
and create conditions
for sustainable relief
and reconstruction.

Precipitated a humanitarian crisis
of immense proportions,
the international community
should encourage the government
to prosecute all
those who may have caused criminal
negligence leading to alleged deaths,
value-laden
and judgmental.

Value-laden
and judgmental.
Consequent sanity
which now prevails countywide.
This is not a one-off thing,
in the previous five years,
groups within Zimbabwe
have made sustained
and detailed allegations
of gross human rights violations

like extrajudicial killing
and torture.
When you look at Operation Murambatsvina,
it's not an aberration by the government,
but part of systematic abuses of the rights
of Zimbabwean citizens,
one would hope that the security Council,
looking at the report
and the seriousness of the report
and looking at it in the context
of sustained human rights violating
that have taken place,
would then be obligated to take action.

It's high time the United Nations
security Council took some action
against Zimbabwe,
I knew there's great reluctance
and a great indifference
in the United Nations,
when it comes to Africa.

South Africa

UNITED NATIONS

Rape

I was raped by my own dad,
when I was sixteen.
The love I had for him
deteriorated after that
and I could not stand
the sight of him...
I called him yesterday.
He is very sick
and wasn't able to say much.
He said,
"sorry if I was the one..."

The problem with rape
and AIDS are recent,
but they derive from a similar source:
the little girl has no value
in the society of Africa;
she is an object to be used
to fulfill the lives of the men.
The problem is definitely there
and it is staring at us in the face;
unfortunately,
we have no way of tracking it.
We are not actually checking
for the Human Immunodeficiency Virus
when the patients come in
and they usually don't test for it
when they are referred to a clinic.

We see girls as young as eight
or nine
with HIV.
We see a lot of abuse in the rougher areas
of South Africa,
surrounded with violence;
but also in the rest of Africa.

Cross generation infection
is a difficult area to address.
In some places,
it could be a sugar daddy;
while in other places,
coercive sex.
There is a cultural component
that is different across Africa.

Sophie's choice—
it sometimes seems
that we do nothing,
but rape cases
and we see only the tip
of the iceberg.
We even have cases of children
still in diapers being raped.
It is a society gone upside down.

Space Explorer

AMERICA'S NEW TRIUMPH

Contact.
Wormholes,
closed time,
like curves—
time machines.
That far out on the edge.
Ideas are crazy
if they don't have any chance
of being right;
only through mathematics
can you test
whether your insight is '*right*',
but if you had to work strictly
on the basis of mathematics,
you'd move at a snail's pace.
See some distance downstream,
to figure out which direction
you should explore mathematically.

Private eye.
Mortified.
Partly for fun.
Then if you need a substantial
amount of money,
you have to have a certain ability
to deal with politicians,
like Queen Isabella
or the National Science Foundation,
asking for a very large amount of money
for something that has never been seen.

I'd lay moderately heavy odds,
the spinning holes are like two tornadoes,
not made of whiling air,
but whirling space
and warped time—
orbiting around each other
inside a third tornado
made of whirling space

and we're asking what happens
when they come together.
We don't throw spacequakes
we make it different.
It's not as much fun anymore.

Space.
Playing around with Einstein's equations,
negative guesses,
based on knowledge
and past experience,
mostly shapes
and curves.
Mouth,
mouth,
the equations say unequivocally
that in the simplest case
if you had such a wormhole,
it would convert itself into a time machine.
Embarrassingly simple
it is not hopeless,
but I'd give heavy odds
that explosions destroy all time machines,
so we needn't face the conundrums;
you can't see air with your eyes.

Chronology protection keeps the world safe
for historians,
this is tough stuff
that I don't understand
very well at all.
I get enjoyment
out of probing ideas like time machines,
but it's not clear
whether that's ripe for real success.

SpaceX

AMERICA'S NEW TRIUMPH

The rocket landed
instead of putting a hole in the ship
or flipping over;
so we're really excited about that,
at least the pieces were bigger.
When it becomes boring,
when it's like,
'another landing',
no news there.

USA!
I have a confession to make–
I did,
indeed,
hug Hans…
the whole SpaceX team
was super excited.
They've all worked incredibly hard
to get to this day;
making the landing
and re-flight easy–
is hard.

Ultimately it was Maherol time,
he was totally committed to this.
He's committed to reusable technology.
Pretty much everybody
will be eating his dust.
A great step forward.
The next step for SpaceX
would be to take a good look
at this engine
and stage
to see what needs to be done.
Does it need an overhaul
or does it test out
and just need a new paint job?

I think you'll see

a potential cost savings
of 30% off the original launch cost
and that price will continue to drop
with the success of this.

He doesn't consider
them failures,
he considers everything research
and development.

Spain

UNITED NATIONS

        Peace

Pakea behar dugu,
we need peace.
It's not just the prospect
of less business
or fewer visitors,
but the way we feel inside.
When people lose
hope in peace,
they lose energy
and a sense of purpose
in their work.
They get depressed.
The pessimism contaminates everything
for a definite peace!

The truce is over.
Once again we are under terrorist threat.
Nobody is against peace,
but it must come with a recognition
of the Basque people's right
to make their own decisions
without interference of any kind.

The violence radicals,
those people with the flags,
are here for us.
The important thing
is that we're here together,
asking for a chance
to express our differences in peace.
I hope Euskal Herritarrok is listening
sooner rather than later.
Euskal Herritarrok was in a bad way
a year and a half ago
and it's not much better now;
as long as they are able to kill.
I will not use the word '*weak*.'

José Maria Aznar
and his government
took Euskal Herritarrok's truce as proof
that they had won the war,
not as an opportunity to resolve
a complex conflict.
They thought Euskal Herritarrok was finished.

Special Games

SPORTS

Shandel took his buddy,
Sophia right away,
he held her hand
through every event.
It was so neat to see him try
and be allowed to try things
that he wouldn't normally be able to do.

One of our therapists for Shandel
told us a long time ago
just to treat him
like any of the other children.
Love on him
and help him
keep trying,
we are his biggest fans.
We will support him
and love on him
as long as we can.
He continues to amaze me
every day.

His buddy Sophia
had the colorful cards
with pictures
of every activities available.
She used the colorful visual aid art
with all the games on there
and Shantel could just point
to what he wanted to do,
it was a great change for him
to go
and have fun.

In 2016,
we offered new games
for the participants
and had more sponsors at the event
with great information

for parents
and caregivers.
The athletes at our Special Games
range from age four
to sixty years old.

The Star Spangled Banner.
Shantel loved playing the baseball game,
we play in the backyard all the time.
He's got an arm
and he can swing.
I know that he can do all of these things,
but other people don't get to see that.
It feels wonderful to share
with the world
that Shantel can hit a ball.
He swung
and the bell rang
and this was awesome.
We all cheered.

When I first learned
my son would be affected
by a chromosome disorder
or a heart defect,
I didn't want to believe it,
I just wanted a healthy boy,
I didn't understand how my world would change
forever in the best of ways.
I get to wake up every morning
and fall in love all over again.
I wish someone would have told me that.
This little boy can make you feel
that you will burst
with so much love
and pride
to see him accomplish so much,
it means everything.

St. Tropez

UNITED NATIONS

France

...And God Created Woman,
remarkable natural preserve.
How can you say to thirty thousand visitors a year:
"This goes back to nature?"
"No toilets."
"No parking."
"No food."
The case is deeply troubling.
The environmentalists went too far.

The image of France.
I know that sounds pretentious,
but St. Tropez is a part of the French image.
St. Tropez is life–
Men
and women
with all the weaknesses that make life.
It is a strong symbol
and one of youth
and vitality.
Having fun,
doing what you please.

Magic.
A few bamboo cabins
have gotten bigger
and bigger
and they have been selling off
to each other–
making a fortune.
There has been an anarchy
that the local officials
have closed their eyes to.
No one asked whether it was legal
or not,
because they were making money.

Removing westwards from Pampelonne
would be like banning Waltzes in Vienna
or beer in Munich.
Natural
we will have to find a solution
that is lawful,
but takes into account
the reality of the thing.

Stimulus Checks

ECONOMY

Internal Revenue Services

You can expect to see
a lot of the rebate money going into gasoline,
most of which is imported from overseas,
so the simulative impact on the economy
will be less than what it could have been.

Our nation has been living on debt
under the label of consumerism
for far too long.
When we have an economy
that's just based on spending
more money,
we get into trouble.

I think I'll keep my money in serving
or maybe in my mattress...
It's probably a better interest note
than any bank is offering anyways.

Have a nice vacation,
some fun
and buy some stuff we don't need!
Before you splurge
on that new high-definition television
or some other consumer item,
consider switching from the shopping channel,
to the Third World hunger channel.
There you'll be treated to scenes
of Haitian children eating dried mud cakes,
because they can't even afford rice.

Does that stimulate our country?
The tax rebate is a bad policy:
this should be going toward re-building
our infrastructure
or helping the poor,
so we sent our rebate to a food bank,

where it should have gone
in the first place!
It's not like we couldn't have used the money
and of course the car
went into the shop this week
for the miraculous coincidence
of $1,200 worth of repairs–
but it was the right thing to do.

FINANCE

Stocks

New York Stock Exchange (NYSE)

This calls to mind
my favorite saying,
the market will do whatever it has to do
to prove most people wrong,
correction,
surviving?

Market psychology
was bordering on euphoria
in late January
and is coming back down to earth now,
this is an important reminder to investors
that 2018 is not 2017
when it comes to the stock market.
Expectations were high
and they needed to deliver,
so thankfully they have delivered,
as long as earnings continue
to follow through
and economic data doesn't roll over materially,
stocks can keep going.
People will say that valuations are expenses,
but I would say,
'*Yeah,*
but not relative to fixed income.'

The stock market
would be completely normal,
we went over 400 trading days
without a 5 percent pullback.
They really had been no volatility
in the market.
Nothing is wrong economically,
the economy is doing better now
than it has at any time
in the past decade.
This is just some healthy

and overdue,
volatility
to wring out any excess.

Still seems like a very reasonable projection.
To me the X factor
in all of this,
are strong
and will be getting stronger,
could be a by-product of that success.

We were due for a correction,
we're putting a lot of money to work.
I think the market is going to end
the year much better.

Sudan

UNITED NATIONS

Now people are afraid to come
together for ceremonies;
it's too dangerous.
This day is supposed to be a day
of celebration,
but it's the opposite,
we're living in fear.
You just have a meal
and that's it.

They hit me there,
on the side of my hand.
It is just beyond
that dried river bank,
we dug in a hurry,
we mourned them,
but we did that in a hurry too.

All options are open,
it is playing with fire.
I swear to God,
I swear to God,
I swear to God,
we will not hand over any Sudanese;
to the International Criminal Court.

We take the situation quite seriously,
if genocide is the charge
that the ICC prosecutor is pursuing,
he has sit himself a high hurdle
to get over.
Charging a sitting head of state
is going to generate a lot of commentary
and controversy,
but given what has happened
in Darfur since 2003,
it is hardly a surprise
that the trail of evidence leads

to the head of state.
It is an important step
toward the end of impunity.

In principle,
I believe that peace
and justice
should go hand in hand.
The government
wants it as a showcase,
it's still a thorn
in Sudan-American relations.
It will always be a point
for the Sudanese government to bring up.

Damaged the development efforts
of my country
and deprived my people
of basic medicines.
Today,
from this rostrum,
we reintegrate our calls
to the United Nations
to take the necessary
and just measures within the framework
of international law
and appeal to the international community
as a whole to support
this just
and legitimate demand.

My government labeled this
as anti-Islamic aggression,
but I regret that,
if Shifa was involved
in such an evil program,
it deserved to be attacked.
I would have to sit with him,
we all make right decisions
and wrong decisions
based on the advice we get,
but whenever you are wrong,
you have to make it right.

This was a very bad decision.
When a person attacks you
in your home,
what do you call him?
Is he a friend
or an enemy?
We don't want to hate you.

Super Bowl City

VENUES

There's going to be events
going on all over town,
we're so excited,
because there's going to be so much energy
everywhere.

We are the entertainment capital
of the world.
We should be at a movie studio
of some sort.

Media day.
You want the entire city
to have Super Bowl fever
and I think that's what the design reflects,
in this era of mass amounts of content,
everything changes,
your goal is always that the event reflects well
on the entire city,
the citizens,
the transportation hubs
and the stadiums,
it's a complete effort.
From the moment you land
at the airport as a guest,
to the moment you get back on the plane,
did you enjoy
the Super Bowl city experience?

Super Bowl City,
Super Bowl Live.
We want to see what everyone else is doing,
but we want it on a different level,
because of our city
and the fact that the weather
is so great here.
We have so much to offer
and we're so spread out.

Superbugs

BABIES

We want the strategies we employ
to work 100% of the time,
but that's not always possible.
Broad use of antiseptic strategies
deployed over many days
or weeks
may only partially help
and many in turn induce
unintended consequences,
universal decolonization.
Methicillin-resistant staphylococcus
reuses (MRSA).

We did this to answer the question,
'Can we reduce the number of infections?'
It wasn't,
'Can we lower the cost?'
Great caution should be exercised
in transferring the study's results
into clinical practice,
indiscriminate use
should be discouraged.
we wonder how many other
patients were not told
what was going on.

Supersonic Airliners

ECONOMY

Aerospace Industry

Flower of the aerospace industry.
We're benefiting from 50 years of progress
in fundamental aerospace technology.
Since the Concorde was developed,
the amount of international business
and international travel has skyrocketed.
You can find a huge market.

I think its main customers
world be very wealthy individuals
who would look at
it as the ultimate prestige aircraft,
it very much would have its own specific niche.

The reason why Concorde
prices were so high
is fuel economy was poor
and there was no economy of scale,
we have technology for that today.
We're now able to bottle physical
features in a computer
that a short decade ago
were unheard of,
I think the market's
always there,
we just didn't have the right pieces
and parts to fit it.

Taiwan

UNITED NATIONS

*"Five thousand years
of Chinese culture
has been best preserved
in Taiwan,
many mainland girls lack
proper Confucius respect
and will resist serving
their in-laws,
a long standing part
of Taiwanese culture."*

Marriages

If the Chinese President Hu Jintao
had a Taiwanese wife
and the Taiwanese President Chen Shui-bian
had a mainland wife,
they would be a lot better off with their lives.

I feel we're a really important link,
mainland girls,
especially northerners;
like strong,
spicy food…
while other Taiwanese
prefer their food
mild.
These preferences are so important
to the Chinese
that it can break up a marriage.
Sometimes the choices
get all blurred in the brain,
we'll talk it through
to help them straighten
things out.

I thought it went all right,
well,
actually not that great.
Producing so many women
is exhausting,
my real job
is a breeze compared to this.
One girl's family in Dalian
demanded $60,000,
but we knocked that down
to $2,200.
Like anything else,
they'll get what they can
out of you.

Five thousand years
of Chinese culture
has been best preserved
in Taiwan,
many mainland girls lack
proper Confucius respect
and will resist serving
their in-laws,
a long standing part
of Taiwanese culture.
We have to provide them lessons.
In ancient times,
warring kings married
their daughters off
to the other side
to settle things,
in the same way.
I think these marriages
can also be an important
stabilizing force
between China
and Taiwan.

We met one day
and married the next,
there are probably many
exceptional women in Taiwan,
but I didn't have time.
When you're 45,
I'll be 70,
are you willing to take care
of an old,
frail man,
who wets the bed?

Even if the girls don't talk
about it,
it's definitely competitive,
in my case;
all of the other girls were prettier
than me.
I thought there was no way
I had a chance,

but we hit it off
and he ended up choosing me.
It's great fun.
He seems nice
and my lifestyle would
be better in Taiwan,
but I was very nervous.

In China,
you can't vote;
the leaders vote for you,
here they vote
and the legislature
get into fights.
Many Chinese women,
especially those from rural areas,
see marriage as a vehicle
for getting rich,
in many ways
it's a business transaction,
his money for her beauty.

Colleagues say,
*"why would you want
a wife from China?"*
I've learned to ignore them;
she's my wife.

We try and convince them
it's about the personality,
but they don't always listen.

Taliban's Little White Book

FAITH

Official gazette.
Islamic Emirate of Afghanistan.
In the name of God,
the compassionate,
the merciful,
while we are in charge,
the universal decree
is that wherever has the power
is to prevent the people
from doing these big sins,
Emir al Momeini.
Every woman who goes out
without the hijab,
head covering,
will be followed to her home
where the woman
or her husband will be punished,
depending on the amount
of unveiling she is guilty of.
If the above mentioned woman
is in vehicle
the driver must be imprisoned
up to five days,
depending on the amount
of unveiling.

Women who wash clothes
in a desert
or near a spring
must be prevented
from doing such acts.
The owner of the house
where the woman lives
must be punished.

Women who have their clothes made
by a tailor
must be chastised
and the tailor imprisoned

up to ten days.

They've implemented some laws
that don't have the color
or smell of Islam,
nor any basis in Islam at all,
what I've read so far is very stupid
and childish they've mixed traditions
with Islam
and their own misinterpretation of it
and then imposed it on the Afghan people
in the name of Islam.

This makes no sense,
if you look at the life of Muhammad,
he used to get down on his hands
and knees
and put children on his back
so they could take pretend Camel rides.
He did this to make them happy
even when his grandson,
Hussein,
used to climb onto his back while he prayed,
he didn't push him off.

It has always been said an ignorant friend
will damage you more than a wise enemy.
We laugh at what it says now,
but those laws
for a long time
made us cry.

Tax Havens

DEBT

Your deep dark secret.
Do you wish to own land
or other assets
without anyone becoming aware of it?

Offshore.
We often say
that the United States
is one of the easiest places
to set up so-called anonymous
shell companies–
the mechanisms
are pretty much the same here,
there's nothing special
happening in Panama.
Panama is pretty much a microcosm
of what the United States
is a willing partner in.

From the states' perspective,
the end game is to raise revenue
for the state by creaming off fees
from a large number of companies
incorporating there–
and the consequences be damned.
This thing called the expression
'follow the money'?
Well,
when the money trail leads
to a Delaware Corporation,
it is almost a dead end
for law enforcement.

Nominees.
The State of California
does not know
who the owners
of a California Limited Liability Corporations
are if the owners don't want them to know.
News Plus Media Capital Group.

Teen Drivers

SOCIETY

Knowing the risks
can help parents
and teens make smart decisions
about which sides are safe
and which ones are off-limits.

Teen drivers don't always think.
Sometimes they think
they're just in this little bubble
where they can't get hurt
and they don't really think
about the consequences.

I've told her flat-out,
that in regards to some of her friends
who I don't believe
have been taught well enough,
in certain areas of driving,
that she is not to get in a car
with them behind the wheel.
This reminds us that raising teens
means having to constantly speak
to them on all the kinds of things
in life that are important.

Terrorist Attacks

UNITED NATIONS

After being confronted
with the results
of different expert examinations,
he confessed
his presence
at the crime scene,
here's what we do
to make sure
that doesn't happen here,
there's a lot more patrolling
of public areas here
than I believe
was the case in Brussels.
We have explosive-sniffing dogs
moving through the fronts
of the big airports.

The only person
that is going into their airports
to get the airports off their duff
and to limit the access
into their airports
is going to be you
and your administration.
There's some things
you have to do after Brussels
and one of them
is to realize
that public areas of the world
are vulnerable,
by definition.
It helps
that we have a vast national intelligence network.
I'm comfortable
that the United States,
in particular,
is doing about as much as we can
do to track,
to identify

and to pay attention
to people of concern.
If you've made a reservation,
your name
is automatically bounced against data bases.

Thailand

UNITED NATIONS

Fifth tiger.
When I heard that Indonesia
gave five-million dollars,
I felt so ashamed,
so embarrassed.

Seminars this year
I just want to survive.
I don't think it will be better
next year either,
because this is the worst
I've seen in twenty years
in this business.

Exporters have no complaints,
but for the long term,
if the economy is not good,
everybody loses.
We are not really confident
of the situation right now—
the government is not stable…
the baht is not stable.
If I have money now,
I don't invest.
We keep it in the bank.

One thing I think
is the need for trust
in our financial institutions
and even Thai politics,
we feel we can't trust
them anymore.
I blame the whole economic system
and not just this government,
but the government before that
and the one before that.
On top of that,
the Thai people themselves are spoiled.

When the economy was growing fast,
they spent more
and more.
They paid for imported brands…
people just looked ahead,
but didn't take care
of their own backs.

When this kind of situation happens,
people feel it's unbearable,
a shock.
Yesterday you were rich,
but today
you have to be poor.

Before,
I think,
Thai people were proud.
They thought
we were quite successful,
but now everything's just collapsed.
You cannot sell houses
and condominiums,
because people don't have enough money.
Cars cannot be sold,
yet they will have to raise the price,
because of the devaluation of the baht.

It's uncomfortable for me to say,
but I don't have as much income
as you'd expect.

Thailand

UNITED NATIONS

You need to wait
and see,
I'll be there in court
to the last day:
we will meet there.

It is now difficult
for us to analyze
what to do next,
we want to hear from her
and what her role will be now.

Thailand has been stuck
for two decades now,
the country remains divided
and polarized.
Yingluck's flight was a victory
of sorts
for the generals,
her running away
reinforces their rationale
for the coup
that the rice-management scheme
was corrupt
and that she knew about it,
they key will be
what the military regime takes away
from all of this.

We believe she left on Wednesday,
but we don't know how,
we haven't tried to find out.
What happened?
It is better to let her inform the public.

We haven't heard
from a government official
or from Khun Yingluck herself,
we have to wait a little bit longer

to be sure
that she is actually leaving
the country.

Madam,
you should have fought to the end,
they issued an arrest warrant
against you.
They announced
they took your bail money
of 30 million Thai Baht.
This is like stepping on my heart.

Thailand

UNITED NATIONS

    Thai Resort of Phucket

The Deadly Face of Shame,
the booking rate has fallen sharply
by 80 percent
to 90 per cent across the province Phucket
after the boat disaster.
Just how bad can Thailand handle
a disaster situation.

Repeated explanation
of how to claim your loved one's body.
Despicable handling
out of commiseration gift baskets
to those overwhelmed with grief
at the hospitals.

Thai officials
were unable to even keep count
of how many people
were supposed to be missing
in the Phoenix tour boat tragedy–
the worst single-vessel maritime disaster
in Thailand's modern history–
never mind actually attempting to find them.

No compromising on safety.
Nobody wants accidents to happen…
we must have safety
and management procedures in place
and leave no room for compromise.
If we become known
as a country that doesn't compromise on safety,
it will become another plus point for us
to be recognized for not being lax
in our standards.

Setting up checkpoints
at piers

where officials could perform safety checks
before tour boats depart,
checking all passengers
and crews always wear life jackets
and boat pilots have a license,
installing 38 extra closed circuits
television cameras at Chalong Piers
and the introduction
of a voluntary tourist payment
for a 100-baht wristband tracking system
with a Q R code
storing personal details
for emergencies,
which includes insurance
in case of death
or medical expenses.

Mai pen rai,
it doesn't matter.
The law is far too lenient.
Heavy fines must be imposed
and rogue operators
banned for life.
Thailand must put her act together
as far as transport safety is concerned.
So many innocent people,
Thais
or foreigners die each year,
due to the negligence of stakeholders
and operators.
Travel insurance will not make the country safer,
I think tourism in Thailand
is growing very fast
and maybe the government
should spend more money improving
and updating facilities
and providing a safe
and secure place for tourists
to enjoy their holidays.

Three-Toed Sloth

ZOOAMERICA

It is a precious jewel
of tropical biological research,
compared with our wild primate relatives.
Our modern western diet
has gotten us off track in terms of our health.

Sleep is good for human beings.
We perform poorly
if we are deprived of it,
if we can look at animals
and see what purpose sleep is serving,
we can formulate help
or treatments for people with insomnia.

Smithsonian Tropical Research Institute
is an ideal location to study them,
because it offers all the necessary conditions.
It's comfortable,
has the necessary facilities
and I can work with other global authorities.

A frog dies
and people say,
"so what?"...
but if that frog ate mosquitoes
that cause yellow fever,
maybe it's better to find out
what the frog's role in the ecosystem is,
before they all disappear.

Town Hall Meeting

COMMUNITY

Town hall meeting,
non-NATO ally,
we believe
that we should be sending a signal
that this is the policy
that other countries should follow.
The invasion business
we can show
a lot of our drug consumption
is going down.
Voces del futuro–
Voices of the future.

It's true that I tried to win
the reelection,
it's true that I asked
people to support me
and it's true that from time to time
I actually spoke to my supporters.
I think that's how democracy works,
to become part of the strategic
decision-making process
to be perfectly honest with you,
I never thought of it
in that way before…
I would urge anyone else here
who is interested in this,
if you have any ideas,
to write me about it;
I will think about
and see what can be done.

Humane.
The truly extraordinary efforts
that have happened
just in the year of nineteen nineties,
where Argentina has gone with us
to Bosnia,
has gone into Haiti,

is working with British soldiers
in Cyprus,
is working in Mozambique,
we want Argentina to be working
with Chile,
to be working with Brazil.
It would be the height of stupidity
for these countries to go to war with each other.

NATURE

Toxic Chemical

I can't believe
that a chemical we make
and that the stockhom convention
has told the industry
they need to curtail
the production of.
Nature makes the same thing,
why does your sponge
need to be flame-retardant?
It's sitting at the bottom
of the ocean.
That's crazy talk.

Someone swimming by
or crawling by
may not want
to have a mouthful
of brominated chemicals,
toxicologists quickly realized
that these are extraordinary toxic molecules
and they resembled the flame retardants
that we were adding
to our consumer products,
we're trying to connect the dots
of this puzzle
and find the producers
of these molecules,
then we can make our way
up the food chain
and discover
how these molecules travel to us
and if there is anything
we should do
to reduce our exposure.

SPORTS

Triathlon

Cloud.
I apologize to everyone
for being too late
and I am always late.
I wouldn't let them tell me the time.
I told them
if I make it,
I make it;
if I don't,
there's no use worrying about it.

I missed one of these by two minutes,
fourteen seconds
and it's kind of sad.
You're out there seventeen hours
just killing yourself
and believe me,
you do.
The support was unbelievable,
it's always that way.
I always tell people
that if it wasn't for the volunteers,
we wouldn't be here.
You have to give them a lot of credit.

The last six miles
were the toughest part–
it was a tough course
and I wasn't expecting
the sun to be beating down so hard
when we got into Pendleton for the bike,
but I just wanted to finish it.
It was incredible,
I'd been walking for hours,
but you can't help,
but run that last stretch.
The people want it.
It's so emotional.

I had to set an example,
for her–
that girls can do anything.
I wanted to make sure
that my kids saw
that when I start something I finish it.
The swim was so tough,
but by the time I got to the run,
I felt like I could talk to the other runners
and encourage them.
I just felt like the whole day
was a gift.

TV Advertising

ECONOMY

Television advertising in 2017
is in a states of total upheaval.
Rent,
A Christmas Story,
American Idol,
media companies are placing huge
bets on data to prove the value
of television to a greater extent
than in the past;
which has created tons of pressure
on the media companies
to prove that their commercials still work.

We've gone a step further
by saying we're going to guarantee
that advertisers are reaching
the right people;
audience targeting platform.

This Is Us.
Even if it was,
because their wife
or girlfriend was making them,
This Is Us.
Where do the advertisers get
the biggest reach
and the biggest return
on their investment?
We nail that.
This Is Us.
Empire.
Certain shows
that you put out there
seem to bring back audiences
that have gone away,
we have to find more %
those kinds of shows.

Working around the clock
to ensure that your ad shows up
in the right place.
You never have to worry about
your brand showing up next
to something objectionable,
television is the most effective
medium ever.
We know it,
you know it
and our friends in Silicon Valley
know it.
We have premium content
that can be trusted.

More relevant ads
are a good thing for everyone,
we are focusing on
metrics that matter.

TV Guide

ECONOMY

Magazine Industry

We were profitable for the first time
after 15 consecutive quarters of losses
and we're extremely excited about that.

There's more of a need
for this magazine than ever,
given the explosion
in the number of TV Channels.

We are in the process of a major redefinition
of our company.
We are moving into the business
of enabling consumers to find their media,
wherever they are.
I'm looking for topicality
and newness;
urgency.

Twitter Age

ECONOMY

Our great country
has been divided for decades,
sometimes you need protest
in order to heal
and we will heal
and be stronger than ever before!

Decades as decade.
Heal as heel.
Third Times the charm!
What a heel.
What a heel.
Counsel as council,
gas instead has.
Tap for tap,
unpresidented for unprecedented,
honered for honored.
Covfefe.
Heel instead of heal.
You should listen to you wife.

Texture.
LOV
OMG
Alien
Confused
about human language.
Herby as hear-by,
hear-by.

Potato was potatoe,
does spelling matter?
Fort Sumpter instead of sumter;
inaugural as inaugural.
Suddenly it became a badge
of your education
and status,
it mistakes what good spelling is about.
It's essentially a memory test,

an exercise in not learning–
but we now take it
for so much more than that.

Bigger texture.
You'll see this often on Twitter,
someone will post something
that's terrible–
racism
or homophobic
or something–
and a lot of people
will respond to it with,
aha,
I see you have misspelled
the word '*its*'
and do I will not even engage
with your argument.
It seems to me
that you're missing the point.
A racist tweet
is a racist tweet,
whether it's spelled correctly
or not.

Uber

COMMUNITY

*"As a woman
who often travels alone,
I feel safer."*

It's convenient
and quality.
Rental car centers
are not at the airport,
they're miles away;
if a business traveler is in a city
they're not familiar with…
to let somebody else do the driving
while they work in the back seat
is a much more efficient use of time.

Lyft for work.
As a woman
who often travels alone,
I feel safer.
I love being able to secure the ride
inside a building,
in a safe location,
instead of having to hope to find one…
I also love the electronic receipt
and that there's no cash
changing hands.

Uganda

UNITED NATIONS

Invisible Children

Invisible Children.
Two years ago,
all we had was passion,
drive
and we knew how to make a movie.
Now we really are making a difference
in people's lives
thanks to a lot of help
from a lot of young people
who are just like us.
One thing we have learned
is that illiteracy
and violence go hand in hand.
Education is key
to creating leaders
in Uganda who,
hopefully,
can skip the bloodshed.

Roadies.
Our generation
has been given a bad rap,
that we only know about video games
and pop culture,
but we are the most educated generation
in American history,
the most tech-savvy–
Kids graduate today
with insane skill sets.
We want to show the world
what we can do.

The Oprah Winfrey Show.
When movies like '*Hotel Rwanda*,'
and '*Blood Diamond*' come out,
they do a great deal
to release awareness,

but we think it's unfair
to show people
and tragedies,
but not really give them
a direct way to do something about it.
Nothing gets us more excited
than to screen our film
for high school kids,
to see them laugh away
and scream in frustration.
Then we tell them,
they can make a big difference
in the world.
The number one question
we get is:
*"How can I help Uganda
and help you guys?"*
It's very gratifying.

Invisible Children.
It was shocking to me.
I couldn't believe what was happening
to these kids in Uganda.
I live in such a protected,
sheltered world,
but these kids
were cheated out of their childhoods.
I made up my mind
to do something about it.

Undocumented Workers

THE QUAKERS

Under the employer sanction
provisions act,
we must act as the government's agent
in denying employment to a whole class
of people
and driving them underground;
opening them to ruthless exploitation
by the unscrupulous.
We find ourselves ordered by the government
to cast out the very people
we've been seeking so long to help.
A lot of the staff has said
they would not provide us documentation,
on moral grounds;
we're aware
we're vulnerable,
and this would release us
from a burden,

I can't imagine the conscientious objector concept
being any kind of a valid reason
to disobey the law.
The law says everybody,
whether you're Quaker,
Catholic
or member of the Jewish faith,
has to comply.
Another way to try to resurrect
the dying sanctuary movement,
this is a typical twist that
the sanctuary people would use,
it's clever,
but I don't think it's anything;
i'm concerned about.

Unidentified Flying Object (UFO)

NATURE

I couldn't believe it,
at first.
The shape
was about 100 ft. long
and there were four lights
coming from it;
initially,
the shape moved slowly
and it seemed to pivot
on a certain axis.
Then,
without warning,
a sudden flash of light
like a shooting star
went across the sky.
It was very strange.
I have been an amateur astronomer
for the past three years
and I've never seen anything
like it before.
It's unexplained.

Unification Church

FAITH

A bit surprised.
Declared to all heaven
and Earth:
that Reverend Sun Myung Moon
is none other than humanity's savior,
Messiah,
Returning Lord
and True Parent.
Father.

I remember the king
and queen thing,
but we have the king
and the queen of the prom,
the king
and the queen of 4-H,
the Mardi Gras
and all sorts of other things.
I had no idea
what he was king of.

I never saw Reverend Moon present
during the time I was there,
I did not stay
for any formal program.
It's my understanding
that what they were doing
was recognizing Mr.
and Mrs. Moon as parents.
They call it true parents,
as parents who provide
parental guidance
or parental direction.
That's what it meant to me.
It meant nothing more,
nothing less.

Reverend Moon has been very international
about promoting his activities

within the African-American church community.
Flimsy excuses,
you had what effectively amounted
to a religious coronation
in a government building
of a man who claims,
literally,
to be the savior.

I'm conservative,
I'm delighted
that we have
a middle-of-the-road-paper
in Washington.
From his spiritual perspective,
that is how he sees his role,
as ordained by God.
This is not the first time
the man has been on Capitol Hill.

Nobody sent it to me,
I discovered it
and I thought,
"Oh, my God."

United Automobile Workers (UAW)

ECONOMY

Source: John Schwartz
N.Y. Times Writer
MotorIntelligence.com

Concessions,
I used to cringe at that word,
but now,
why hide it.
That's what we did.

It is a historic
and awful difficult moment
for the United Automobile Workers.
The story of the industry
seems to have shifted a little bit
from potential buyers
being able to close the deal,
due to the credit tightening,
towards a widespread reluctance
to purchase durable goods at this point
and continued very weak.
Consumers confidence,
looks worse than it really was
to try to make the case to Congress,
"look we're desperate."
There's a bit of consumers
that postponed buying a car
in the past year,
they're waiting for the dust to settle.

Desperate.
On the other hand,
it's a shame
it wasn't of their own violation.
You don't defuse outrage
with cute little stunts.
Most of my clients,
have corporate jets;
if the C.E.O.

of one of the world's largest companies
is dealing with a product recall
in Europe
and he's futzing around at Dulles,
waiting for his shoes to be scanned,
it's ridiculous,
three Asian countries in three days?
I would have flown commercial,
maybe coach.
Why don't they ride bikes?

A more serious set of plans.
We don't have a good sense
from our members that this is something
they want to do,
it's going to take Bush
and Obama calling people;
I just don't think we have the vote
to do that now.
Couldn't you all have downgraded
to first class
or jet pooled
or something,
to get here?
It would have at least sent a message
that you do get it.

Not only should bankruptcy be an option
for domestic automakers,
but it is considered by most experts
to be the best option.

You have to be sensitive
to the symbolism,
this is a hot-button issue.
It's as much to showcase product
as it is to get to D.C.,
optics.
Sell its corporate aircraft
as part of its overall cash improvement plan,
as a sign of his confidence
in the company's transformation plan
and future.
Our industry is in a much more severe situation

than the rest of the economy,
it is in an unsustainable position
for all manufacturers.
We cannot continue to operate
at these levels
or else the entire industry's going to go down.

Let me tell you something folks,
we've got much better products
right now in every single category
than we did in June of 2005.
Buy one,
get one free.
We believe the economy
will continue to weaken in 2009,
our near term production plan
reflects this view,
as we continue to align capacity
with customer demand.

UNITED NATIONS

United Kingdom

Queen Elizabeth II

She's doing engagements
in Windsor
on her birthday,
she has provided
the single greatest blueprint
of any other monarch.
She is a study of how it's done,
in every capacity–
she is a study
in how to be queen.

United Service Organization (USO)

MILITARY

We are a non-profit
and yet here is a man
in a for-profit company
who has gained such a role
over the decisions
and policies of this organization.
Who is running this organization,
the senior leadership
and employees
or this outside vendor?
In most institutions,
a vendor would have a vendor client relationship,
in the U.S.O. it is stronger than that.

Worth Linen is considered
to have a quasi-executive function.
He has extraordinary clout
and he is taking management decisions
never given to an outside vendor.
He tends to exercise a sort of veto power
over what other vendors can offer
to the U.S.O.,
basically,
other vendors report to him;
he's a vendor who is considered
to have executive authority.
Hire
or fire vendors.
Worth has no ability to hire
or fire any staff;
he is similar to a general counsel
or to an ad agency.
To be effective,
you have to treat them as partners.
I had met him three
or four times before
and just,
because someone is a friend
doesn't mean you should exclude him.

There appears to be some confusion
as to who has responsibility
for the management of the U.S.O.

Data Base,
I wish to set the record straight,
once and for all.
Please accept instruction
for the management of our data base
from only one source.
That source will be Worth Linen.
All inquiries
or asking for access
to the data base
must be approved in advance
by Worth
or his designee.

It's very easy to upset donors
and I don't want people
sending out junk mail,
It's all a matter of coordination.
I just want to make sure
that we are all on the same page.
Worth isn't the easiest person
to get along with,
but he has performed beyond
our wildest expectations.

I wish I did have an inordinate
amount of influence.
We have a very clear relationship
with the U.S.O.
To be very specific,
we have no management role
whatsoever.

Allowing someone
with a personal allegiance
to obtain a no-bid contract
raises questions.

I concluded that,
under these conditions,

the only development programs
that can survive at the U.S.O.
are those controlled by Worth Linen.
Worth has a long
and effective background
and I think we are fortunate
to have him working on our behalf,
we have dramatically improved
our marketing efforts,
both in terms of donations,
as well as in terms of building mailing lists
and positive communications.

United States

UNITED NATIONS

Global Terrorism

Terror 2000.
Outrageous.
Terror 2000.
There's only been one,
but then we haven't
yet hit the year 2000.
Super terrorism.
Future terrorist will find
they need ever more spectacular horrors
to overcome this American capacity
to absorb what previously
would have seemed intolerable.
We must be prepared to defend
against dangers that only a few
years ago seemed impossible.
Terror 2000.
Tumult and transition in the future.
We expect peace settlements
in many areas where violence has originated-
in the Middle East,
Northern Ireland,
Yugoslavia,
Russia and its neighbors,
but it will take time
and during that time
terrorism is going to get worse,
before it gets better.

In some ways,
we're victims
of our own success.
As we've made it appreciably
more difficult for terrorist
to reach their traditional targets,
they've just calculated how much larger
their bombs or weapons have to be
to reach their targets

or how many lives
it will take to have an impact.

Terror 2000.
Pattern of Global Terrorism 1997.
We are concerned that terrorist
will push this trend to its most awful extreme
by employing weapons of mass destruction.
Terror 2000.
Cells.
The greatest terrorist threats
to the United States' interest today
come from extremist groups who claim,
however falsely,
to act on behalf of religion.

The means and methods of terrorism
are readily available at bookstores,
from mail-order publishers,
on CD-ROMSs
or even over the Internet
and therefore accessible
to anyone with a grievance,
purpose,
agenda
or any idiosyncratic combination
of the above.
Easy access to biological,
chemical
and nuclear technologies
will bring many new players.

Universal Studios

VENUES

Universal has worked,
very hard,
to listen.
Listening is sometimes very hard
and painful.
We think this reduced project
is appropriate,
is less big,
but it will also work
and it allows us to grow our core businesses;
we've gone more than the extra mile.
There will always be a naysayer,
but we're ready to invest in Los Angeles.
Let's move on.

Just because it goes down 40% in size
doesn't automatically make it
so that it takes care of everything.
Independent third party
do an analysis
of all these noise controls.

We don't want Universal to expand
their theme park at all,
if you can hear amplified noise,
within 200 feet,
it's too loud.
Absolutely would not solve the noise problem.
They said no new theme parks.
If they are expanding
their existing entertainment venues,
I have a problem with that.

U.S. Mexico Borders Mayors Association (USMBMA)

GOVERNMENT

I will NOT attend a function
That is sent to me in Spanish/Mexican.
one nation means one language
and I am insulted
by the division caused by language.
I didn't want to pick a flight.
The purpose of the Border
Mayor Association
is to speak with one voice
in Washington, D.C,
and Mexico City about issues
that impact our communities,
not to speak in one language.
My humble apologies if
I ruffled your feathers.
Giving away our sovereignty
To benefit others is Not a way
to strengthen our Nation
and our homes;
it is an idea that is probably
doomed to failure
for the Common man.
If Mexico is NOT stopping
drugs,
crime
and terrorists from coming
INTO our country from Mexico,
then Mexico is not a friend
and I don't care to help.
I have better things to do
in fighting the problems
they export to us.

Has anyone informed
Huachuca City Mayor
or Ken Iaylor that
Mexican isn't a language?
Learn some regional history,
Mayor.

He should really set the example
by speaking English
while in the United States.
America is going
'Down Hill' fast,
because we spend more time
catering to others
than we are concerned
with their own self-interest,
it is far past time to remember
that we should be
'America first'...
there is NOTHING wrong with that.

I am a Veteran who served
in other countries FOR America,
this has nothing to do with
a lack of patriotism
from my side;
horrified at how badly
I have been misrepresented
to the public.
Produced literature putting
America subservient to Mexico.
Address to opportunities
and challenges facing the United States
and Mexico in a global economy.

Union of Soviet Socialist Republics (USSR)

UNITED NATIONS

War of Words

Will be coming.
Russia vows to shoot down
any and all missiles
fired at Syria.
Smart!
You shouldn't be partners
with a gas killing animal
who kills his people
and enjoys it!

We are working
with our allies
on how we can ensure
those who are responsible
are held to account.
If there is a strike
by the Americans,
then the missiles will be drawn
and even the sources
from which they were fired
and therefore we are ready
to hold negotiations.
What the ambassadors are actually saying
is that they're going to try to sink ships,
sink submarines
and shoot aircraft
out of the sky—
that's war.

Is it the idea
to use the smart missiles
to sweep the traces
of the provocation under the rug?
They are fighting like street bullies.
The time is not one for competing.
It is time to heal the wounds
of the region.

To our very foolish leader,
do not attack Syria.

Vladimir Putin
is provoking the West
by encouraging Mr. Assad
to use chemical weapons
to see how far
we can be pushed.
A decisive response is needed.
Why is killing someone with gas
worse that killing them with a bomb
or a bullet?
If we get involved in Syria,
it should be
because of the inhumanities happening;
full stop.
Innocent Syrians
don't deserve to be attacked
with air strikes
when they already have Mr. Assad
gassing them.

Some who want to interfere
in Syria
talk of upholding international law,
but international law
is quite clear:
Article 2(4) of the United Nations Charter
expressly forbids interference
in the internal affairs of states
on any grounds.
All members show refrain
in their international relations
from the threat
or use of force
against the territorial integrity
or political independence
of any state.

U.S. Theater

VENUES

This movie is something very personal
to people
and it feels like a bigger movement
than just the movie itself,
'Crazy Rich Asians'.

There's this whole notion
of the movie being a triumph
for representation,
which is very problematic.
The only Indians
and Malays you see are servants.

To us,
Crazy Rich should not just be about the opulence
and luxury showcased in the film,
but Singapore's actual richness
in terms of our diversity.

We want to see Asian actors
on Asian topics,
we're hungry
and ready for this type of film.

U.S. Trade Tariffs

FINANCE

China is still the biggest market
for many California exporters,
how can you ignore it?
Nobody wants to pay more
for the same thing
they paid for six months ago.
Innovation is key for the future,
it is a lesson for everyone.
We do not like it,
products are blocked for political reasons.
Tax on online shopping
is considerably lower in China,
which effectively means
the total tax including the tariffs
could be the same
as that of traditional imports.

We are testing the Hong Kong market
for our Christmas wine
for the first time,
but we cannot switch markets overnight.
The trade war will hurt economic growth,
which in turn hurts consumers' spending desire.

As the largest importer
of United States soybeans,
China is a vital
and robust market
we cannot afford to lose,
strongly complimentary
in agricultural trade,
Chimerica.
Over time,
I suspect that this co-dependency
will diminish as Chinese rebalancing shifts
the structure of demand away
from exports toward internal private consumption,
this '*asymmetrical rebalancing*'–
with China saving less
and the United States squandering

the opportunity to rebuild savings–
was always the greatest risk of codependency,
I think he genuinely believes
that bilateral trade deficits are bad.
He is not the only one.
He is just the loudest voice.

So the United States
imposes tariffs on China,
half of that pain
will be felt by other countries.
This is highly regrettable
and will cost both countries
in terms of innovation
and economic performance.
It's called '*delinking*'
the two economics.
I don't think either government
realizes what the price of this might be.
Yes,
as we joined with our partners
in creating China's first investment bank,
we shared our business practices,
proprietary products
and distribution systems.
Yet,
contrary to the assertions
of the US Trade Representative,
we were hardly forced
into these arrangements.

Cease
and desist.
Tariffs are bad–
there is no such thing as a good trade war,
a trade war is good
and easy to win.
The longer the current dispute festers,
the greater the chance
those beliefs become deeply ingrained
in the collect conscience
of both nations.
The urgency to resolve
the current tensions
cannot be emphasized enough.

Unsafe Refurbishment

HOUSING

Grenfell Tower,
as original built,
appears to have been designed
on the premise
of providing
very high levels
of passive fire protection.
The original façade
of Grenfell Tower,
compromising exposed concrete
and given its age,
likely timber
or metal frame windows,
would not have provided
a medium for fire
to spread up the external surface.
There would have been little opportunity
for a fire
in a flat of Grenfell Tower
to spread to any neighbouring flats.

None of the materials used
would be capable
of providing 30 minutes'
fire resistance.
Fuel considered in combination,
as opposed to when they occur
in isolation.

The Grenfeell Tower fire,
which claimed 71 lives,
would not have spread
had it not been for refurbishment
of the building.

Utility Rates

ECONOMY

Economic terrorists
we have to recognize
that we have an enormous job
on the home front
in building a 21st century state
and in jump-starting an economy
that hasn't really grown
for almost five years,
we have to resolve problems
related to poverty
and social exclusion.

I live alone,
I'm never home
and I got bit with a 300% increase,
totally crazy,
I think this government has made a mistake,
it will be hard to reverse the rising trend
that we're seeing in urban poverty
and indigence rates.

Venezuela

UNITED NATIONS

*"International force.
Restore
the Constitutional order
and protect the lives
of our citizens.
We've seen that happen
when the free world
and freedom-loving people
Unite around
a single cause."*

Humanitarian Aid

Conspiracies
and provocations.
There are a lot of generals
and a lot of readers
on Maduro's illicit payroll
through illicit drug trafficking,
money laundering
and any number of businesses
in the oil industry,
Maduro has bought their loyalty.

We are prepared
to protect
the United States lives
and protect
the diplomatic facility
in Venezuela,
there are a range of options
that are on the table.
This shows that we're serious—
this humanitarian aid
must reach the people
of Venezuela
no matter what Maduro says.

Of course they can invade us,
they are used to killing millions
in Iraq,
Libya,
Syria
and elsewhere,
they've spent seven years
helping Syria already
and look how the country is,
but are we ready to die
defending the fatherland?
Yes,

we are ready to do it.
Invasion.

5,000 troops to Columbia.
All options are on the table
very likely.
Any unilateral military intervention
in Venezuela
would be a huge mistake.

Welcome to my country.
We Venezuelans need help.
We are fed up.
Economic war.
Blockade.

International force.
Restore
the Constitutional order
and protect the lives
of our citizens.
We've seen that happen
when the free world
and freedom-loving people
unite around
a single cause.

Venture Capital

ECONOMY

It's a debate we're constantly having:
does the world need a cure for cancer
or another e-commerce start-up?
In the old days,
the Valley went for moonshots
in part because of,
well,
moonshots;
Venture capitalists invested in
and nurtured companies doing these things,
because very small companies could grow large
by building sophisticated little devices.
It took a while for these firms to develop
their reputations,
they had to figure out
which business models worked for them.

You don't always need tech
to be transformative,
I don't think anything is game-changing tech
in what we do,
we were born online,
so digital was part of our DNA
(Deoxyribonucleic Acid)…
I don't define us as e-commerce
or retail.
Rather,
I define the company as a way of life.

It's almost like these things
are so commonplace
you forget how revolutionary it is,
I don't think the mission
of Venture capital is more prosaic–
investing money in companies
that will have more value
in the future
than they have today.
Frankly,

I find most venture capitalists
are investors more
than risk takers;
as I like to say,
I'm okay with a 90% chance
of failure,
if there is a 10% chance
of a world-changing technology,
in some large area.
We don't do e-commerce
and the reason is,
because they aren't tech companies,
in our view,
they are about marketing the products.

I wish more of my students
would spend more time thinking
about start-ups based on solid technology,
as opposed to
meeting the next consumer trend;
I believe the pendulum has swung
too much toward consumer-oriented start-ups,
I don't think it benefits
the long term vitality of our economy.
Strong tech that creates
something unique
and a competitive advantage
is more sustainable.

Video Games

SOCIETY

The big market,
the eight to twelve year old kids,
with game makers increasingly aiming
their products at that market.
In these games
you become a character.
It's a much closer identification
than television.
We usually identify
with someone in the family.
Games allow them to identify
with some very violent
characters.

It's pretty apparent what the attitude
of the Duke Nukem doll is.
If there are people
who find it offensive,
they shouldn't allow
their kids
to play with them.
Ten years ago,
the intent was violence,
but the graphics were so poor
it just looked like pixels,
kicking other pixels.
Now you get screams
and blood…
that's what the people
are asking for.

Not letting the games
get into the young people's hands,
with the rating system,
you have that.
People don't really get in their cars
and drive over the pedestrians.
Postal Dude.

It's always funny
until someone gets hurt
and then it's absolutely
friggin' hysterical!
We were excluded from some channels,
but we really didn't lose anything
by not having the distribution.
It instilled more interest
in the product.
Ultimately,
it's all fantasy.
How each child deals
with fantasy
is something parents
need to decide for themselves.

Virtual Reality

ECONOMY

Virtual reality is going to fundamentally transform
the human experience of shopping.
Lift sales for those retailers
who get ahead of the curve.
If you don't think
about the way people conceptualize
remodels now,
it's really abstract–
they go
and get a much more '*holistic*'
and immersive view
of how a slab of marble
or different paint colors
can change an entire room;
drastically increasing the likelihood
that they will go with Lowe's
for their project.
It removes five steps along the way,
anyone who has done a renovation
has a really visceral reaction.
You can stand in your own kitchen
and overlay a fridge on top of your own fridge,
it's uncannily real.

Retailers have been down
for so long,
they have got to differentiate themselves
to get people to shop.

That's amazing,
you want to wave back,
pretty incredible.
It's like you're there.
It just touches more of your senses,
it gives you a more immersive experience–
you really get the feel of motion.

There is so much e-commerce today,
you have to come up

with a new reason to go to stores,
let people see the beauty of these places,
one unique way we can introduce
and encourage people to get outside.

Unless virtual reality devices
come down in price
and are widely accessible,
the truth is,
you can probably get
a good enough way of simulating somethings
just with photography.

Voter ID

IMMIGRATION

The health of our state
is based on the health of our democracy
and Voter ID is an attack on our Democracy.
I think Democrats
probably underestimate women,
sometimes.
Initialing an affidavit
is really not that big of a deal.
We won't slow them down
in the elections next year.

Urban legend.
Everyone who's eligible is going to vote,
period,
it's not an overly complicate step.
It's not much to hang your hat on
in terms of a complaint
about limiting suffrage rights.
If no one is denied the right to vote
and the sole impact is they have to check a box…
that's unlikely to resonate outside
of the party faithful,
for me,
the voter ID law's principal impact
is the impact you can't see:
the person who doesn't turn out,
because they lack documentation.

COMMUNITY

Voter's Registration

    Civic Engagement

This award
and every single award given out tonight
were voted on by the people?
It is the midterm election
on November 6.
Get out
and vote.
I love you guys.

Taylor Swift's visibility on this issue
is driving a lot of coverage
of voter registration
and it's reaching many of her fans
who would not otherwise
be following news like this.

You never know
what issues will free you
in a year
or two years
or four years–
so you need to make sure
that your representatives are good proxies
for your positions,
for an individual
to be really promoting the vote,
it needs to start with their own circles
of friends
and relatives.
That's the most effective place
they are going to be.

What we know
is that we influence the people
in our lives–
we're the biggest influencers of them
when it comes to voting,

our family,
our friends,
our communities
listen to people that they love
and trust the most about these things.

It's vital right now
to look at states
that your friends are in,
look at those dates
and then encourage them to register
if they're not.

Wage

ECONOMY

*"The economy is booming
and profits are increasing,
we ought to share
that with the people
who need it the most."*

We can't survive with five dollars
and seventy-five cents
and we can't survive with six dollars
and seventy-five cents.
The economy is booming
and profits are increasing,
we ought to share
that with the people
who need it the most.
They want you to believe
that the kids who graduated from high school
are washing dishes
and that's not the case;
they are adults.

Six dollars
and seventy-five is not enough.
Imagine how difficult it is for me
at seven-dollars
and fifty cents an hour;
then think about those who earn five dollars
and seventy-five cents,
how do they survive?

A driver might have a salary
of eight dollars an hour,
but with tips that
climbs up to thirteen dollars an hour.

West Nile Virus

NATURE

> Sources: California Department of Public Health
> Centers for Disease Control and Prevention
> San Diego County Department of Environmental Health
> SDFighttheBite.com
> WestNile.ca.gov

2007:
San Diego: 15
California: 380
United States: 3,623
3,700 Nationwide / 124 people died, 20 in California.

Most of those 12 days
I don't remember...
I had fatigue,
muscle weakness
and was unable to do anything
by myself.
Climbing stairs is still a challenge.

All it takes is one bite
from one mosquito
to effect your life
in ways you can't imagine.
Sometimes it takes story telling
from people like this
to get the message out.
All had backyard
mosquito breeding sources.
It doesn't take long
for mosquitoes to set up house.

Western Education

FAITH

My daughter is alive,
but they wouldn't release her,
because she is a Christian.
They told her
they would release her
if she converted,
but she said she will never become a Muslim.
I am very sad,
but I am also overjoyed,
because my daughter
did not denounce Christ.

Leah Sharibu will not be abandoned,
Western education is forbidden.
President Buhar:
should engage his negotiating machinery
to get Leah released unconditionally…
since it is obvious
that the federal government
negotiated to get
the other Dapchi students released,
it is unfortunate
that Leah is being subjected
to further physical
and psychological trauma,
because she insisted
on holding onto her religious faith,
it has now become a crime
to become a Christian in Nigeria.

My heart was broken
when I searched
through the released girls
and could not set my eyes
on my dear daughter,
Leah.
What her schoolmates told me
was that my daughter was told
she must recite the Kalima Shahada,

the Islamic profession of faith
and she said she does not know how to recite it,
that she was not brought up as a Muslim.
She had already boarded alongside others
who were ready to come home.
They said my daughter
would only be brought back home
the day she knows how to recite
the Kalima Shahada.
If Leah were home,
she and her little brother
would attend to everything in this home;
she would not let me do anything.
Since we were told that the negotiation was done
for all the schoolgirls,
why did the government accept
that only my daughter be left behind
when others were freed
and even brought home?
If they negotiated
as if they loved all the girls
as their own,
then they should do everything
to help release my own girl.

Whales

WILDLIFE WORLD

We have the animal,
off the bow,
at eleven o'clock!

A deaf whale,
is a dead whale.
If you're in the ocean
and you rely on hearing
for navigation,
to avoid predators
and to find your mate,
I don't think nature is
going to let you live
too long,
if you're deaf.
Whale watching
and fishing boats figure in,
not,
because a lot of them
can be around at one time,
but,
because we are conditioning
the animals
not to be fearful of ships.

It was partly loud.
What I suspect,
is that in the St. Lawrence
there are times of the year,
days
and sites that are
potentially dangerous to
the hearing of whales.
We don't know
what a whale hears;
for whales
there are no hearing standards.
It's a very complex problem that
isn't one that will be solved

within the next year.
Whale watchers
are good people,
they want to do
what's right for the whales.
We need good scientific proof.
The purpose is not to put
somebody out of business.

They breed
and show off their calves.

Occasionally,
you'll get a wild guy
in an outboard motor,
he'll tear over to where
a whale is
and really harass it.
There is a much greater
threat from tankers,
oil ships
and military ships.
Whale watching is very incidental.

Wicca

MILITARY

      Source: John Bourdrecue
                      Contra Colt Times

The base provided us
with what we wanted,
equality;
we didn't want special treatment,
we wanted exactly
what everybody else had.

Sky clad,
minority.
Intro to Wicca.
They want to learn
how to turn people into frogs
and toads.

She was telling me
we were all going straight
to hell
as we were desecrating the Church,
and it harm none,
do what ye will.

Picket Fence
if you make a mistake,
fix it,
don't ask the Guards.

I feel comfortable here;
I've had almost no trouble.
Back home,
I'd be in physical danger
if I walked around
with my pentagram
around my neck.

We may not agree with them,
but we have to defend

their right to worship,
it's part of our diversity,
you have to accept people
for who
and what they are
to get the mission done.

Decisions to accommodate requests
to hold meetings
or conduct ceremonies
on military installations
do not constitute endorsement
of a particulate belief
or practice,
there are incidents of harassment
or discrimination,
but they are linked
and usually dealt with quickly.

Make no mistake:
The status quo is unacceptable,
the United States Armed Forces
is not a seminally in camouflage.
It's not a forum
for compulsive religions.
There is no question
that the presence of the groups
diminishes readiness,
good order,
discipline
and morale.

We believe God hates witches,
I'd like to see them saved,
but they are a bunch
of wicked witches.
They are Pacifists.
They are nature lovers.
They admit this.
We don't need those kinds
of people in the Army.
March for righteousness…
Obviously
it's a concern,

it causes people
to have a dim view of the military.
They are promoting it
by allowing it.
It's a product
of the political times–
a moral.

Wildfire Disaster Relief

COMMUNITY

It was very frustrating,
obviously I volunteered,
because I wanted to help,
but I was just wasting my time.
We weren't helping anyone at all.

These are very large incidents
and it's tough to coordinate,
when disaster is uncertain,
sometimes it's a moving target.
We want to take as much responsibility
and be as humble about this
as we can,
it's in the best interest of our donors
and our clients.
For the most part,
people are told to stay at the airport
and wait for someone else coming in.

The national Red Cross volunteers
from out of town didn't ever have directions
or know where they were going,
they would go out and assess damage
where the firefighters had already been.
They were just wasting resources
and it was crazy.

That mistake
seems like it would be hard to make,
you'd think they would have learned
their lessons
after the Katrina situation.

They didn't have significant knowledge
and experience to do their jobs,
it's in the American Red Cross'
best interest
and it was to be able to reassure the public.

They are good stewards of the donor dollars,
it's something that neither we
or this chapter had any control over,
I'm just very confident that it did occur.

Wildfires

NATURE

Global Warming

The fires
that are getting everybody's attention
right now
are not about forest management.
The major factor
is climate change
across the West,
regardless of fuels management,
we just wouldn't be burning like this,
especially in Northern California,
in a normal year.

We've got to do something smarter
than what we've been doing,
this is very clear.
Get people out of there.
Go back to the cities
and towns
and counties,
planning boards
and zoning commissions
and have a very different approach.
Our experience shows wildfires
burn right into the city
of San Diego's long established neighborhoods,
so halting new suburban home building
is not panacea,
the projects the board has recently approved
meet stringent,
modern fire safety standards
and during our public,
televised deliberations,
five authorities responded positively
during extensive questioning
about their confidence
in the safety of those developments.
Autumn precipitation

has been decreasing
and is likely to decrease in the future
as global warming continues,
so when those winds occur,
they're occurring
over a backdrop
of record dry vegetation.

Radical environmentalists.
You have dead
and dying timber
you have years of neglect.
It was like a flame thrower
of embers shooting through
the forest.
In the name of protecting
endangered species,
we placed increasing tracts of land
off limits to forest management,
allowing our forests
to become dangerously overcrowded
and overgrown,
the fact is
that managing the forest
is part of it,
they're a lot of denser
than they were 200 years ago.

Jackstraw.
People will say
that usually those big logs
don't burn,
but 10 years from now
you could get a fire
in the concentrated down wood
and if that happens,
we're going to see fires
that we've never seen the likes of before.
I have to say
that it's shocking to me
that scientists
funded by the Forest Service
would push snag removal
as fire management right now.

After the Camp Fire
just blew through everywhere
the Forest Service
had removed nearly all of the snags
and burned down most of Paradise.
It's for restoration
of the forest ecosystem,
to protect it from catastrophic wildfire
and insects
and disease
and outbreak,
it's a combination
of everyone rolling up their sleeves
and working together.

There has been a downward trend
in timber harvesting
in California
since the '70s
and '80s,
so you cannot turn that around
on a dime,
it takes time to attract new sawmills
to certain parts of the state
and attract the workforce,
but I think the grants will help that.

We could before the fuels,
there to a more appropriate density
and structure
through thinning
and prescribe fire.
We could make them
much more resilient
to climate change,
but it's getting harder
and harder
to get ahead of that.
It requires a lot of resources.
Reestablishing fire
has been the finding
of the fire science community
for the last 25 years.

Wildflowers

NATURE

Geraea canescens.
Cryptantha angustifolia.
Pectocarya heterocarpa.
All right,
Ok,
I think we are finally taking off here,
if you don't track it numerically,
you can't really compare year to year
or even know for sure
where you are in the bloom cycle.
There's a garden around here,
it's the only spot it exists
in the county.

Out of this world.
We had the highest volume
of annual germination
I've ever seen;
we're seeing a fascinating adaption,
the volume is tremendous,
but they are pygmies.
The plants are in a race
to get their flowers out.

To be owned by the desert,
you have to get down
on your knee,
it's all there.
May you see the desert
with new eyes.
Do you have
your Global positioning system
on it?
I'll go get it,
Ganderi!
Yay!

Wildlife Corridor

WORLD WILDLIFE

Wildlife corridor.
P-22.
Can get around,
meet P-23
and P-24.
Will this stop development?
Will this impose undue burdens
on developers?

Developers have to move over
a little bit
so that the wild animals
in fact
can have their pathways.
These are relatively modest changes
to the planning code
that will make a massive difference
to the health
of our bobcats
and mountain lions
and raccoons
and other animals.

Witchcraft

FAITH

Not much comfort
to those hanged,
by a judicial system
made of men
who felt divinely inspired.

One of Windsor:
The Untold Story
of America's First
Witch Hanging.
Historians of New England
have long treated events
in Massachusetts
as if they represented
the entire history
of New England,
this has only begun to change
significantly
in recent years.

Never heard any commentary
or expression on this topic.
Town leadership would investigate it.
Never had occasion to consider.
There should always be an effort
to right all injustices,
the exhibits about the Salem Witch Trials
are some of the most visited
tourist attractions
in New England
and bring an enormous amount of cash flow
into Salem,
great potential for bustling tourism.

Many of the exact locations
of particular events
are either unknown
or have been effaced
through the centuries.

There are also very few artifacts
remaining
from the period
of the witch trials,
so this would have to be a created story
largely presented in imaged
or stimulated spaces.

Physical place
or venue that speaks to the events.
So,
really,
there isn't there,
there.
Witch trials were a part of the state's history
that we are not very proud of
and therefore not greatly interested
in promoting.

Women's Fourth Amendment

JUSTICE

Crack baby.
Epidemic routine in today's world
agents of the police.
This was being done for medical purposes,
the police didn't show up
and say,
"*we want to find a way
to bust your patients.*"
True medical epidemic
in only one hospital?
You can't prevent anything
when...
the child is already born.

A policy of destiny.
Everyone may be more sustainable,
which became in effect,
the police.
This program was designed by
and for law enforcement.
Probably,
because the doctors used the promise
of confidentiality
they took on the mantle
of the police.

Special needs,
child abuse.
We were trying to stop a woman
from doing irreparable harm
to her child.
It happens all the time that
a doctor has to turn someone in.

Women's March

COMMUNITY

       Women's Rights

Hear Our Vote.
Last year after the march,
a friend of mine said,
'Now what do we do?'
This is what we do.
Each of every day it's up to us
to make our voices heard.
We do not stop.
We march forward,
because of you,
the revolution is rolling!
Everything is at stake
we've got to give it all we've got.
Time is up!
Speak out
and change things.

He says what the voter looks like,
your voice is your superpower,
he'd say,
'Don't cancel my vote',
but I'd go into the voting booth
and vote
for whoever I wanted to anyway,
I was afraid.
Now,
though,
I have reclaimed my voice
and I am speaking
for those who are afraid to speak
their truth.
I am speaking today
not just for the MeToos,
because I'm a MeToo,
but when I raise my hand;
I am aware of all the women
who are still in silence,

the women who are faceless,
the women who don't have the money
and who don't have the constitution
and who don't have the confidence
and who don't have the images
in our media
that gives them a sense of self-worth
to break their silence.

Grab them by the midterms,
Access Hollywood.
We still believe in civil discourse,
we're here,
because we're strong,
erudite
and sick of being led by people
with no compassion,
no morals,
no character
and no intelligence.

I have three sons—
three sons who know better
than to act like President Trump.
Dreamers.
Empathy is an American value.
Protect the Dreamers.
I'm out here today,
because…
enough already,
it's important that we do not lose hope.
We're here,
because it's making a difference
not just for us,
but for any kids
we have in the future,
somos semillas.
We are seeds.
They tried to bury us,
they didn't know we are the seeds.
We couldn't be here.
We're here for our students
whose parents have been deported.
The dreamers.

We're here for our LGBT friends
who are afraid.
We're here for our husbands.
We are here for them,
it's overwhelming how many reasons there are
to be here.

We have seen
a tremendous amount of momentum,
men of quality are for equality,
we see women coming
into the workplace
that are incredibly skilled,
men need to change the culture,
wisdom is experience gone wrong.
Hey,
look up #GoodGuysWearWhiteHats,
We have just been so,
so distressed this year
with what's going on in our country,
we just feel
they're sucking us down the drain,
these divisive,
racist,
misogynist hatemongers
who are trying to make it us
versus them,
instead of we.
We want to go back
to where we're hopeful again.

World Bank

ECONOMY

One of the things
that could destabilize us is,
in fact,
social unrest around the world
and I believe
that the numbers are getting so compelling
that it is a real risk.
These inequities can't exist.
If someone signs me a blank check
for seventy billion dollars,
I'd be happy to forgive
all that debt,
but that's not likely
to be forth coming.

No one can doubt
President Wolfensohn's personal commitment
to the poorest people in the world,
but the World Bank
and its board,
continue total to deliver on its mandate
and his vision,
most likely on debt relief.

World Chess Championship

AMERICA'S NEW TRIUMPH

In the chess world,
this is huge;
it shows that United States chess
is on an upswing,
it gets kids to fall in love
with thinking–
the country's changed.
It could be like that now,
especially if an American wins,
we have to prepare people for it.

O.K.,
we've seen the computer evaluation,
so we see it's very good,
but over the board
it's very hard to play a move like that.

It's removed me of the poetry of it,
Chess instills in you to work with a plan.
Computers don't do that.
They don't suggest plans.
They just tell you what's the right move.
They rob you of some of the grace of the game.
There's something about someone figuring out
the moves,
a charm for an excitement for someone,
who is not booked up.
If you're not computer savvy,
you're at a disadvantage
and these little kids who come along
are into it tenfold.

If you talk
to some of the older players
they definitely say they see beauty
in certain games,
in my case,
there are certain times when I think,
'*Wow,*

that's so amazing,
chess is so full of ideas,'
but most of the time
I intend to much more pragmatic about it,
as opposed to thinking
about it as art
or something exquisite.

There were a lot of times
when his understanding of chess
from when he grew up,
his intuition,
or feel,
was simply wrong
according to the computer,
it showed how much different chess is now,
because computers are the ultimate authority.
You just automatically accept what they say
and you move on.

Y2K

GOVERNMENT

"It now appears
*that a number of countries
will experience
Year Two-Thousand
failures in key structures;
such as electric power,
telecommunications
and transportation.*"

Compliant

The biggest problem
with the Year-Two Thousand
is not all the worries about January first
and people buying groceries
or generators
in the United States,
but with all the companies
with dependencies around the world
and the countries
that could see serious problems—
just in time.
It's an area of uncertainty,
after a while,
the numbers of supplies
just get astronomical.
This is an international problem,
unfortunately.
Russia
and other nations
may lack the resources
to fix the computers
that control their nuclear weapons—
monitoring the problem is not enough—
the problem needs to be fixed
in the United States
and Russia.
The Pentagon should make every effort
to reach the Russian government
and other governments
to make sure all nuclear weapons systems
are Year Two-Thousand compliant.
It now appears
that a number of countries
will experience
Year Two-Thousand
failures in key structures;
such as electric power,
telecommunications
and transportation.

Y2K

ECONOMY

Millennium Bug
"*00*"
Zero zero
Final Jeopardy
"*00*"
Zero zero
Turn of the millennium,
century,
eternal,
no expiration date–
epoch.

It's another one of the gotchas,
it's part of the complexity
of the technological age.
There is no way
we can know about everything.
Global Position System epoch.
By having the problem occur
every twenty years,
people just didn't think about it.

A year ago,
there were people who still arguing
about whether it was a leap year.
There's no more confusion now.
It's going to be a problem
for small companies
that have taken a nonchalant approach
to fixing it.
No doubt about it,
they'll have eight thousand years
to figure it out
and yet still mess up.

Sixty-four bits
literally gives you
some multiple of the life
on the universe,

that's pretty good.
We're not going to have
this problem again.

Real
and serious,
"00"
bug,
the United States securities markets
are very aware of the need
to correct their systems
and are making a strong,
widespread commitment of time
and money for this effort;
deep recession
probably a stretch…
some of the stuff we're getting from
outside contracts aren't working.

Disrupting the flow of information
could be just as distressing
as the disruption in the flow of oil
in nineteen seventy-three
and seventy-four,
there's a sixty percent chance.

Personal Computers are in good shape
computer Basic Input-Output system chips
give the impression that PCs are way down
the food chain compliant with minor issues.
We were late in delivering the depth of information
that our customers needed,
we've now made sure
our customers understand
that we are taken very seriously
from the top down.

Yahoo

INTERNET

Very open-minded.
It was very disappointing to us
that they didn't want
to defend this deal.
At the right price,
did we want to close the deal
with Microsoft to sell the company?
Yes,
had we been able to do so,
we would have been very happy.
It was not meant to be.
My job is to figure out
How to find the right path
for Yahoo.
I don't know
what else we could have done.

However,
after a four month review...
it's clear that government regulations
and some advertisers
continue to have concerns
about the agreement.
Pressing ahead risked
not only a protracted legal battle,
but also damage to relationships
with valued partners.

Everyone recognized
that Yahoo was committing itself
to a very costly addiction
in return for their flood
of Google dollars–
illegal deal,
continuing opportunities.
There is no interest in acquiring Yahoo.

The loss of the Google deal
is going to cause cascading problems

for Yahoo.
It's hard to see
how Jerry Yang survives it.
Just like one
never wants to have an IRS audit,
even if you haven't done anything
wrong.
At some point,
there needs to be someone
to step in,
because Yahoo
is still a valuable asset.
They need to do something
prior to researching a point
when it is not a leading
Internet asset.

The arrangement
likely would have deemed consumers
the benefits of competition:
lower prices,
better service
and greater innovation.
Become collaborators
rather than competitors
for a significant portion
of their search advertising business.

Yellowstone National Park

NATURE

If that becomes the norm,
where there's no time
for these forests to take a break,
to grow for 150 years
or so without burning,
you could see some widespread changes
to the forests,
but what we're seeing now
is more homogeneous burning
throughout the forests,
with fewer islands
of unburned areas,
when that happens,
there are fewer seed sources
to replace the stands.

Found One!
When fires burn at short intervals,
we have a lot fewer trees
coming back,
it's still enough for a forest,
but it will be sparser than before.

It's an example of linear thinking
to say that warmer
and drier
and bigger fires,
the question were asking now is,
'What does the future hold
for these forests?'
Are we entering an era
in which things
aren't going to behave
like they did before?
Change is going to happen,
but we'll still have forests.
We'll still have a wide variety
of native species.
It will still be Yellowstone.

SOCIETY

Young Girls
Like a Girl.
Throw like a girl.
Play like a girl.
For young girls specifically,
a sense of empowerment
and having opportunities
can be protective
against many risks
in their lives
and facilitate positive development
and well-being.
Girls who think positively
about their future
are less likely to engage
in high risk behaviors;
such as unprotected sex
and substance use
and are more likely to engage
in healthy behaviors,
like going to school
and playing sports.
Also,
studies of all-girl curricula
and schools,
along with programs
that give girls a meaningful voice,
have been found to be beneficial.

If a healthy foundation
has been established
by a positive environment,
it is very likely that the young girls
will have higher self-esteem
and be empowered
to make good choices
in their school life,
excel in academics,
athletics
and be impactful leaders.

www.ingramcontent.com/pod-product-compliance
Lightning Source LLC
Chambersburg PA
CBHW021436070526
44577CB00002B/187